# Luis Leal

Mario T. García

# Luis Leal

## An Auto/**Biography**

University of Texas Press, Austin

Requests for permission to reproduce material from this work should be sent to
Permissions, University of Texas Press, P.O. Box 7819, Austin, TX 78713-7819.

♾ The paper used in this book meets the minimum requirements of ANSI/NISO Z39.48-
1992 (R1997) (Permanence of Paper).

Library of Congress Cataloging-in-Publication Data
García, Mario T.
    Luis Leal : an auto/biography / by Mario T. García — 1st ed.
        p.     cm.
    Includes bibliographical references (p.    ) and index.
    ISBN 0-292-72828-X (alk. paper) — ISBN 0-292-72829-8 (pbk. : alk. paper)
    1. Leal, Luis, 1907–    —Interviews.    2. Critics—Mexico—Interviews.    3. Critics—
United States—Interviews.    I. Title.
PQ 7109.5.L43    G37    2000
860.9—dc21
[B]                                                                                              99-052635

Cover: (front) Luis Leal at age 18 in his hometown of Linares,
Nuevo Leon, shortly before leaving to study in the United States.

Frontispiece: Leal at the Center for Chicano Studies,
University of California, Santa Barbara, 1981.

Design by José Clemente Orozco

*To Luis Leal and Gladys Leal*
*for being wonderful human beings*

# Contents

*There are three times—a present of things past,*
*a present of things present,*
*and a present of things future.*
—The Confessions of St. Augustine

# Acknowledgments

I am totally indebted to Professor Luis Leal, who so graciously agreed to cooperate in this project. I want to thank him for his support and patience and for simply being "Don Luis." I also wish to strongly thank Gladys Leal for making her home accessible to me for my interviews with Don Luis and for being a wonderful and caring person. I want to acknowledge UC MEXUS and the University of California, Santa Barbara (UCSB) Academic Senate for providing research funds for this project. A very special thanks to Roberto Trujillo and Adan Griego of the Green Research Library at Stanford for their support of this project.

For transcribing the taped interviews, I wish to thank Jonathon Burgoyne, Tairi Gould, and Darla McDavid. Donna Ryczek O'Toole expertly typed the manuscript.

Professor Ellen McCracken kindly and generously took time from her own busy research schedule to read the manuscript and provide valuable suggestions for changes. She also graciously compiled the index.

In addition, I want to acknowledge the support and highly professional work of the University of Texas Press. I particularly wish to thank Theresa May for her enthusiasm and support, and Leslie Tingle and her staff for the editing of the manuscript. Moreover, gratitude goes out to the two anonymous reviewers of the manuscript, whose suggestions for changes were very much welcomed.

As usual, I want to acknowledge my two growing children, Carlo and Giuliana, for just being their wonderful selves. They are very fortunate to have had the opportunity to know both Don Luis and Gladys.

# Introduction

Professor Luis Leal is one of the most outstanding scholars of Mexican, Latin American, and Chicano literature—he is the dean of Mexican American intellectuals in the United States. Don Luis, as he is affectionately called by those who know him well, is now in his early nineties and has devoted his long life to scholarship, teaching, and to helping others with his unassuming but effective leadership.

Born in Linares, Nuevo León, in northern Mexico on September 17, 1907—the eve of the Mexican Revolution of 1910—Don Luis spent his early years with his family surviving and adjusting to the turmoil and hostilities of Mexico's most profound political crisis. The temporary dislocations of the civil war and, more importantly, the Revolution itself, represented a defining period for the young Luis. As well-to-do ranchers, his family emerged from the conflict in better shape than most other Mexicans. The Leals supported the uprising against the longtime dictator Porfirio Díaz and embraced the progressive liberalism espoused by particular factions of the alliance against him. This implanted in Don Luis a humanistic world view and a sympathy for social justice. In addition, the Revolution would come to be an important research theme for Leal.

As a *norteño*—a man of Mexico's northern region—Don Luis was influenced by the proximity of the United States. Following the Revolution, he desired to pursue his post–high school education north of the border. He applied and was accepted in 1934 as an undergraduate at Northwestern University in Evanston, Illinois, just outside Chicago. Coming to the American Midwest was an important juncture for him. It would mean that his future life would be spent mostly in the United States, with a good portion of it in the Midwest. Although it took him longer than average to graduate due to his need to master English,

Don Luis did so in 1940. By then he had settled on the goal of pursuing a Ph.D. in Spanish and of becoming a college professor. To achieve this objective, he entered the graduate program at the prestigious University of Chicago. Staying in the Midwest was also important to him, since as an undergraduate he had met and married Gladys Clemens of Chicago, a marriage that has endured for some sixty years. Don Luis received his M.A. in Spanish in 1941 but had to postpone his doctoral studies due to the outbreak of World War II; as a naturalized American citizen, he was subject to the draft. Don Luis loyally served his new country and saw active duty with the U.S. Army in the Pacific, including the retaking of the Philippines from the Japanese. Fortunately, he returned home unharmed.

Reunited with his wife and two young sons, Don Luis devoted the next few years to completing his Ph.D., which he achieved in 1950. He expressed his interest in Latin American history and literature by writing a dissertation on the colonial chronicles of New Spain as fiction and as the origin of the Mexican short story.

In 1952, two years after completing his graduate work, Don Luis began his career as a university professor in the Romance languages department of the University of Mississippi. He recalls often seeing the famous American writer William Faulkner on the streets of Oxford. Not completely happy there in the mid-1950s, a time of increasing racial tensions, he accepted a position at Emory University in Atlanta in 1956. In this period Don Luis, already a published scholar, accelerated his research to focus on studies and anthologies of the Mexican and Latin American short story. Indeed, he became the premier scholar of the Mexican short story as highlighted by his books *Breve historia del cuento mexicano* (1957), *Antología del cuento mexicano* (1957), and *Bibliografía del cuento mexicano* (1958).

As his career progressed, Don Luis received opportunities to teach and conduct research at larger and more research-oriented institutions. In 1959 he accepted a tenured position at the University of Illinois at Urbana, where he would work until his retirement in 1976. There, Don Luis matured and flourished as a scholar and teacher. He published numerous books and articles and read at countless scholarly conferences papers encompassing his interests in both Mexican and Latin American literature. In addition to his work on the short story, Don Luis began to write on a variety of major Mexican and Latin American writers, such as Mariano Azuela, Juan Rulfo, Octavio Paz, Carlos Fuentes, Gabriel García Márquez, Jorge Luis Borges, Mario Vargas Llosa, Julio Cortázar, and Juan José Arreola. He knew many of these writers personally, some of whom achieved international recognition in the 1960s as part of the so-called Latin

American Boom in literature. As a significant part of his Illinois years and as a testimony to his own growing reputation as a scholar, Don Luis mentored to completion some forty-four Ph.D. students of Latin American literature.

In addition to his work on the Mexican short story, some of Don Luis's major publications in the area of Mexican and Latin American literature include *México, civilizaciones y culturas* (1955 and 1971), *Mariano Azuela, vida y obra* (1961), *Historia del cuento hispanoamericano* (1966), *El cuento hispanoamericano* (1967), and *Juan Rulfo* (1983).

It was also at Illinois that Don Luis became interested in Chicano literature. Mexican Americans, as Don Luis would stress, could trace a literary genealogy within the borders of the United States as far back as the Spanish colonial period. However, it was not until the 1960s and the ethnic revival associated with the militant Chicano movement of that period that specific attention came to be focused on Chicano cultural and artistic contributions, including literature. Beginning with his participation in one of the first sessions on Chicano literature at a meeting of the Modern Language Association, Don Luis, as an "adopted Chicano," commenced a significant new direction in his research. He believed in the viability of Chicano literature and saw the need to turn his talents and leadership to legitimizing it and its criticism. Don Luis became not only one of the first senior scholars in the country to champion this new writing and research, but he also became one of its first scholars. His previous work in Mexican and Latin American literature contributed to helping establish the cultural linkages between Hispanic literature south of the border and Chicano literature north of it. Moreover, his stature and importance in the early days of Chicano literary criticism made it difficult for others to dismiss this research area as nothing more than political rhetoric.

Don Luis's involvement in the founding of contemporary Chicano literary criticism was further advanced by his permanent relocation to Santa Barbara in 1976. He and Gladys initially chose Santa Barbara for retirement, but the move would come to bear a whole new career of research and teaching focused primarily on Chicano literature. Within a couple of years of arriving in California, Leal began to teach courses in Chicano literature and Mexican cultural traditions for the Department of Chicano Studies at UCSB. He was named a senior research fellow in the Center for Chicano Studies and even served as its acting director for three years in the early 1980s. To this day, Don Luis teaches two courses per year for the department, plus an occasional seminar in the Department of Spanish and Portuguese, and maintains a research appointment. During this fresh and active period, he has written and published widely on a variety of·

topics in Chicano literature. In recognition of his contributions in this field, the National Association for Chicano Studies named Don Luis as its scholar of the year in 1987. At UCSB he was further honored with the establishment of an endowed chair in Chicano Studies in his name. This is the first and only such chair in the United States. The first recipient of the Luis Leal Endowed Chair in Chicano Studies is another outstanding scholar of Chicano literature, Professor María Herrera-Sobek.

Among some of his most important works in Chicano literature, in addition to his numerous articles and reviews, are *Corridos y canciones de Aztlán* (1986), *A Decade of Chicano Literature, 1970–1979* (1982), *Aztlán y México: perfiles literarios e históricos* (1985), and *No Longer Voiceless* (1995). In all, Don Luis has published close to 250 articles and over 30 books.[1]

But Don Luis has never been just an ivory-tower intellectual. As an undergraduate at Northwestern he became involved in Latino community-based organizations; he has always been willing to assist the community in any way he can, especially the Latino one. In recognition of this service and of his outstanding academic achievements and leadership among Latinos, the Santa Barbara Hispanic Achievement Council named Don Luis the recipient of its 1984 Hispanic Achievement Award. His leadership and record as an American scholar was recognized more recently by his adopted country when President Bill Clinton honored Don Luis by awarding him the country's most prestigious humanities award, the National Humanities Medal, in 1997. The Mexican government, still claiming him as a native son, presented Don Luis its nation's highest honor, the Aguila Azteca Award, in 1991. One more feather was placed in Don Luis's illustrious cap in 1998, when he was elected to the prestigious North American Academy of Spanish Language.

During his six decades of research and writing—a career that is still ongoing at the end of the millennium—Don Luis has exhibited certain key characteristics as a scholar that I believe serve as outstanding examples for others. First, he has always seen his research not in isolation from the community or from social issues but as very much a part of a dialogue on how to advance those interests. He has seen his research as a way of better understanding human relations and of promoting social justice (that is the humanist and the citizen in him). To this end, he has always attempted to study literature and writers within a historical context. For Don Luis, literature does not exist outside of history but is a part of history and the making of history. His interdisciplinary orientation, even in his earlier years when the term was not yet in vogue, has been indicative of his nontraditional approach. He is a scholar who understands the complexity of the world and of the intricacies of human social relationships—which are not subject to easy judgments. He was an anti-essentialist even before postmodern scholars took up the theme. Don Luis has never remained static.

Perhaps his most exemplary characteristic as a scholar is his sense of tolerance and support for the work of others. As he told me more than once in our interviews, everyone contributes something—every scholar produces some useful knowledge that is of benefit to other scholars. Discouraging elitist and ego-driven competition among academics, through his work and his example Leal has encouraged a humanistic tolerance among the scholarly community. In this day of one-up-manship in the academy, Don Luis's kind and gentle approach is a refreshing alternative.

A word about how this book came to be and about the working relationship between Don Luis and myself is in order. I am not a literary scholar but a historian. I came to the production of this *testimonio,* or oral history, from several perspectives. As a practitioner of oral history, I understand and appreciate the importance of recording the history and stories of our elders. I have done many oral histories over the years, including a book-length *testimonio* about the life and times of Bert Corona, an outstanding labor and community leader in this country.[2] Due to his activism, Corona would never have had the time to write his autobiography. I realized the same was true of Don Luis: his active research and teaching schedule, and undoubtedly his own modesty, would never have allowed Don Luis to produce his life story.

When I approached him about the possibility of working on a *testimonio,* he graciously agreed to the project. As a historian who has focused on the role of leadership in Chicano history, I recognized that Don Luis's life and career are important aspects of the leadership that has emanated from the Latino intellectual community. Finally, I have always been interested in literature and understand the significant ideological and artistic contributions that Chicano literature has made. For all these reasons and more, I chose to devote time and energy to producing this *testimonio* of a remarkable individual.

Don Luis and I conducted our conversations from the fall of 1993 until the winter of 1999, with various breaks in between. In all, some thirty-five hours of interviews were taped. These tapes, along with the unedited transcripts, are deposited in the Luis Leal Collection in the special collections of the Green Library at Stanford University. We worked—if work is the correct word for what were in fact delightful and stimulating conversations—in Don Luis's modest but comfortable home in the Santa Barbara suburb of Goleta. There we spent many memorable afternoons, never exceeding more than two hours and refreshingly interrupted by Gladys's thoughtful hospitality of coffee and *panecitos,* or baked goodies. In these afternoon conversations, Don Luis in English recalled some of the details of his own life and of the many episodes and periods of his career. We went back in time and relived the Mexican Revolution, the Great Depression, World War II, the Eisenhower 1950s, the turmoil of the 1960s, the challenging spirit of the Chicano movement, and Don Luis's California years. In this voyage, or pilgrimage, of memory, we visited with a bevy of writers and critics from both sides of the border. This list reads like a *Who's Who* of Mexican, Latin American, and Chicano literature: Martín Luis Guzmán, Mariano Azuela, Samuel Ramos, Octavio Paz, José Revueltas, Carlos Fuentes, Jorge Luis Borges, Gabriel García Márquez, Julio Cortázar, Mario Vargas Llosa, Juan José Arreola, Octavio Romano, Tomás Rivera, Alurista, José Montoya, José Antonio Villarreal, Rudolfo Anaya, Rolando Hinojosa, Ron Arias, Joseph Sommers, Juan Bruce-Novoa, Miguel Méndez, Oscar Zeta Acosta, Ernesto Galarza, Américo Paredes, John Rechy, Estella Portillo Trambley, Elena Poniatowska, Arturo Azuela, Gustavo Sainz, Alejandro Morales, Richard Rodríguez, Gary Soto, Arturo Islas, Sandra Cisneros, Ana Castillo, and Denise Chávez.

When most of the interviews were completed, I began to write up the text based on the transcriptions of the tapes. Very early on, I decided that the best way to write the narrative was not as a disguised monologue but in the form of a dialogue, which is what in essence a *testimonio* is all about. In this sense, the text is neither a traditional autobiography nor a traditional biography, but instead a synthesis of the two genres, an "auto/biography." I chose to include both our voices because this particular *testimonio* is actually more of an intellectual autobiography than, as in the case of Bert Corona's, a full life story. From the beginning both Don Luis and I understood that our project would be centered on his career and work as a literary scholar. Some aspects of his personal life would be covered, but in respect for Don Luis's privacy and that of Gladys and his family, the project would focus predominantly on his career. As a result, I did not believe that a first-person, singular narrative was appropriate. Don Luis's career—his comments and thoughts about his intellectual world view, about his own projects, and about the many writers and critics who have crossed his path—is best represented by maintaining the original (though edited) dialogue format of the interviews. Although I want to minimize my own voice in the dialogue, this format shows how a *testimonio* is produced and how it is clearly the result of dual voices. Don Luis's contributions to the text are obvious in the dominance of his voice throughout the narrative, but he also went over each draft of the text and made corrections and additions.

I want to close this introduction by reemphasizing what an exceptional and memorable experience it was to have participated in these *charlas,* or conversations, with Don Luis. His career is a model and an inspiration of how to be an intellectual and scholar with dignity, honor, integrity, and the highest of standards, commitment, kindness, consideration, and respect for others. The importance of Don Luis's life is not how long he has lived but simply *how* he has lived his life.

# Luis Leal

*Leal (right), about 2 years old, with brother José.*

# Chapter One

## Linares

*Leal with his father, Luis Leal Ardines, about 1912.*

# Family Background and
# Early Life

**MG:** Don Luis, when and where were you born?

**LL:** I was born on September 17, 1907, in Linares, Nuevo León, in northern Mexico. Linares is located southeast of Monterrey, the capital of Nuevo León. I was named after my father.

When I returned in 1985 after many years to receive an *homenaje* [homecoming award] from city officials, I discovered that Linares had not changed very much over the years. In fact, it struck me that it had not changed at all.

At the luncheon for me, I was seated next to the *presidente municipal* [mayor], who asked me, "Why did you leave Linares all those years ago?"

I said, "Well, I left because I had to study and so I went to the United States. I had the intention of coming back, but I never did." What I politely didn't tell the mayor was that at that time nobody stayed in Linares. They all went someplace else.

**What is Linares like? What is its economy?**

The economy is mostly agriculture, especially oranges. Most of the oranges in Mexico are grown in this region around Linares and Montemorelos. It is a very productive agricultural region. There has also been some cattle raising. When the railroads entered this region during the period of Don Porfirio Díaz's rule [1877–1910], this expanded agricultural production.

**Is it an arid climate?**

Yes, it's dry, but it's not as hot as in Monterrey. Linares sits not far from the Sierra Madre Oriental, which means it is at a higher elevation than Monterrey and is cooler. It's very fertile land and is similar to Southern California.

**Were your parents originally from Linares?**

My mother, Josefina Martínez, was born in a town called Galeana, which is up in the Sierras not too far from Linares. It's a town made famous by the

*Leal, about 2 ¹/₂ years old.*

exploits of General Mariano Escobedo, who was born there and later fought bravely with Benito Juárez against the French intervention in the 1860s. Escobedo received the sword of the French-imposed Emperor Maximilian after the capture of Maximilian. My mother's family—the Martínez family—was distantly related to General Escobedo. I don't know how far my mother's family goes back. It was a ranching family. I know, unfortunately, less about my mother's side of the family.

On my father's side, the Leal family can be traced back to the seventeenth century—specifically to 1636—when that family left the center of Mexico and settled in what came to be Linares. I have a land map of Linares from the eighteenth century that contains the names and locations of particular family homes. It indicates the existence of the Leal family. The family home was right in front of the marketplace—the *parián*—in the center of the town. The term *parián* is a word from the Philippines, and the market is referred to as *el parián*. Our home existed in this exact location—although periodically it was rebuilt. Unfortunately, today it only partially exists, or some of the walls do. When I visited in 1985, a very large theater had been constructed in this place, along with a furniture store.

We had a very large home. It occupied an entire block. It was a typical Spanish-style house with an interior central patio surrounded by the various rooms and the kitchen. I had my own bedroom as a child. Much of our time was spent in and around the patio.

Linares was a very small town. It had its central square with its church and marketplace. In the evenings families and young men and women would go to the central plaza. There the young men and women would participate in the *serenata*, which consisted of the young men walking around the plaza in a clockwise direction and the young women in a counterclockwise one. This tradition goes back to Spain and was a way for young people to socialize with each other but still be under the eyes of watchful parents or elders. Boys and girls never walked together unless they were engaged. I remember by around age fifteen walking with my male friends and looking and smiling at the girls. The girls would walk on the inside and the boys on the outside of the plaza. This would take place for an hour or two each evening of the week.

I also remember attending as a young man dances at the *casino*. This was not a gambling casino but the central social hall in Linares. It was designed by Germán Leal, my father's brother, and was two blocks from our home. This is where the traditional, more middle-class families socialized. At these dances the young women would sit on one side of the hall and the young men on the other side. I didn't have a girlfriend, but I enjoyed dancing with all of the girls. A band would play, and we would dance a variety of dances, including the Charleston. Other dances would include *boleros*, waltzes, and the tango. I never took dancing lessons. I just observed and learned.

Another thing that I remember about the *casino* was that it contained the very first radio in Linares. My Uncle Germán had bought it in the early 1920s. There was no local station in Linares, so we listened to the ones in Monterrey. People would stop by the *casino* to hear the news.

**What did your family do? Were they farmers?**

They were cattle ranchers. They would sell the cattle to the local slaughter-house. People, including my family, would then purchase fresh meat at the central market. My grandfather, and later my father, owned significant parcels of land, although the family lived in Linares. My father had studied engineering in Monterrey, which is why I first wanted to study mathematics before turning to literature.

**Did your father have the equivalent of a college degree?**

Something like that. I think that he studied in the Colegio Civil in Monterrey.

**What else do you remember about growing up in Linares?**

Well, what more is there to say? It was just a regular small town.

**Would you help out on the ranch or farm?**

No, no. I never had to help out. We were city or, at least, town people. My father employed workers for the ranch. At home we had several servants who did the cooking and the cleaning. I remember that one of the servant girls would accompany my aunt to the market carrying the *canasta* [basket] where the purchased food would be placed.

**Did you have other brothers and sisters?**

Yes, although I was the oldest. I had two younger brothers, José and Antonio, and two younger sisters, María Teresa and Ángela.

**Does longevity run in your family?**

Yes. I have an aunt on my father's side who died at the age of ninety-six. I remember her and my other aunts on my father's side, who lived with us for many years. There were five aunts along with my mother, so that women completely dominated the household.

**So you had an extended family?**

Yes; it was a big household. We would sit down to large *comidas,* or main meals, around two in the afternoon. This would consist of several dishes: *caldo,* or soup; *sopa de arroz,* or rice; then meat, beans, vegetables, and fruits; and *postres,* or dessert. The meat was usually cooked as a stew. At the meal everyone conversed, including the children. My father was not strict about that. After I started school, I would come home for *comida* and then return to my classes. The adults would have their *siestas,* or afternoon naps, after the meal, but I couldn't due to school.

**What stands out the most about your childhood activities?**
The *carpa,* or traveling circus, when it came to town. I would always go. I especially liked the one-act plays, something like the *actos* of the later Teatro Campesino and Luis Valdez. One particular circus I'll never forget because my shirt caught on fire. Somehow someone threw a match while I was standing in front of the tent entrance, and it landed on my shirt, setting it on fire. I was close to home, so I ran there on fire. My mother quickly put it out before I was seriously hurt. I'll never forget this!

One other attraction of growing up in Linares was going to the local movie house, which by the early 1920s was showing American silent movies. I liked all of them but especially the comical ones, such as those featuring Charlie Chaplin. Besides American films, the theater also showed a few Italian ones, which were very popular in Mexico. All of the films would be shown about three times a week, including weekends.

Sometimes I would go with my father to Monterrey and go to the movies there. There were many more theaters in the capital city. Another attraction in Monterrey was the bullfights. My father was a real *aficionado,* or fan. These trips to Monterrey we did by train and were about two hours one way. During my last trip to Linares I discovered that this train no longer operates.

**Did you have a happy childhood?**
Yes, although we were dislocated during the Mexican Revolution of 1910 – 1920. We had to flee to Mexico City around 1915 or 1916 due to the conflict. I was still quite young then. We left Linares due to the fighting in the surrounding area. Not everyone left, but of those who did, some went to the United States and others, like my family, went to Mexico City. Some of my relatives went to New York City. We first went to Saltillo and then to Mexico City.

**What do you remember about the trip?**
We went by train. I remember nights in a hotel in Saltillo where I could hear the hoofs of the horses as they passed by on the street. I'll never forget the

train that we were on running over and killing a young boy and the terrible shout by the boy when this happened. And I remember the train being very crowded.

**What happened to your father's ranch?**

He abandoned it and the cattle were stolen. He left our home in charge of my aunts, who refused to leave. When we returned we resumed living in it.

**What other conditions do you remember about the revolution?**

What impressed me the most were the *fusilamientos*—the executions. I remember witnessing some of these.

**Was your father political? Did he support the revolution?**

He was very much in favor of the revolution. He didn't participate in the military fighting, but as an engineer he helped build bridges for the revolutionaries. He was with a group that followed Lucio Blanco, who is not a very well-known revolutionary general but an important one. No one has studied him, as far as I know. During the early phase of the revolution, he captured Matamoros on the Texas-Tamaulipas border. He was also one of the first northern leaders who tried to make an alliance with Emiliano Zapata, the leader of the peasants in the south. Lucio Blanco was later deceived and killed in Laredo, Texas, by some of the other revolutionary leaders.

**Do you remember your father talking to you about the revolution?**

Yes. He said that the revolution was the only way for Mexico to change and to progress.

**How long did your family stay in Mexico City?**

Not a very long time before we went back to Linares. This was some time after 1918, when things had calmed down.

**What were your parents like?**

Both of my parents were very kind people. They rarely punished us.

**Would you say that you grew up in a patriarchal household?**

Yes, to an extent. We had an extended family with many adult women. My father let the women run the home. I particularly remember my Aunt Josefina, who seemed to be the dominant figure in running the house, even more than my mother. But I'm sure that my father made the ultimate decisions regarding our family.

**What was your relationship with your father?**

It was a wonderful relationship. He always wanted me to learn and to improve. By the time I had learned to read in school, my father always made sure that I read at home. He would have me read part of the newspaper each evening. This was *El Porvenir* from Monterrey. He would then have me discuss what I had read with him. This practice went on for most of my childhood.

Reading was very much a part of my home life. My father had lots of books. Many were technical books, but he also possessed many nineteenth-century Spanish novels. At one point, he bought for us children an encyclopedia set. I remember being fascinated by it and reading many of the entries, as well as being impressed by the pictures.

When I was about fourteen or fifteen, I read most all of *Don Quixote* on my own outside of school. I loved it and was particularly attracted to the humor of the novel. Much later in my career, when I formally studied it and taught it, I appreciated many other aspects of this great classic. But in my youth, it was the humor that I liked. In fact, I would read a part of *Quixote* to my younger siblings in the afternoons when we returned from school. They would laugh at the humor.

**And what was your relationship with your mother like?**

Just as wonderful. She was a loving mother. She and my grandmother, Mamá Lola, were very religious—very Catholic. My mother would read the catechism to us once a week. We accompanied her to Mass every Sunday. My father, however, didn't go to Mass. He wasn't antireligious, but he just didn't go to church.

**In what other ways was religion a part of your life in Linares?**

I remember the *posadas* at Christmas time, when for the appropriate nine days all of the families of Linares participated by visiting different homes to commemorate the search by Mary and Joseph for shelter in which the baby Jesus could be born. Besides Christmas, the other major religious feast was the *semana santa*, or Holy Week, leading to Easter. In fact, all throughout the forty days of Lent we fasted by not eating any meat. On Good Friday we would go to our church—San Felipe—and recite *el rosario,* the rosary. There was no reenactment of the crucifixion. On Saturday—the *sábado de gloria*—large cardboard human figures representing devils would be hung up in the plaza and filled with firecrackers. That morning they would be exploded. Then on Easter Sunday we all went to church, including my father, and then went home to a big *comida*.

In our home, I don't recall a home altar, only pictures of the *Corazón de Jesús* [the Sacred Heart of Jesus]. I don't think we had pictures of the *Virgen de Guadalupe*. My aunts belonged to the *Hijas de María* [the Daughters of Mary], who helped out in the church and organized some of the religious festivities.

I guess I was as religious as any other young Catholic in Linares. I learned my catechism. I went to Sunday Mass and attended the other services of the church. Of course, I was baptized and confirmed. In a small town such as Linares, everyone knew if you went to Mass or not. I remained religious until I came to the United States. I found the American Catholic church too foreign and different from what I was used to—including the use of English in the sermons. So, little by little, I stopped going to church. However, I still consider myself a Catholic.

**What schools did you go to? Did you go to public schools?**

I attended a small Catholic school. It was close to our home. Most of the traditional families sent their children to it and not to the public school, where the poorer children went. The school consisted of *primaria* [elementary school], up to and including the sixth grade, and *preparatoria* [a combination junior and senior high school], up to and including the ninth grade. My teachers were priests, whom I believe were Jesuits, although they didn't wear their clerical robes while teaching. The school was coed, but boys and girls were separated in their own classrooms. The girls were taught by nuns. We didn't wear uniforms, but had to go to school nicely dressed. The teachers were good, but very strict. I remember one time I must have done something wrong and I was punished by a hard slap of a ruler on my palm. One teacher taught all of the different subjects in each class. However, sometimes a teacher would have two grades in one class, and alternated instruction.

**Who decided that you would go to Catholic school?**

My mother. She was very religious. She didn't care for the more liberal education in the public school, including the fact that the government chose the required textbooks.

**Did you start at this school before you had to flee Linares?**

Yes. My education was interrupted due to the revolution. I was in about the third or fourth grade when we had to leave. In Mexico City I didn't attend school. When we returned to Linares, the Catholic school also resumed, and I started my classes again.

**Did the anticlerical provisions of the Constitution of 1917 affect the Catholic school?**

I was not aware of any change. The anticlerical movement was not very strong in northern Mexico.

**What kind of education did you receive?**

A very general education. I still remember some of the books we read. I remember one especially that had a great influence over me. It was a translation of a book of short stories, *Cuore,* written by the Italian writer Edmundo de Amicis—who was a very famous late-nineteenth-century and early-twentieth-century writer.

**Why did this book have a particular influence on you?**

Because the characters in the stories were boys like myself. There was one story about a boy who came from Italy to the Argentine plains, and his description of the pampas reminded me very much of Linares. I remember another story called "El pequeño vigía Lombardo," about a boy who dies when *guerilleros,* or revolutionaries, attack his town. It reminded me of events around the Mexican Revolution. In fact, I was later surprised to learn that I had read a Spanish translation of an Italian story. I had thought it was a Mexican story. I think that this exposure to these stories and my later discovery that they were Italian ones influenced me to study Italian—especially the Italian short story—as a minor when I went to graduate school.

**Is this when your interest in literature began?**

Yes, in these younger years. I always liked to read as a young boy. I was always reading. I still remember many of the books I read as a boy. Many of them were adventure stories, including Victor Hugo's *Les Misérables,* which I read, of course, in translation.

**You've mentioned books in translation, but did you also read as a young boy books written by Mexican authors?**

Yes. One writer in particular I very much enjoyed. This was Rosas Moreno, who wrote rhymed fables during the nineteenth century. These fables were used to teach ethics, and we had to read and memorize them in class. Later I discovered that the famous American poet William Cullen Bryant had translated Rosas Moreno.

**Is Rosas Moreno a forgotten writer in Mexican literature?**

Yes, because fables are unfortunately not used in schools anymore.

**But was Rosas Moreno an important Mexican writer?**

Yes. He also published a little book called *Los chiquitines,* or *The Young Kids,* which is now a very rare book. I'm fortunate to own a copy of it.

**What else did the curriculum consist of at your school?**

Arithmetic, grammar—lots of grammar—history, geography, but no foreign language. I was particularly good at mathematics.

**What did history consist of?**

It was primarily the history of Mexico, although we also studied the history of Latin America and of Spain. In geography, we had to learn all of the states and districts of Mexico, including the capital cities.

**What about religion—was that taught?**

It consisted of going to the church once a week, where some of the parents, such as my mother, would teach catechism.

**Did you have social functions at school?**

We had poetry recitals and we put on plays, especially during religious and civic *fiestas*. I remember once in sixth grade being asked to recite a poem for Columbus Day, only to forget the poem as I stood up in front of the students and parents, including my own. I was so embarrassed!

**As you look back on it, how important was your Catholic education?**

It was very important. In addition to the subject matter, I learned discipline. I learned to do my work. I learned punctuality—to be on time. All of this has stayed with me all of my life.

**After *preparatoria*, what additional education did you have in Linares?**

The *preparatoria* was equivalent to high school. There wasn't anything beyond it, at least not in Linares. You could get more education in big cities such as Monterrey, but not in small towns such as Linares. In Monterrey, for example, you could go to *escuelas normal,* or normal schools, to become a teacher. You have to remember also that in Mexico at that time most kids didn't go beyond *primaria,* or sixth grade, if they even went this far.

I was fortunate because I was able to continue my education at home. It was a kind of home schooling. Not only did I continue reading, but my parents structured my education at home. I would work in my father's study for several hours. He would select certain texts for me in mathematics, history, and other subjects. When he returned home in the evenings, we would discuss my day's assignments. My mother participated in my home education by selecting literary texts for me. "Read Amado Nervo," she would say and give me one of his collections of short stories and poems. My father also chose literary selections, in particular from his collection of Spanish novels. He gave me readings from Pedro Antonio de Alarcón, José María de Pereda, and Benito Pérez Galdós. One Mexican writer that he assigned was Federico Gamboa.

In history, I continued reading on the history of Mexico. My father especially wanted me to read about pre-Colombian history. I think this is where I developed my interest in this period. He also had me read *México a través de los siglos,* which is a multivolume history of Mexico edited by Vicente Riva Palacio.

All of this studying at home meant that I had to develop my self-discipline, which I did.

**What about your religious education?**
That consisted of attending church.
**How long did this home schooling last?**
For about two or three years.

## The Mexican Revolution of 1910

**MG: Don Luis, you experienced the Mexican Revolution. How much influence did the revolution have on your sense of identity?**
It certainly influenced my ideas. I have always felt that it was a good thing for Mexico to have had the revolution. Before the revolution, for example, there was really no such thing as Mexico. There were regions and various political factions, but there was little sense of national identity. The revolution helped produce such an identity. It linked the north and south and other regions together. The revolution worked toward the incorporation of the Indian. Despite the fact that over a million Mexicans died during the revolution, Mexico comes of age as a result of the revolution. Now, what happens after 1940 or so is another matter.

**As you know, some historians, such as Ramón Eduardo Ruiz, argue that the Mexican Revolution was not really a major social revolution. Ruiz contends that it was largely a political rebellion led and dominated by the middle classes, who were disenchanted with Díaz because he wouldn't share political power with them. What do you think of this thesis?**
I admire Professor Ruiz and his work. However, I don't agree with his analysis of the revolution. Of course, the revolution was made by some prominent landowners, such as Francisco Madero, but at the same time there were also many other, smaller landowners. In other words, it wasn't just an elite middle class who benefited from the revolution. Many other groups also benefited.

**If Ruiz is correct in his conclusions, then this implies that the only major changes the revolution produced were political ones. But it begs the question whether there weren't other major changes.**
Well, I think the revolution changed many things. Some of the Indians were integrated. But more significantly the revolution represents the ascendance to power of the mestizo. The common people come to power in many small communities. In Linares, for example, it wasn't the aristocrats or a new aristocracy who came to power after the revolution, but the common people.

So perhaps we need to look at the revolution not just from the top down, as Ruiz does, but from the bottom up, especially at the local level.

Right. In many towns, previous *caciques*, or local political bosses, were replaced by citizens' committees. These changes, as I mentioned before, were also racial. Previous *criollos*, or "white" elites, were replaced by mestizos.

And, as you also mentioned earlier, one of the changes has to do with a new national identity.

Yes. Before the revolution there was no national unity. The revolution created a sense of being mexicano. There is that wonderful little book, *Juan Pérez Jolote*, which deals with a Chamula Indian who becomes a part of the revolution and in so doing becomes a mexicano. Not only Indians but many rural people before the revolution had no sense of what Mexico was. The revolution had the effect of bringing people together in a common cause and developing nationalism.

Do you think that Mariano Azuela, one of the great writers of the Mexican Revolution, captures much of the essence of the revolution?

Well, Azuela captures some of the essence. But in order to understand Azuela you have to know that Azuela was a Villista, a follower of Pancho Villa. If you don't know that, you can't understand Azuela, because his critique of the revolution is not aimed at the Porfiristas, Porfirio Díaz's dictatorship, but at the Carrancistas, the followers of General Venustiano Carranza, who detested Villa. Of course, in his very early writings Azuela criticized Díaz.

But a book such as *Los de abajo* [*The Underdogs*] is really a critique of the Carrancistas.

That's right. *Los de abajo* is a statement about those who, unfortunately, took advantage of the revolution for their own personal gains. Azuela called these people *los tejones* [the badgers].

Do you think that Azuela would agree with Ruiz's assessment of the revolution?

Yes. Although I think that the revolution was more complicated than just the idea that it was only a middle-class and cynical revolution. There is an ultimate betrayal of the revolution, and both Ruiz and Azuela are correct in this, but this doesn't mean that the revolution was only for one class and that only one class benefited from it.

It's interesting that Azuela first published *Los de abajo* in a Spanish-language newspaper in El Paso, Texas, *El Paso del Norte*, which serialized the novel.

Azuela lived in exile in El Paso for a short period of time during the revolution. He had an interesting background. He was a medical doctor who had studied in Guadalajara. For a long time no one knew where Azuela had studied to become a doctor. But in researching my book on Azuela, I discovered his actual transcripts, which conclusively prove that he trained in Guadalajara. He then joined the revolution with the Villistas. When Villa was defeated by his rival, General Alvaro Obregón, at the battle of Celaya, many of the Villistas, including Azuela, crossed the border. Azuela found himself in El Paso. There another Villista, Fernando Gamiochipi, was publishing *El Paso del Norte*. He befriended Azuela, let him live at his print shop, and it was there that Azuela finished *Los de abajo,* which he already had been writing. This led to its publication in Gamiochipi's paper. After the entire novel was serialized, it was published as a book in 1915. A second edition of *Los de abajo* was later published in Mexico, in Tampico I believe, in a newspaper called *El Mundo,* which serialized this edition. Unfortunately, no copies of this newspaper have survived. I have never been able to find it. Azuela wrote a third version, which came to light in 1923. Up to this point, no one knew of the existence of the novel. However, after the revolution, when there was an effort to promote a new national literature in Mexico, the novel received attention.

**Why was the novel not known in Mexico before this?**

Because the newspaper *El Paso del Norte* was not distributed in Mexico.

**Could one make the case that because *Los de abajo* was first published in El Paso, it has a linkage to Chicano literature?**

Yes, I think so. In fact, some who don't know much about Chicano literature think that *Los de abajo* is Chicano literature. It can be considered to be a part of early Chicano literature in that it not only was written by a Mexican in the United States, but it deals with the Mexican Revolution, which is a central experience for many immigrants and refugees who crossed the border into the United States and formed the nucleus for many contemporary Chicano communities. Besides *Los de abajo,* other novels written by Mexican exiles were produced in Texas and other southwestern locations during the period of the Mexican Revolution. We're just beginning to discover the extent of this literature, which I believe has a link to Chicano literature. Many of these novels were published in San Antonio by the newspaper *La*

*Prensa.* These are novels of the revolution. For example, one is called *La patria perdida* [*The Lost Homeland*], by a Teodoro Torres. The first part of the novel takes place in Kansas.

**So there is a link or genealogy between the novel of the Mexican Revolution and Chicano literature?**

There's no question about it. I would say that the real link is with the Chicano novel, not with Chicano literature in general. Part of this linkage concerns the structure or themes in the Chicano novel, where the protagonist is a Villista who comes to the United States. You see this in the novel *El Coyote the Rebel* by Luis Pérez and, of course, in *Pocho* by José Antonio Villarreal.

**Do you consider Azuela to be the greatest writer of the Mexican Revolution?**

I would say that he is one of the two most important writers of the revolution, the other being Martín Luis Guzmán, who wrote *El águila y la serpiente* [*The Eagle and the Serpent*]. In his work, Guzmán sees the revolution from the perspective of its leaders, such as Villa, Carranza, and Obregón, whereas Azuela saw it from the perspective of the soldier.

**Which of the two was the better writer?**

Guzmán was the better writer. He was more conscious of style than Azuela was. I prefer Azuela to Guzmán, however, because I think that Azuela was more sensitive to common people than was Guzmán, who held many elitist notions.

**Don Luis, after experiencing the revolution, and after going through high school in Linares, you decided to come to the United States to continue your education. Why did you decide to do this?**

I didn't have many choices about my education. The times into the 1920s were very uncertain. The national university in Mexico City was not functioning, nor was the state university in Monterrey. I had some friends who had already gone to Chicago, to Northwestern University, to study. So I followed them.

**Did you or your family know English?**

My mother knew a little bit, but not my father. I also knew a little but not much.

**Did they teach English in the school at Linares?**

No, but I had studied a little English from books. I could read some, but not converse in it.

**Was there any American influence in Linares?**

Not much, although the owner of the electric company was an Englishman.

# The Norteño Type

**MG: Before discussing your coming to the United States, I wanted to discuss, in relationship to your growing up in Linares, whether you think there is such a thing as a *norteño* type or a specific northern Mexican personality or character.**

As a matter of fact, I have written a few recent papers on just this subject. I have been analyzing the literature from northern Mexico. What distinguishes the north from other regions of Mexico? What distinguishes its literature? I don't know whether it is really possible to conclusively determine that there is a *norteño* type, but I would suggest the following that might be used to consider this issue.

The first is that the Spanish explorations and settlements in the northern area of New Spain—in what is now part of northern Mexico—was accompanied by much fighting against the Indians. This continued well into the colonial period, after the Aztec empire in central Mexico had been pacified. This produced in the north a type of strong frontier character somewhat similar to the western figure in U.S. history. But this frontier influence on the Mexican northern personality has not been studied very much, whereas in the United States this has been done much more extensively, beginning with the work of Frederick Jackson Turner.

A second factor in possibly influencing a *norteño* type would be the climate and geography of the north. They are more distinct and rugged than in other parts of Mexico.

A third characteristic is the influence of the United States on the north because of the proximity. This, of course, raises a question of what constitutes the north of Mexico. Is it only the states adjacent to the United States, or does it include other states, such as Durango, that don't have a common border with the United States but are certainly geographically situated in the north?

A fourth characteristic concerns the Indian customs of the north, which have been and are different from Indian cultures in other parts of Mexico. Then there are some linguistic differences in the north. People from the north—the *norteños*—speak Spanish somewhat differently than in other parts, or, at least, their accent gives them away as being from the north. And, finally, there are certain cultural differences, such as in the food consumed in the north. Unlike in other parts of Mexico, for example, where the corn tortilla is the basic staple, in the north it's the flour tortilla because wheat is grown more in the north than is corn.

And what about in literature? Is there such a thing as a *norteño* writer?
Well, this can become a complicated question. For example, who qualifies as
a *norteño* writer? Is it just writers who were born in the north? Writers who
live in the north, whether they write about the north or not? Does it include
writers from the north who live in Mexico City but don't write about the
north? In my opinion, a *norteño* writer is someone who is from the north and
who writes about the north.

**And what themes do these writers develop?**
This is something I am researching now. One of the key themes concerns
the cultural struggle in the north, which is sandwiched between the rest of
Mexico and the United States. They write about the interconnections with
the United States and the conflicts with the northern neighbor. Then there
are those who write to preserve the cultural traditions of the north, such as
its folklore and legends. Alfonso Reyes, who was from Monterrey and who
is without question one of Mexico's greatest writers, wrote about the legends
of Monterrey and the landscapes of that area, the Cerro de la Silla. Reyes, of
course, was also a very cosmopolitan writer and wrote about Greek literature
and French poetry. But he also associated himself with *el norte*.

**Can *norteño* literature be distinguished from literature of *la frontera*, or
border literature? Are they one and the same?**
Juan Rulfo wrote about the border but had never lived along the border.
Luis Spota wrote novels that deal with the border, but he also never spent
much time on the border. But to answer your question, to me *norteño* literature and border literature are the same. You can say that border literature is
an aspect of *norteño* literature.

**Do you identify yourself as a *norteño*?**
Yes. I along with other *norteños* speak Spanish in a particular way. This is
true all over Mexico. You can distinguish people by their speech patterns
and dialect. For example, you can distinguish a Yucateco—someone from
Yucatán. Yucatecos are also very nationalistic about their region. They even
wanted to secede from Mexico at one point.

**Has there been much interest by literary critics who work with Mexican
literature on both sides of the border in *norteño* literature—or in the
regional literature of Mexico, for that matter?**
Unfortunately no. The work I've been recently doing on *norteño* literature is
among the first in this area. There are references to *norteño* literature but no
substantive studies.

**Who would you consider to be the best contemporary *norteño* writers?**

There are writers such as Carlos Montemayor, who writes about the mines of the north. There is Jesús Gardea from Ciudad Juárez, who writes short stories about border life. These two are among the best.

**Do writers such as Montemayor and Gardea have much *éxito* [success] in Mexico City?**

Yes, to a certain extent. Montemayor lives in Mexico City, which helps him. Gardea, on the other hand, still lives in Juárez, which doesn't help him. The problem over the years has been the "brain drain" of writers leaving the north or other regions and going to Mexico City—the center of the country. Mexico City has a way of attracting and co-opting many of these writers, who forget about their roots and begin to write about the urban Mexico City experience.

# Chapter Two

## Chicago

*Leal in Chicago, Illinois, early 1930s.*

# Northwestern University

MG: Let's go back to your migration to Chicago. You left in 1927 to come to Northwestern University because some friends were already studying there. You went to study mathematics. Why was there this Linares connection with Northwestern? Why didn't these students go to a closer American school, such as the University of Texas?

LL: I don't know exactly why there was this connection. These were young men also from the traditional families and who had gone to the Catholic school. I think that the connection may have had to do with the Englishman who operated the electrical plant. He had been in Chicago prior to coming to northern Mexico and he probably had arranged for these students to come into contact with Northwestern.

What do you remember about making your decision to apply and go to Northwestern?

I was in touch with these young men. I would talk to them about their experiences when they returned during summertime. They would talk about their classes, the football games, and the girls! They encouraged me to join them. I wrote to Northwestern and they sent me an application form. I was provisionally accepted until I learned sufficient English to become a regular student.

What do you recall about your initial journey to Northwestern?

I was nineteen and ready to go. My father accompanied me to Monterrey. From there I was on my own. I took the train to San Antonio and then transferred to the Missouri Pacific line to St. Louis. There I changed to the Chicago and Alton Railroad, which took me into Chicago. During the trip I had difficulty ordering a meal due to my very limited English. I would go into the club car, be seated, and then just point to an item—any item—on the menu. Somehow I got by!

*Leal in Chicago, 1944.*

**Where did you first live? On campus or off campus?**

I moved in with my friends from Linares. They were renting rooms in a boarding house off campus managed by a Mexican family by the name of Morales who were from León, Guanajuato. They had come to Chicago a few years before to work. They had either bought this house or were renting it. It was on the north side of Chicago not far from Evanston, where Northwestern is located.

**How did you learn English?**

My friends helped me. I read or tried to read on my own. I sat in on classes, including one on English phonics. I went to the movies and concentrated on the subtitles until the "talkies" appeared, and then I listened to the dialogue. Little by little my English improved, until after a few years I began to take classes in math, science, English, and other undergraduate courses. After I was formally enrolled I even took a course on Shakespeare. But it took me seven years to master English, which is why I didn't complete my B.A. until 1940.

**What was the most difficult thing about learning English?**

The pronunciation. I found that learning to read English was not as difficult as learning to speak it. Even after half a century I still have problems with pronunciation. Writing English was not that difficult.

**Did you have to work after you got to Northwestern?**

I had a part-time job. I worked with a fellow who was from Colombia. He ran a business translating from English to Spanish and vice-versa. He hired me to proofread the Spanish. He did a lot of work for the John Deere Company, which manufactured tractors and sold many to Latin America. My parents also would send me money to help pay for my room and board. The tuition at Northwestern was relatively inexpensive.

**Were Northwestern and Chicago a big change from Linares?**

It was a tremendous change. The idea I had of Chicago before arriving there did not coincide with what I found. I had visualized something entirely different, something more modern. I had seen the film *Metropolis* in the 1920s and thought Chicago was a futuristic city of the type presented in that film. But this is not what I found. There were slums and there was much poverty. Of course, this was during the Great Depression. If you went downtown you would see people selling apples. On the South Side there were the black ghettos. All this was a shock to me. I also didn't care for the cold weather.

**Were there other mexicanos or Latinos, besides your friends, who attended Northwestern?**

There were also a few other students from Latin America. Not many, but a few. Several of us lived together in the same boarding house.

**Why did you eventually change your major from math to Spanish?**

I found myself taking a number of Spanish classes rather than math classes. But the major reason was the influence of one of my Spanish teachers, Professor Roberto Brenes Mesén. He was from Costa Rica. He had been Costa Rica's ambassador to the United States before teaching at Northwestern. He taught Latin American literature. He interested me in literary criticism and in literary history. I studied modernism with him.

**What did your father think about this change in major?**

He was supportive. I never had a conflict with my parents over such matters.

**Would you return to Linares for visits?**

Oh, yes, especially during the summer. But I always returned to Chicago.

I had thought about returning to Linares after my B.A., but I was becoming more comfortable in Chicago and establishing more friends. The only thing I couldn't get used to in Chicago was the food. I didn't like American food. I tried cooking for myself but there were no adequate Mexican ingredients to cook with. This was one of the cultural shocks I experienced in Chicago.

**Chicago, of course, as well as other areas of the Midwest, had already been experiencing a significant migration of Mexicans in the period following World War I. Where did most Mexicans live in Chicago?**

There were large numbers of Mexicans in Chicago as well as in certain other nearby areas. In Gary, Indiana, for example, many Mexicans had been working in the steel mills. Gary was very much a Mexican town. In Chicago, most Mexicans lived on the West Side. They lived on Halsted and Roosevelt Streets, close to the Virgen de Guadalupe Church and also close to Hull House, which had been founded by Jane Adams to assist earlier immigrants from Europe. After World War II these Mexican neighborhoods around Hull House were destroyed, and the Mexicans were forced to live elsewhere so that the University of Illinois, Chicago Circle, could be constructed. It was also after the war that many Puerto Ricans began settling in Chicago. They moved into the North Side.

**When you first went to Chicago in the 1930s, what were the conditions of the Mexicans there?**

It was very bad. In fact, many of these conditions haven't changed very much. There was a great deal of poverty and people working for low wages. There were also a number of Mexicans who had no documents because they had entered the United States without permission.

**Was there hostility toward Mexicans?**

This was especially the case in 1938 after Mexico expropriated the oil industry, which affected many American oil companies. There was a big reaction against Mexican people. There was talk of invading Mexico.

**Did you ever personally experience discrimination in Chicago?**

No, I didn't, and I don't recall that my friends did either.

**But was there a clearly defined Mexican barrio in Chicago?**

There was. You could find Mexican restaurants, barber shops, book stores, grocery stores, and, of course, the Church.

**Did the presence of the Mexican barrio in Chicago help ease your transition?**

Yes, it helped very much. As I said, there were a number of Mexican shops and businesses there. I remember going to a Mexican barber shop where the barber kept a machine gun. These were the days of Al Capone and gangsters. This barber was somehow involved in some of these activities.

**And what was Northwestern like as a campus?**

It was a beautiful campus just like here at UCSB. It was by Lake Michigan.

**What kind of students attended Northwestern?**

It was mostly Anglo-American students with a few foreign students, such as those of us from Mexico and Latin America.

**So students were still going to college even though there was a depression? They had enough money, or their parents did, to send them to a private school such as Northwestern?**

Oh, yes. In Evanston, you didn't really notice or feel the Depression. It was only when you went into Chicago, especially in the downtown area.

**When you decided to major in Romance languages, specifically in Spanish, did you have any idea then of becoming a university professor?**

No, not really. I remember taking one of those aptitude tests which are supposed to give you an idea of future career possibilities. Most of the ones suggested for me I wasn't interested in at all. However, one was to become a teacher. I did know that I enjoyed reading and studying literature and that I hoped I could continue to do so.

**When you decided to switch to Spanish, was this also done because that department could provide you with a sense of cultural community in an otherwise Anglo campus? Perhaps it was a way of dealing with whatever cultural alienation you were experiencing in Chicago.**

That's right.

**What was the state of Latin American literature at Northwestern?**

It was not stressed very much. Most of the professors were in Spanish pen-

insular literature. There were only two professors who taught Latin American literature. There was Brenes Mesén and then there was Professor William Berien, who came to Northwestern during my senior year. He specialized in South American literature and had studied with Arturo Torres-Rioseco at Berkeley. Berien had done a dissertation on José Enrique Rodó, the famous Uruguayan writer. He later went to Harvard and then to UCLA. **What were some of the texts in Latin American literature that you read in your classes with these professors?**
At this time, there was a heavy emphasis on *modernismo* as well as what was called *la novela de la tierra*, the novel of the land. Examples of this form of novel were *Los de abajo* and *Doña Bárbara* by Rómulo Gallegos. We also read some of the nineteenth-century writers, such as Blest Gana from Chile, Ignacio Manuel Altamirano from Mexico, Amado Nervo, also from Mexico, Jose Martí from Cuba, and, of course, the great *modernista* poet from Central America, Rubén Darío.

## Rubén Darío and Amado Nervo

**As an undergraduate, I believe that you wrote a paper on Darío. What interested you about him?**
I was fascinated by Darío's use of language in his poetry and the images he created. Darío created new forms of poetry influenced by the French writers. He broke with the romantic tradition of writing poetry. The paper that I wrote concerned Darío's experiences in Mexico during the turn of the century, when Porfirio Díaz was still in power. I later published this paper. I also wrote another paper on Darío's *nocturnos*, which are a form of lyrical poetry. In his poems, Darío always expressed his fear of darkness and death. That attracted me very much. I later revised these papers and published them.
**What would you say is Darío's place in Latin American literature?**
He was the creator of a new style of poetry beginning in the late 1880s. In addition, with his book *Azul . . .* (1888), he also introduced a new form of prose and short story which had a very important influence on the contemporary short story in Latin America because Darío breaks totally with the earlier *costumbristas* and *realistas*. The *costumbristas* were interested mainly in describing the customs of the period and characterizing the types prevalent in society, without giving their *cuadros* any plot. The *realistas* went beyond that and painted society in all its aspects, not just the picturesque.

**Can you say that Latin American literature begins with Darío?**
Modern literature, but not all of Latin American literature.

**When you wrote your paper on Darío, what professor did you write it for?**
For Professor Brenes Mesén.

**Do you remember his response to your paper?**
Yes, he liked it very much.

**You also, I believe, wrote an undergraduate paper on Amado Nervo. What was the attraction of Nervo for you?**
Of the Mexican *modernistas*, Nervo was the most important. The fact that he was from Mexico attracted me. Darío is the greatest *modernista*, but Nervo is also one of the key writers of this literary movement. Nervo was still quite popular in the 1930s. Today nobody reads him.

**Why was Nervo important? What was it about his writings that brought him attention?**
Nervo introduces into *modernismo* a new style, which you could call the spiritual aspect of life in his poetry. This was not characteristic of other *modernista* writings, which were more objective. The *modernista* was not subjective, but Nervo was. This distinguished him from the other writers, including Darío.

**What do you mean by *objective*?**
Describing things as you see them. Things that are material are objective. By contrast, Nervo is spiritual. He writes about the spiritual aspects of life. By doing so, he expanded *modernismo* into a new dimension.

**What did you specifically write about Nervo in your paper?**
I concentrated on his short stories because I was interested in this genre. As a matter of fact, a few years later I edited and published a collection of Nervo's short stories.

**Is Nervo more or less significant than Azuela in influencing contemporary Mexican literature?**
Oh, there's no question but that Azuela is the more significant. Azuela, of course, was not a poet, while Nervo was principally a poet, although he also wrote short stories as well as many essays.


## Modernismo

**Don Luis, could you give me a general definition of Latin American *modernismo*?**

Well, *modernismo* is a form of writing, especially in poetry, but it also includes prose, that is the result of French influence introduced into Latin America. It is also the focusing on a world that is not the everyday world. It is instead a world of the artist. *Modernismo* is not concerned with the political but with the aesthetic. It is less concerned with the local than it is with the universal.

**And *modernismo* emerges in the late nineteenth and early twentieth centuries?**

Yes. There is a first group of poets/writers referred to as the pre-*modernistas*, which includes Manuel Gutiérrez Nájera in Mexico and José Martí in Cuba. Then comes the great *modernistas,* such as Rubén Darío and Amado Nervo. There is a third group referred to as the post-*modernistas,* such as Leopoldo Lugones in the Argentine.

**So, *modernismo* comes to an end when?**

After 1910. Certainly in Mexico the demise of *modernismo* is synonymous with the Mexican Revolution.

**Since *modernismo* aspired to the universal, it obviously was incompatible with nationalism.**

Yes. In the case of Mexico, the nationalism that results from the revolution rejects *modernismo.*

**The one exception, I suppose, to this was José Martí?**

Martí, of course, as one of the great leaders of the Cuban independence movement, was very political and a strong nationalist. In his style as a poet he was seen as a *modernista.*

**You read Martí at Northwestern?**

Yes, especially his *Versos sencillos.*

**What was your reaction to Martí's writing?**

I was very much influenced by his book *Nuestra América.* I particularly liked his essays comparing George Washington to Simón Bolívar.

**How did Martí compare as a writer with Darío and Nervo?**

Martí's prose is better than Darío's or Nervo's.

## American Literature

**Don Luis, as an undergraduate did you study any literature of the United States?**

Yes, I took a course on the American novel that included writers such as

Theodore Dreiser, Henry James, and John Dos Passos.

**Who were your favorite U.S. writers during the 1930s?**

Dreiser was very popular, and I liked his work.

**Why in particular did you like Dreiser?**

Primarily because of his treatment of social problems.

**Were you reading any of the social-realist writers of the 1930s, such as [John] Steinbeck?**

I did read Steinbeck, but I may have read him outside of class. I remember reading *Tortilla Flat*, which I had some problems with in Steinbeck's caricatures of Mexicans in Monterey, California. One of Steinbeck's other novels which was of much interest to me was *The Pearl*. It's set in Baja California. What's interesting is that it is very similar to an earlier story written by Dr. Atl in Mexico.

**You mean that Steinbeck adopted the story from a Mexican writer?**

No one really knows. It's possible he may have just heard about the story in Baja California.

**Dr. Atl was a Mexican writer?**

Yes, he wrote during the revolution. He was also a muralist and painter. I had a student later at the University of Illinois who wrote a dissertation about the short stories of Dr. Atl. She even came to California to try and solve the mystery of whether Steinbeck knew of Dr. Atl's story. But she couldn't solve this.

**What about Hemingway? Did you read him in the 1930s?**

I read Hemingway—especially *For Whom The Bell Tolls*, which was very popular when it came out.

**Were you comparing U.S. writers with Latin American writers at this time?**

Not systematically, but I do recall recognizing the influence of some Spanish writers on the work of Eugene O'Neill, the great American playwright. One of his plays—I forget which one—had the same story line as a Spanish play, and I don't recall this play any longer. But the point is that it was obvious to me that O'Neill must have been acquainted with these Spanish writers.

**Isn't it amazing, Don Luis, that in the 1930s, at the same time that you're reading U.S. writers such as Hemingway, in Texas Américo Paredes was writing his novel *George Washington Gómez*, which wasn't published until 1991! Had Paredes's novel been published in the 1930s, what a difference that would have made!**

Yes. I wrote Paredes at the time the novel was finally published congratulating him and telling him that if the novel had been published in the 1930s he would have been considered as one of the pioneers in Chicano fiction.

**I think you're right. Paredes is part of that period of the 1930s and the writings about social conditions in the United States. I think his exposé of race/ethnic relations in south Texas compares to Steinbeck's work on California.**

## The Spanish Civil War

**Concerning social conditions in the 1930s, I wanted to ask you about the impact of the Spanish Civil War on Chicago. Was there much reaction? What about at Northwestern?**
It had a tremendous impact. In fact, it divided the Spanish department at Northwestern between Republicans and Loyalists, or Franquistas. The split also affected students. Everybody took sides.

**Were you on the Republican side?**
Of course! It was the side of democracy against fascism.

**Was there much activity on this issue on the campus?**
There were numerous meetings and rallies, mostly in support of the Republican cause and against the rise of fascism in Europe. Some students joined the Abraham Lincoln Brigade, which went to Spain to fight on the Republican side. This was a very emotional issue.

Another emotional issue was Mexico's expropriation of the Americans' and others' foreign oil property. Many Americans, including many students, favored U.S. intervention to recover the oil wells. As Mexicans, I and the other Mexican students supported the action of Cárdenas in expropriating the oil wells. We participated in demonstrations in the Chicago barrios defending Mexico.

## Social Life

**What was social life like for you at Northwestern?**
I spent much of my free time with my Linares friends as well as with other students from Latin America. We participated in a foreign film series and discussion group on campus. This consisted of showing French, Italian, and German films. Those of us from Latin America were able to get the organizers to show films from Mexico and Spain. We would also go to movies

in Chicago, including, now and then, Mexican movies, at a theater in the barrio called *Tampico*.

We also went to the theater in Chicago, seeing plays by writers such as O'Neill and George Bernard Shaw. From time to time we also went to the opera, which was inexpensive.

I remember going to the Chicago World's Fair in 1933, which displayed the latest technological inventions. The fair led to the construction of the Museum of Science and Industry in Chicago, which I often visited, along with the many other impressive museums in the city.

We also attended dances both on and off campus. In fact, I met my wife Gladys at one of these student dances.

## Marriage and Graduation

**One of the big changes in your life while at Northwestern was that you got married to Gladys. What year did you get married?**
It was 1936. I had met Gladys, whose family name was Clemens, at Northwestern, where she was also a student. She was from Chicago, a third-generation German American. Her grandmother still spoke German. Meeting and eventually marrying Gladys also helped me with my English.

**How did your parents feel about your getting married?**
They had no problems with it. However, my aunts were troubled because we didn't marry in the Church. It was a civil ceremony. Every time we visited Linares, my aunts wanted to know when the church wedding would take place.

**So, Don Luis, you finally graduated from Northwestern in 1940. It took you about six years, since you first had to learn English. Did you go through the graduation ceremony, and did your family attend?**
Yes. It took me a while to graduate, but I did go through the ceremony, and my parents came up from Linares.

**What would you say were the most significant intellectual influences on you at Northwestern?**
There's no doubt about it: it was Professor Brenes Mesén. Not only did he convince me to change majors, but he was a real role model for me. He was an accomplished poet and scholar and just a very nice and supportive person. I would often go to his home along with other students, and he would talk to us about numerous ideas and subjects. He wrote a book that very much

influenced my intellectual development. It was titled *Crítica Americana* [*American Criticism*] and stressed that Latin American culture and literature had to be seen and studied from a Latin American perspective rather than from the then-prevailing European perspective. This impressed me and helped shape my later work, including that on Chicano literature—the idea of analyzing Chicano literature from a Chicano perspective.

## The University of Chicago

**After graduating from Northwestern, you decided to go to the University of Chicago for your master's. Why did you decide to go to the University of Chicago?**

I decided to apply to the University of Chicago at the urging of Professor Salomón Treviño, who was in the Spanish department there. Students from the Spanish departments at Northwestern and Chicago used to get together, and it was at one of these gatherings that I met Treviño. He was a Chicano from Laredo, Texas. He was a specialist in phonetics. "Come to Chicago," he would say. "It's much better than Northwestern." Well, he was right. It was much better and more prestigious.

**Did Treviño have a Ph.D.?**

Yes, from the University of Chicago. He had taught there for several years.

**So, he's one of those unknown Mexican American/Chicano intellectuals of this early period?**

Yes, from Laredo. But at that time I didn't think of the concept of a Chicano professor.

**How long did it take you to do your master's?**

I finished in one year.

**Can you tell me about some of the papers you wrote that year?**

I wrote a long paper on the seventeenth-century Spanish golden age dramatist, Juan Ruiz de Alarcón, in a course I took on golden age drama. Ruiz de Alarcón was actually from Mexico but lived many years in Spain. He was a contemporary of Lope de Vega and Luis de Góngara, the great writers of the golden age.

**But was Ruiz de Alarcón seen more as a Spanish writer than a Mexican?**

Well, that's a big problem, because the Spaniards claim him and so do the Mexicans. There is no question, however, that he was born in Mexico.

**You were trying to rediscover Ruiz de Alarcón as a Mexican writer?**

Well, I was interested in the fact that he was from Mexico. I read all of his work. He wrote about twenty-four plays.

**Does his drama reflect his Mexican background?**

Only in one play. In this one he writes about Mexico. However, Pedro Henríquez Ureña, a famous critic from Santo Domingo, once wrote a paper noting that Ruiz de Alarcón's style is different from the other golden age writers and that this is the result of Ruiz de Alarcón's Mexican background.

**What were some of the differences between Northwestern and Chicago?**

One big difference was that Chicago was a smaller school. There were many fewer undergraduates, since the emphasis at Chicago was on graduate studies. A major difference also was the presence of Robert Hutchins as the president of the University of Chicago. He was one of the giants of university leaders then and into the future. While I was at Chicago, Hutchins introduced his innovative education reforms, such as the idea of acquiring a university degree in two years.

**This was an undergraduate degree?**

Yes. A bachelor's degree in two years. As part of Hutchins's plan, a student didn't even have to attend classes. All you had to do was to successfully pass a comprehensive exam in the enrolled subjects. You could take the exams any time you wanted to.

**So you studied at your own pace? Did the Hutchins reforms affect the graduate programs?**

To a much lesser degree. Most of his reforms were aimed at undergraduate education. Hutchins's idea was that a four-year undergraduate program involved much wasted time and could be streamlined into two years. But Hutchins's reforms failed because when students graduated under his plan, they would not be admitted to graduate schools elsewhere or professional schools which did not accept the University of Chicago's degree program. After a few years, the campus reverted to the more traditional undergraduate program based on a four-year tenure.

**What was the Spanish department like at Chicago?**

It was a very good department. Like most Spanish departments at that time, however, it stressed peninsular literature rather than Latin American literature. As a result, I studied a good deal of peninsular literature, such as that of the golden age. But there were some Latin Americanists whom I studied with, such as Professor Carlos Castillo, who taught both peninsular and Latin American literature. Castillo had been born in Spain, but had spent a lot of time in Mexico. His specialty was golden age.

**Who were some of the other professors you worked with on your M.A.?**
There was, of course, Treviño, who had recruited me to Chicago. I studied the Spanish essay with Professor Parmenter, who was also the head of the department. Then there was Professor Hayward Keniston, who was an expert on Spanish medieval literature. Some of these professors I studied with for both my M.A. and my Ph.D.

**Since the Spanish department was tilted toward peninsular Spanish, did you encounter any difficulties with your Mexican Spanish?**
I didn't personally, but you were encouraged to speak Castilian Spanish. All of the professors had to do so.

**Did you speak in Castilian Spanish?**
No, I never did. I refused to do so and got away with it. I thought it was unnatural for me to speak in Castilian Spanish. I was never penalized for this.

**For your M.A. thesis, what did you choose to write on?**
I chose to write on Amado Nervo. The thesis was directed by Professor Castillo. It was a kind of literary history of Nervo. I wrote about one hundred pages, but I never published it as a book. I later published several articles on Nervo, on his poetry and short stories.

**When did you complete your M.A.?**
In 1941.

## Doctoral Work

**Did you then go right away into your Ph.D.?**
Yes, immediately. I continued taking classes with some of the same professors. I was fortunate in 1941 and 1942 also to take classes with Professor Amado Alonso, a distinguished scholar who came from Argentina. He came to Chicago for one year. Alonso was a great influence on me. He was a linguist and a literary scholar who was very precise in his work. He was also a role model for me.

**In what way did Alonso influence you?**
In two ways: one, his emphasis on Latin American literature as opposed to peninsular literature. I took a seminar with him on Rubén Darío and Pablo Neruda. He also offered a course on the Spanish language in Latin America. A second way that he influenced me is that I learned much from him about doing research and applying literary criticism. I think that my interest in pursuing literary history was strongly influenced by Alonso.

**In Alonso's seminar, was this the first time that you were introduced to the work of Neruda?**

Yes. He was still a young poet then but already recognized as a major one. He had just published his *Residencia en la tierra*. Alonso had also just written a book on Neruda's poetry.

**What was your reaction to Neruda's poetry?**

I thought it was excellent. I especially was impressed with his new style of poetry. He could take any subject and turn it into a poetic image. Unlike Darío and the *modernistas,* whose images were crystal clear, Neruda produces images that need to be interpreted. His use of powerful topics, such as death, is also very significant. Of course, his later political poetry, such as *Machu Picchu,* was extremely powerful. He reflected a much more Latin American perspective.

**Do you consider Neruda to have been the greatest Latin American poet?**

There's no doubt about that, Mario.

**And when you were a graduate student at Chicago, what were the other students like? Were there many other students from Latin America?**

There were a few from Latin America, but not many. There were also a few Spaniards and Italians. But most were Americans. Actually, the department had few students. It was a small Romance languages department.

**Was there a particular literary tendency in your department or at Chicago as a whole?**

What was big at Chicago at the time was the New Criticism. This was the emphasis on studying the text by itself without regard to history, politics, culture, etcetera. The New Critics said, "Go to the text!" My department, unlike the English department, was not obsessed with the New Criticism, but it was around and you couldn't avoid it. I was never too taken by it because of my own interest in history and politics and their relationship to literature.

**I noticed in your vitae that in 1942 you published a short article entitled "La leyenda guadalupana" in a publication called *ABC*. What was this article about and what was *ABC?***

*ABC* was a Spanish-language newspaper in Chicago. It was published by a Mexican by the name of Armando Almonte. But the history of this particular article is that I belonged to an informal group of Latinos in Chicago, some from the colleges and some business and professional types. We used to get together once a month for lunch and invite a speaker. The Mexican consul in Chicago also would join us. Besides mexicanos, there were individuals in our group from other Latin American countries, as well as from Spain. As a matter of fact, we held our luncheons at the Sociedad Española. The Spanish consul would be our host.

For December of 1942, I was asked to give a talk on the Virgen de Guadalupe in connection with her feast day on December 12, which I did. Almonte was at the lunch, and he liked my talk. "I want to publish it," he told me. So he took my paper and published it in *ABC*. This was one of my first published pieces. I also published other essays in *ABC*.

**Beginning in the 1930s, you were involved in the mexicano community of Chicago. Why did you feel the need to be involved?**

Ever since I was an undergraduate at Northwestern I was active in one form or another in the community. I don't know why. It's probably as a result of this monthly discussion group that I became interested in community affairs.

**In the late 1930s and early 1940s, was the term *Mexican American* used in Chicago? What terms were being used? *méxico-americano*? *Chicano*?**

I don't recall the English term *Mexican American* being used, but the term *méxico-americano* was used. I never heard the term *Chicano* in Chicago at this time.

**What term did you use to identify yourself?**

I still called myself mexicano.

**Did you remain a Mexican national all during this period?**

No. I became a U.S. citizen in 1939.

**Why did you decide to become a U.S. citizen?**

Because I wanted to be able to vote and because I had decided to stay in the United States.

**Did your parents object to your becoming a U.S. citizen?**

No, they didn't have any problem with it.

**When you started your Ph.D. program at Chicago in 1941, I understand that you at the same time were hired as an instructor of Spanish, is that correct?**

Yes. One of Hutchins's reforms had been to separate the college from the division. The college was responsible for basic undergraduate teaching while the division focused on graduate studies. The faculty in the college were separate from those in the division. I was hired to teach Spanish language in the college. Since class attendance wasn't required, my students over a semester gradually disappeared. All they had to do was to pass the comprehensive exam at the end of the semester. I remember that most who didn't attend class in the end failed the exams.

**Was language, including Spanish, one of the requirements the students had to take?**

Yes. Besides a language requirement in a specific language, students also had to take a general language requirement that involved the origins of language and the history of language. This was a very good course because it showed students how languages functioned and how they developed. I once had to teach a section of this course, which was a very good experience for me.

**Was being an instructor a way of getting financial aid for your graduate studies, or were there fellowships or teaching assistantships?**

At that time, there were no fellowships or teaching assistantships. So being appointed as an instructor with an M.A. was the only way to get financial assistance. I was an instructor from 1941 to 1943. One of my duties as an instructor was to teach Spanish to a class of army officers. These were officers who were being trained to be sent during the war to countries such as Spain or to Latin America.

## World War II

*Leal (back, on left) in New Guinea during World War II, 1944.*

**Don Luis, tell me now about when you went to war. How did this happen?**

I was drafted in 1943 during World War II. My department wrote a letter to my draft board that I was needed for instructional purposes. But the draft board said no. So I was drafted. One of the ironies of becoming a U.S. citizen a few years before was that it made me eligible to be drafted into the U.S. Armed Forces. My oldest son, Antonio, was born in 1942, but having a family didn't defer you from the draft.

**Were you drafted into the army?**

Yes, although you had a choice of selecting what service you preferred. However, during my initial medical examination, it was discovered that I was color blind. I didn't know this myself. I could be put only into the army because of my color blindness. I was sent to Camp Blanding in Florida for my initial training. I was then sent to Fort Ord in California in preparation for my unit's being sent to the Pacific. Gladys and my son stayed, of course, in Chicago. They moved in with her mother.

We were put on a huge passenger ship that was being used to transport troops. We embarked from San Francisco. There were ten thousand soldiers on this ship. We went all the way down without escort to South America. From there we crossed the Pacific, first to an island close to Australia and then on to New Guinea, where we stayed for six months.

**Had New Guinea already been taken by the U.S. from Japan?**

Yes. This had occurred a little before we arrived. Many Americans died in the battle of New Guinea. We could see all of the Japanese prisoners. From New Guinea we prepared for the invasion of the Philippines.

We landed with General MacArthur in the Philippines. It was a horrible experience. Many Americans died. Many ships were sunk. When we landed on one of the smaller islands, we came under heavy bombardment. In fact, a big bomb landed right on the transport boat I was on. Fortunately, it didn't go off. Then a Kamikaze plane came in and missed us by a few feet. I was lucky that nothing happened.

**And what about when you landed?**

It was awful. We were bombed every day, every night, until Christmas. From October when we landed until Christmas we were bombed. Everybody was wounded except me. I was very lucky.

**So it took a long time to retake the Philippines?**

Yes, several months. We went from one island to another. There are many islands in the Philippines. We finally landed and took the main island of Luzón, including Manila.

**Did some of your friends die?**

Yes, some of them. Especially when we landed. Fortunately, nothing happened to me. The irony here is that many from my unit received Purple

Hearts for being wounded. I was one of the few that didn't get a Purple Heart!

**What happened after the taking of the Philippines?**

We began to prepare for the invasion of Japan. In the meantime, we stayed in the Philippines. One benefit of this was that I had had the opportunity while a student to have read some Philippine literature. So I knew some of the writers. I met some of them while on the islands. I was also impressed to see the many statues there dedicated to the great Philippine writer José Rizal. He was a great hero because he had written novels against Spain before 1898 and the Spanish-American War, which transferred the islands to U.S. possession.

**In your unit, were there many Mexican Americans?**

No, very few. Most of my unit was composed of young men from the Midwest. There were many other Chicanos, however, in other battalions.

**Were your experiences generally positive in the army, or did you face any kind of discrimination?**

Mostly positive, but there was one incident of discrimination. My lieutenant wanted me to apply for officer's training school while we were on the Philippines. I was given an interview. But during the interview, the members of the committee started asking me all sorts of questions about Mexico and Mexican politics. I must have given the wrong answers, because I didn't pass the interview.

**So they really wanted to get at your political views?**

Yes. But in a way it was okay, because I didn't really want to go to officer's school. I found out that if you did, you had to agree to serve for another two years. I didn't want to spend more time in the army.

**What were conditions like on the Philippines while you were there?**

Very bad. There were hundreds of diseases there. The worst was elephantiasis. If you went into the water you got this disease, because the water was polluted and filled with insects. Some stupid guys would go in swimming, and they would get this terrible disease. We had to take pills for malaria. You had to be careful. You couldn't go around without shoes, leggings, or long sleeves. There were plenty of snakes around. I once opened my trunk and was about to put my hand in when I noticed a big snake inside of it. It had crawled in. But I was lucky again and didn't come down with any diseases.

**So when did you return to the United States?**

I came back in November 1945. I had been in the army for two years. They put us again in a very crowded boat, which broke down in the middle of the

Pacific. It took us a month to cross the Pacific. We disembarked in Los Angeles. I went on to Chicago, where I was discharged.

**When you came out of the service, what was your rank?**
I was a staff sergeant.

**Have you ever been back to New Guinea or to the Philippines?**
No, and I don't want to.


## Return to Chicago

**When you returned from the war, did you immediately resume your graduate work?**
Yes. I had only a month's vacation. Then I started teaching full time again as an instructor of Spanish at the University of Chicago in addition to completing my Ph.D. requirements.

**Did you take advantage of the GI Bill to help in your educational expenses?**
Oh, yes, I took advantage of the GI Bill. It paid all of my tuition, books, and supplies. Many returning GIs did the same. You could even use the GI Bill to study abroad, including in Mexico and Latin America. Some later prominent scholars of Mexican literature used the GI Bill in this way.

**Why did you need to teach full time if you had the GI Bill?**
Because the GI Bill didn't provide enough to cover our living expenses.

**I noticed in your vitae that you contributed to a book published by your mentor, Professor Castillo, entitled _Antología de la literatura mexicana_, during the war years. Was this work you did before the war, and what did this work involve?**
Before I left for the war, Professor Castillo had asked me to collaborate with him in putting together an anthology of Mexican literature to be published by the University of Chicago Press. Besides helping to select some of the entries, I was also responsible for the bibliography. When I was drafted, I left Professor Castillo the work I had done, and he then finished it. The book came out in 1944. It was the first anthology of Mexican literature published in the United States. It was aimed at being used for college courses in American schools.

**Was the book widely used?**
Yes, oh, widely used!

**I noticed that the anthology covered only up to the Mexican Revolution.**

Was there a reason for that?

We felt that the rest was too recent.

**If you had to do a similar anthology over again today, what would you do differently—besides, obviously, adding material since 1910?**

I would, for example, start this time with pre-Columbian literature, which we didn't include in the original text.

**What about including women writers? I noticed that with the exception of Sor Juana Inés de la Cruz, there are no women writers.**

Of course! This would be an additional change.

**Was the exclusion of women writers, except for Sor Juana, due to the fact that many women writers in Mexico were not well known or recognized?**

That's right. There were writers such as María Enriqueta Camarillo de Pereyra, but she was not well known. She lived in Spain.

**Of course, this criticism of the exclusion of women writers only comes as a result of a certain hindsight now. Now, Don Luis, I notice that also in 1944 you assisted in the publication of something called *Cuentecitos: Retold and Adopted from the Spanish of Vicente Riva Palacio* published by Heath. What did this entail?**

This series of texts was conceived by Professor Bond, who was the chair of the Romance languages department in the college at Chicago, and Professor Castillo. They were the editors of a series of readers designed to help American students develop a reading knowledge of Spanish. They had made a study of the teaching of foreign languages in American high schools and discovered that students generally only took two years of a foreign language. They understood that two years was insufficient time to teach someone how to speak a foreign language, but you could teach them to read it, at least on a basic level. They adopted a system used in India to teach English to students there. This system involved only eight hundred basic English words. The readers devised by Bond and Castillo were aimed at teaching reading Spanish with a very limited vocabulary. Before I went to the war, Castillo asked me to prepare one of these readers, which I did.

**So you took stories written by Riva Palacio and adopted them for this purpose. Was it your idea to use stories by Riva Palacio?**

Yes, it was my idea.

**Why did you choose Riva Palacio?**

He was a Mexican writer. He came from a very famous Mexican family, and he had been a general in the Mexican army. He began writing novels in the 1870s. These were historical novels; he wrote about twenty of these. After he was named ambassador to Spain, he began to also write short stories, and he published a collection under the title of *Cuentos del general [Short Stories of the General]*. This became a very popular book, especially among students. They were humorous stories. Many were written almost like anecdotes.

**Was Riva Palacio recognized as an important writer?**

He was recognized at the time as an important writer of historical novels, but no one reads these novels very much now, although his short stories are still read.

**And you thought that these short stories would be enjoyed by students here in the United States?**

Yes.

**Were these readers used very much in this country?**

Oh, yes! This little reader that I did eventually sold over a million copies.

**Did you receive royalties?**

Yes, but it only sold for about thirty-five cents, so I didn't get very much. But I did get some royalties for several years. The reader was used for about twenty years in different high schools. I later did about three or four more of these readers.

**After you returned from the war and resumed your graduate studies, did you also still continue to publish these *cuentecitos*?**

Yes. The series published by D. C. Heath continued, and they wanted me to put together some additional ones. The first that I did after the war was *El periquillo sarniento*, from the novel by Fernández de Lizardi.

**Was this a condensation of Lizardi's novel?**

A supercondensation, because it was a big novel. I just took some of the interesting scenes and rewrote them in a simple vocabulary.

**What is the background of this novel?**

It is the first Mexican novel. It was published in 1816. It can even be considered the first Latin American novel. It's a picaresque novel. It takes place in Mexico City. It's about a young man whose parents want him to be a lawyer or a priest, but he doesn't want this for himself. So he becomes a *pícaro*—a rogue. But the novel is a criticism of Mexican society during the last years of Spanish colonial rule. Lizardi at this time was also writing pamphlets criticizing the Spanish colonial government. He was put in prison for this and used the time to write his novel. It became the most popular book in Mexico.

**Had you read *El periquillo* when you were in school in Mexico?**

Yes, I read it. Every student read it, just like we all read *Don Quixote*.

You also then published a similar condensation of [Domingo Faustino] Sarmiento's famous work, *[Civilization and Barbarism: Life of Juan] Facundo*, which is an Argentinean text concerning the role of the *caudillo*— the strong-arm political leader—in Argentina during the nineteenth century. Why did you choose *Facundo*?

I don't remember. The first part of *Facundo* is very interesting because it is a biography of Facundo, the *caudillo*. The second part is mostly political theory. I concentrated on the biography.

Sarmiento, in this text and in others, juxtaposed the themes of civilization and barbarism in Argentina. He sees civilization in Buenos Aires but barbarism in the *pampas*, in the countryside. What was your reaction to Sarmiento's perspective?

Well, you're correct in this. Sarmiento sees in the *gaucho*, or the Argentine cowboy, the prototype of the *caudillo*, or as representing barbarism. He sees the *gaucho* as the result of the Arabic or non-Western influence in Spanish culture. He sees the *gaucho* as symbolizing the nomadic, non-Western life in Argentina and thus the barbaric. This is a traditional theme also found in Spain itself. It goes back to at least the fifteenth century. It's a romantic theory which I, of course, didn't accept.

What were your objections to Sarmiento's theory?

The problem with Sarmiento is that he does not take into serious consideration the important role of popular culture. He didn't appreciate or understand the culture of the *gaucho*, or of the Indian, for that matter. The counter to *Facundo* is the great epic poem by José Hernández, *Martín Fierro*, which sees the *gaucho* as a great hero.

Is the theme of civilization and barbarism a theme that is also visible in Mexican writings of the nineteenth century?

No. For example, Altamirano is the most famous Mexican writer of the nineteenth century, but he doesn't write about this theme.

When you returned to your graduate program, did you still have to take seminars?

Yes. The department didn't have a well-planned program which prescribed a certain number of seminars you had to take. They kept asking you to take additional seminars. Whenever your major professor thought you were ready to take your qualifying exams, then you took them.

How long did it take you after you returned to your program in early 1946 to take your exams?

I took my exams in 1949. I probably should have taken them earlier, but with teaching full time and with family obligations, I felt that I couldn't take them any earlier.

**What were the fields in which you were examined?**

You had to have four fields, including your major one. In my case, my major field was Latin American literature, and my secondary fields were Spanish golden age, contemporary Spanish literature, and Italian literature. In addition, I had to take two language exams outside of my major field. So I took these exams in French and German.

**Did your qualifying exams include both written and oral exams?**

For the major field it included an oral and a written exam, but only a written exam for the other three fields.


## Origins of the Mexican Short Story

**After you passed your exams, what did you choose to work on for your dissertation?**

The origins of the Mexican short story, under Professor Castillo. The title of my dissertation was "El cuento y la leyenda en las crónicas de la Nueva España." What I examined were the fictional elements contained within the chronicles written by the Spanish after the conquest of the Aztec empire. My thesis was that these fictional elements constitute the origins of the Mexican short-story form. I read all the chronicles of the conquest from the sixteenth century to the eighteenth century and extracted all of the fictitious portions.

**The chronicles are usually considered to represent factual and historical texts. How is it that you distinguished between history and fiction in these texts?**

Because history and fiction were in fact not distinguished at that time. The *cronistas* did not differentiate between history and fiction. When you read the chronicles you immediately realize that most of them are fiction rather than history.

**Did you already realize this fictional aspect to the chronicles before you started the dissertation, or is it something you discovered while researching the dissertation?**

I can't remember if I already had the idea or if I discovered this as I researched the chronicles. But when I recognized these fictitious elements in them, I decided to concentrate on this topic.

**Which chronicles did you study?**

All of them. In my later book *Breve historia del cuento mexicano*, I summarize these chronicles in the first chapter. I also included some of these short stories contained in the chronicles in my later anthology of the Mexican short story, *Antología del cuento mexicano*. Some of these stories by the *cronistas* are very good.

**And which of these chroniclers were the better or more interesting writers?**

Well, the most interesting is Bernal Díaz del Castillo, although he doesn't have as many stories as some of the others, or his stories are more incomplete. Some of the most interesting and complete stories are found in the chronicles written by Diego Durán. He tells the story of the Aztec emperor Montezuma sending some of his *sacerdotes*, or priests, to look for Aztlán, the original homeland of the Aztecs. This story is clearly fiction. The *sacerdotes* are transformed into animals, and when they get to Aztlán they discover a hill that if you climb it, you return as a young man. It's all fiction or myth or legend.

**But these chroniclers are reporting these myths as fact?**

Yes. Although, if the stories are about Aztec deities, then they are reported as myths. However, if they are about persons, then they were reported as fact even though these accounts are fiction also.

**Where did fiction end and history start in these chronicles?**

That's impossible to tell.

**The *cronistas* reported what they were told by the Indians?**

Yes, but it's difficult to separate reality from myth. In my estimation, much of this narrative was fictionalized. You have to remember that the chronicles represented a medieval genre. The medieval writers didn't make a distinction between history and fiction. They tell you fictitious things as if they were historical. It's not until the Renaissance that you get a distinction between fact and fiction. Bernal Díaz del Castillo represents more than the other *cronistas* a Renaissance perspective. That's why he calls his chronicles *La verdadera historia*, or the true history, of the conquest. He doesn't want others to think of his work as fiction. But most of the *cronistas* simply accepted what they heard about Aztec history or the history of the conquest as fact, even though much of it was more legend than fact.

**Does this fictional element include the *cronistas* who wrote about the northern frontier of New Spain?**

Yes. For example, Fray Marcos de Niza in his chronicles describes Indian cities without having seen them. He just heard about them from Indians. So he reports that somewhere in the north there exists the Seven Cities of Cibola, the Seven Cities of Gold, but this is fiction. All of these *cronistas*, influenced by medieval tradition, were, in their minds, inventing the Americas through their eyes.

**When you were working on this dissertation topic, were you aware of other scholars working in this area?**

No—very few, if any. Now the study of the *cronistas* has become very popular—but not then. There was very little attention being paid to Mexican colonial literature.

**Where did you do most of this research for your dissertation? Did you have to go to Mexico?**

No. I was fortunate to have had access in Chicago to the Newberry Library, which contains one of the major repositories of the Spanish colonial chronicles, in the Adler Collection.

**How long did it take you to research and write your dissertation?**

It took me one year to write, but even before I began the dissertation, I had already been studying the chronicles.

**Did you have to defend the dissertation?**

Yes. At that time you defended the dissertation before a very large committee of faculty, somewhere around ten or fifteen people. The day before the defense, you were given a question out of the dissertation which you had to lecture on. My question concerned the Indian influence on the *cronistas*, or something like that. After this short lecture, committee members asked questions.

**Were some of the *cronistas* Indians?**

Yes, and some were mestizos. For example, when Sahagún wrote the *Historia general de las cosas de la Nueva España*, all of his informants were Indians, some of whom had written their accounts in Náhuatl, which Sahagún translated into Spanish.

**So in many respects, the Indians were also the authors of these *crónicas*?**

Yes, although many weren't acknowledged as authors.

**So the *crónicas* can be seen also as a part of Indian literary history, not just Spanish.**

That's true.

**Was this defense of your dissertation a good experience?**

Yes; it was a very good experience. They passed me right away, and I was awarded my Ph.D. in 1950.

# Community Involvement

**After you returned from the war and resumed your Ph.D. work, you once again became active in the Mexican American community of Chicago. Can you talk about this community involvement?**

Before the war, there had been organized in Chicago what was called the Mexican Civic Committee. Before the war, the Mexican Civic Committee had attempted to organize mexicanos who worked at the nearby steel mills, in the stockyards, and in the West Side. We had an office in Hull House. The key organizer for the Civic Committee was Frank Paz. We also published a newsletter.

After the war, Paz resumed the work of the Civic Committee but changed its name to the Mexican American Council. I served on the educational committee and was responsible for securing scholarships for Mexican Americans to attend college. I was able to get the scholarships, but had difficulty finding suitable candidates for them. I would go on the radio and appeal for parents to apply for these scholarships. I also made the same appeal in the newspapers. But there were so many problems in the schools, and the kids were not being encouraged to go to college. In addition, among most Mexican working families, there was no tradition of going to college. So it was difficult finding students for these scholarships, but we were able to send a few students.

**Where did the money for these scholarships come from?**

It came from the universities in the Chicago area.

**During this time you also began to write essays for a publication called *Vida Latina*. What is the history of this publication?**

*Vida Latina* was a bilingual magazine published in Chicago by Ernesto Quiroga. He was a mexicano who operated a print shop on Roosevelt Avenue.

**Was it a publication of a particular organization?**

No. It was an independent publication, and you could buy it for ten cents. It was sold in many stores which catered to the Mexican population.

**In *Vida Latina* in 1952 you published a two-part essay on the contributions of Mexican Americans to U.S. culture. Why did you feel the need to write such an essay in the early 1950s?**

Because people didn't know about the many contributions of Mexicans and I wanted them to know. Much earlier, in 1942, I had published an article about the contributions of Latin American culture to the United States.

Was the 1952 article in any way influenced by Carey McWilliams's *North From Mexico*, which appeared in 1949?

Yes, in part, and also because I had met McWilliams in Chicago when he was researching his book. He came to Hull House and interviewed me and Frank Paz. In his book he mentions Paz. I don't think I made an impression on him.

What kind of questions was he interested in?

He wanted to know what was happening in the community.

What was your impression of McWilliams?

He was a very nice and kind man. He was also very knowledgeable.

Did you read *North From Mexico* when it first came out?

Yes, and it made a very good impression on me. I much later was a bit critical of McWilliams because in the book he says that Mexicans in the United States are incapable of producing literature such as novels or autobiographies, which is not correct.

Of course, *North From Mexico* was way ahead of its time. It's the first to suggest that Mexican Americans have had a history in the United States and that it goes as far back as the Spanish colonial period. Did you have any sense if it was widely read when it first came out, and did it influence community people?

It was not widely read by the community, which didn't read much sociological literature, especially in English. But some community leaders did read it and were influenced by it.

Were you surprised when *North From Mexico* was rediscovered in the late 1960s with the Chicano movement?

I wasn't surprised because it was one of the few texts that discussed Chicanos. There was also Octavio Paz's *Labyrinth of Solitude*, in which he wrote on the *pachuco*, but there wasn't much more.

Yes, and the added importance of McWilliams is that he helped provide many of the themes that a new generation of Chicano historians would pursue into the 1970s. For example, he has a very strong theme of social conflict, such as labor struggles. I also noticed in your vitae, Don Luis, that in 1952 you were interviewed by the *Chicago Daily Tribune* concerning the issue of Mexican "wetbacks." Was this a significant issue in Chicago?

Many undocumented workers from Mexico as early as the 1940s were being attracted to work in the Midwest, in states such as Iowa and Michigan. They came to work in *el betabel*—in sugar beets. Many first arrived in Chicago because of the labor agencies there who hired them and then shipped them out to work in particular locations. Then, during the war, we had the Bracero Program, which brought thousands of Mexican contract workers to the United States. But the undocumented continued to come, because those who couldn't enter the Bracero Program entered without documents. Employers wanted them because they could pay them even less than they paid the braceros.

**Did many undocumented work in Chicago?**

Some did, but some went on to work in the nearby steel mills or packing houses. Most, however, worked in agriculture.

**Did the Mexican American Council deal with the issue of the undocumented?**

We tried to see that these people were treated fairly. Martín Ortiz, who took over the council after Frank Paz left for California, interviewed many of these undocumented workers and passed on information about their treatment to the American labor unions.

*Leal receiving his Ph.D. from University of Chicago, 1950 (with wife Gladys).*

# Chapter Three

## Mississippi and Emory

*Leal (left) with colleague William Strickland, Oxford, Mississippi, 1955.*

# Oxford, Mississippi

**MG:**  Don Luis, after you finished your Ph.D., did you apply for teaching positions elsewhere?

**LL:**  I taught one more year at Chicago, but during this time I also looked for a new position because I couldn't stay at the University of Chicago. I attended the MLA [Modern Language Association] in 1951, which was in Detroit that year, to see about other positions. I unexpectedly met up with Professor Arthur Campa, who was at the University of Denver. I had read some of his studies on popular culture in New Mexico and admired his work.

**Were you introduced to him?**

No. I introduced myself. As a matter of fact, I asked him if he had an opening in his department. But he said, "We don't have anything now, but give me your address and I'll write to you if we do."

**So you knew of Campa's work?**

Yes, because I was interested in folklore and Campa had written extensively on this subject. I also had read the work of Professor Aurelio Espinosa from New Mexico. Both were pioneers in studying the *cuento popular*—the folk stories of Hispanic New Mexico.

**Did you ever meet Espinosa?**

No, but I later met his son, J. Manuel Espinosa, who is also an important folklorist.

**What was your reaction to Espinosa's and Campa's work?**

Their work was very similar. They both were interested in folk tales, folk poetry, folk theater.

**You know that I have one chapter on Campa in my book *Mexican Americans*.[1] One of the things that struck me about Campa was that he had a critical perspective on the folk culture of New Mexico. Specifically, he**

*Leal (back, standing) with Jaime Torres Bodet (on extreme left), Secretary of UNESCO. Chicago Westside Committee, Hull House, Chicago, 1952.*

questioned the "authentic" Spanish culture in New Mexico. He saw more of the Mexican influence because he found similar examples of folk tales and folk songs not only in New Mexico but in northern Mexico as well. He recognized the connection between Mexican and New Mexican cultures.

You're right. In Espinosa you can also see that he recognizes that not all of New Mexican folk culture comes directly from Spain. But Espinosa has not been studied very much, especially by Chicano scholars, because he is seen as stressing too much the Spanish connection.

Yes. What I also found interesting about Campa's work was his emphasis on popular culture. It is this emphasis that the Chicano cultural movement of the late 1960s and early 1970s would also stress: the culture of the people—*la cultura de la gente.*

So, Don Luis, when you went to the MLA in Detroit, you were interviewed by the University of Mississippi?

No, I didn't have an interview at the MLA. What happened was I had this friend, Jean Autrei, who was from France and who was also a student at Chicago. He was writing his thesis on the influence of artists on Proust. He attended a meeting someplace and met the chair of the Romance languages department at the University of Mississippi, a Professor Harrison. Autrei recommended me to Harrison, who wrote to me asking if I might be interested in going to Mississippi. As a result, I went for an interview in Oxford, where the university is located. They right there offered me a position with tenure! Associate professor right away! They did this because I already had publications. So I accepted and agreed to start in the fall of 1952.

Did you know any of the faculty there?

No. They were all Anglos. No one there was from Spain or Latin America.

Was the offer from Mississippi the only one you had?

I actually had two offers. The other one was from Emory University in Atlanta. But by the time I got the offer from Emory, I already had accepted at Mississippi. I told Emory that I had signed with Mississippi, but if they were willing to wait a couple of years I would go to Emory. Of course, Mississippi was offering me tenure, while Emory was not. But Emory agreed to be patient and to see if I would later accept their offer.

How did Gladys feel about moving to Mississippi?

She didn't like it, because Chicago was a big city while Oxford was a small town.

What was Oxford like?

Well, William Faulkner lived there. We used to see him every day. We used to see him fishing.

**Had you read Faulkner?**

Yes, but everyone hated him in Oxford because of how he depicted the South in his novels. I read more of his novels while I was in Oxford.

**What did you think of his writing?**

I loved it. Faulkner, you know, had a great influence on Latin American writers.

**What is this influence?**

The way Faulkner describes the small communities in the South. This localism and regionalism would influence writers such as Rulfo and García Márquez.

**You arrived in Mississippi in 1952. What was this experience like?**

Well, it was four years, but they were not complete years because we returned each summer to Chicago. I taught summer school at the University of Chicago for three years. As soon as classes in Mississippi were over, we would go back to Chicago.

**What was it like teaching Spanish in Mississippi?**

It was like teaching anywhere else.

**Did you teach both language and literature classes?**

I taught Spanish language classes and one class on Latin American literature. I even taught one class in Italian, but I did this only once because it took too much preparation. It was not a heavy teaching load, and I had a lot of time to write. Since I didn't have as much community involvement in Mississippi, this also allowed me more time to write.

**How many students did you have in your classes?**

They were small classes, between fifteen and twenty students.

**What was your department like?**

It was a Romance languages department chaired by Professor Benjamin Harrison. He was a very nice person. He was a professor of French. There was a Professor Andrew Sullivan who taught Spanish, had spent time in Perú, and who knew all about Latin America. There was another fellow, Professor Frank Halstead, who taught contemporary Spanish literature.

**But you were the only Latino on the faculty?**

Yes.

**Did you teach graduate courses in Mississippi?**

No; they didn't have a Ph.D. program in Romance languages. I think there may have been Ph.D. programs in some departments, such as history. I did direct three or four M.A. theses. I remember one of them compared the works of Sarmiento and Fenimore Cooper.

**Were there any Latino students at the university?**
Very few. I had some in my classes. They were mostly Cuban.

**How big was the university?**
Oxford was a small town. It had a population of about six thousand. Then there were about another four thousand at the university.

**African Americans, of course, were not allowed to attend the university.**
No, although there were some from the Caribbean.

**They were students?**
Yes. The university didn't know that they were blacks when they were admitted. I used to have coffee with some of them.

**What were race relations like in Oxford?**
There were very few blacks in Oxford. There was a mechanic near our home, and I used to bring my car to him. But the separation was total in everything—bathrooms, restaurants, hospitals—everything.

**During the time that you were in Oxford, was there much civil rights activity?**
Yes. Not only in Mississippi, but all over the South. Things were beginning to change.

**But since there was no Latino community in Oxford, you couldn't participate in community affairs in the way that you did in Chicago. This gave you more time, as you say, to write. In 1953 you published in *Historia Mexicana* an article entitled "El Códice Ramírez." What was that article about?**
This was a piece that came out of my dissertation project. In the nineteenth century a Mexican scholar by the name of Ramírez discovered a manuscript in Spanish which was an interpretation of a pre-Columbian text on the history of the Aztecs. Because Ramírez discovered it, it was called the *Códice Ramírez*. No one knew, however, who had done this interpretation, so its author remained anonymous. What I did was to prove that the author was a Mexican priest by the name of Tovar. I compared the manuscript with the writings of other *cronistas*, such as Sahagún, as well as with other work done by Tovar. Through this comparison, I showed that Tovar was the real author of the *Códice Ramírez*.

**While you were at Mississippi, did you publish materials from your dissertation as articles?**
Yes.

**Did you consider publishing the dissertation as a book?**

No, I didn't.

**During these four years in Mississippi, did you have a plan or an outline of the major research projects you wanted to pursue for the next several years?**

I was too ambitious. That was my problem. I wanted to write about Mexican literature, Latin American literature, especially the short story, Spanish literature, Italian literature, and about the history of the early colonial chroniclers. But I couldn't do everything. So I decided to give up work on Italian literature, on Spanish literature, and on historical work on the chronicles. I decided to concentrate on Latin American literature and specifically on Mexican literature.

## Research Projects

**So what were some of your major projects at Mississippi?**

My first major project was my book on Mexican culture called *México: civilizaciones y culturas,* which was published in 1955. It was based on my lectures for a course I had taught on Mexican culture at the University of Chicago.

**Was this a book more on culture than on just literature?**

Yes. It has a chapter on literature, but it also covers other aspects of culture. It was used for college courses. As a matter of fact, I wrote the book at the request of a Professor James Babcock at Chicago, who was an editor at Houghton Mifflin. He thought the book could be used in Spanish classes. It did quite well. I revised it in 1971 and added a chapter on Chicanos. It still sells about a thousand copies a year.

**How did you define civilization and culture in this book?**

I stressed that Mexico has been the product of not just one culture, but of many. You have the pre-Columbian cultures, the colonial cultures, popular cultures, and contemporary cultures.

**You suggested that each of these cultures possessed its own notion of civilization.**

Right.

**This is not the Sarmiento version of civilization?**

No! No!

**So you were saying that Mexico is not just one culture but a constellation of cultures?**

Exactly. Even today, for example, if you go to a state like Oaxaca, you can see the presence of Indian culture. Arnold Toynbee, in his book on world civilizations, observed that Mexico was a good example of how one culture, Indian culture, was replaced or substituted by another culture, Spanish culture. But then when Toynbee actually visited Mexico, he saw that he was wrong, and he had to revise his observations on Mexican culture. The Indian cultures had not been replaced, nor had they disappeared. They had survived. Mexico has more than one culture.

**Was there another major project that you worked on while at Mississippi?**
I worked on my history of the short story in Mexico. It was published in 1956 as *Breve historia del cuento mexicano*. I also organized it with the same pluralistic viewpoint. That is, I noted the evolution of the short story form through different historical periods: the pre-Columbian, the colonial era, the nineteenth century, and the contemporary. The first chapter was a summary of my dissertation.

**Besides these two major projects, you were also writing articles. One, which you published in *Vida Latina* in 1954, was on Vicente Mendoza, the Mexican folklorist. Was he already recognized as a major scholar then?**
He was very well known. I wrote this short overview of Mendoza and his work to reciprocate, because Mendoza had published some of my work. He was folklore editor of the *Revista de la Universidad de México*. I had sent him a piece on "La Cucaracha"—on the Spanish origins of this popular song— and he published it. I also visited him in Mexico and got to know him well. He and his wife, who was also a major folklorist, made me a member of the Sociedad Folklorista de México.

**Was Mendoza the first Mexican scholar to concentrate on folklore? Was he a pioneer in this area?**
There were a few others before him. However, Mendoza's major contributions were his studies of the *corrido* [ballad]. He was a great musicologist. He focused more on the musical form of the *corrido* than on its literary content. He knew everything about the *corrido*.

**How did you decide to do this article on "La Cucaracha?"**
I forget the inspiration for it. I probably was researching something else and then stumbled on this particular subject. This is not uncommon for scholars. But the point of this essay was my discovery that the song "La Cucaracha," which everyone thought originated during the Mexican Revolution of 1910 because it sang of heroes such as Pancho Villa, was actually a song that originated in eighteenth-century Spain during the Carlist wars.

**How did you prove this?**
By quoting from the original song. It has the same meter, the same music,

and even the same words, although the original proper names were later changed to fit the exploits of figures such as Pancho Villa during the Mexican Revolution.

**What was Mendoza's reaction to your article?**
He immediately published it.

**Was Mendoza an influence on your work?**
Yes. I had read all of his books on the *corrido* and on the history of the Mexican *canción* [song].

**Did you maintain contact with Mendoza?**
I corresponded with him. I only found out recently that he had reviewed my book on Mexican culture, but I had never known this. I never received a copy of the review. It was a good review. In a recent volume of *Aztlán,* the periodical published at UCLA, I have an article on Mendoza, to whom the number—about the *corrido*—is dedicated.

## Leaving Mississippi

**Don Luis, why did you decide to leave Mississippi in 1956 and go to Emory University in Atlanta?**
There were two main reasons. First, Emory had been wanting me to go there for some time. I would have gone to Emory sooner had I not already accepted Mississippi's offer. We had bought a house in Oxford, so I felt I had to stay there for a few years; I asked Emory if they would wait, which they did.

The second reason I left Mississippi was that I didn't like the growing tensions concerning integration there. I supported integration, but the university did not. I remember that the president of the university called a meeting of all of the faculty and told us not to discuss the racial problem in the classroom. I felt uneasy about this because I couldn't teach about Mexican and Latin American culture without discussing race. So it was the tense and difficult conditions concerning race that also moved me to leave Mississippi. They tried to keep me there, although they didn't match Emory's offer. I had a meeting with the president of the university, who told me he wanted me to stay, but that they couldn't offer me more money since I was already at the top of the salary scale. It didn't matter to me, because I already had decided to leave.

**Did you tell your chair and the president that one of the reasons you were leaving was over the race issue?**
Yes, but they only said, "It's going to blow over." But I knew that it wasn't. I also left because I thought Emory was a better university with a better library.


# Emory

**So you started at Emory in the fall of 1956?**
Yes. I went as an associate professor with tenure in the Romance languages department. The department didn't have a Ph.D. program, but it had an M.A. one, along with its undergraduate degree. An interesting thing at Emory was that they had me teach the golden age in Spain, which included Cervantes and *Don Quixote*. They didn't have a specialist in the golden age. But even after they hired one, I was still asked to teach this course. I taught it three or four times.

**What was Emory like?**
It is a private institution. It was, at the time, church related. I forget what Protestant affiliation it had. Once a week the entire faculty had to attend a religious assembly, although they discontinued this shortly after I arrived.

**Did they ask you about your religious background when you were hired?**
No. But you couldn't teach during that one time each week when this assembly was held.

**How big a campus was Emory?**
It had about six thousand students. It is similar to Stanford. It was considered to be the best school between North Carolina and Texas. It had very good students that came from all over the South.

**Was it an integrated or a segregated school?**
There were some black students there. They were let in because the Coca-Cola Company, which is based in Atlanta, provided the money for these black students to attend Emory.

**Did Emory provide you with housing?**
Yes. They gave us a house just across the street from where I taught. I think the rent was only about sixty dollars a month. I could stay home until five minutes before my class, and then just walk over. It was a very nice arrangement.

**What was your reaction to Atlanta?**

It was similar to Chicago. You had, for example, some very wealthy African Americans. Atlanta had all of the aspects of a big city, including an opera house. Emory is a suburb of Atlanta.

**So you found Atlanta to be very different from Oxford?**

Oh, yes. Oxford was very provincial, while Atlanta was a modern city. Another thing is that Atlanta had a large Hispanic community, including some very wealthy people.

**And this community was already there in 1956?**

Yes, and we used to have an *Asociación de Latinos,* which met once a month, where we invited different people to give lectures.

**Who were the people who belonged to this group?**

Most were businessmen. Not many were from Mexico. Most were from Cuba, the Caribbean, and from other parts of Latin America.

**Did their children attend Emory?**

Some did. There were a few Latino students at Emory.

**How many other professors of Spanish were there at Emory?**

There were four of us, including Professor Bruce Gordon, who was the chair of the department. I was the only Latin Americanist.

**Was it a congenial department?**

Yes. I was very happy there. They gave me all the support I needed for buying books, research material, and for inviting scholars from Mexico. At my suggestion they invited Professor Justino Fernández, the well-known Mexican art critic.

**Besides golden age, what other courses did you teach at Emory?**

I taught Latin American literature, including courses on the introduction to Latin American literature and on the Latin American novel. These were all seminars.

**You mean most of the courses at Emory were seminars and not lecture classes?**

Yes. We had just a few students in our classes. That was the type of course we offered—small classes.

**Was this the case for both graduate and undergraduate classes?**

In my undergraduate classes I never had more than fifteen students. In my graduate seminars I averaged around four or five students.

**That was a wonderful teaching arrangement! Was there an interest in Latin American literature?**

Yes, and several of my students went on to write master's theses on Latin

American literature. Emory was a wonderful school. Everything was much better than in Mississippi.

## Research Projects

**Now, Don Luis, during the three years you were in Emory, what was some of your key research?**
I finished a bibliography of the Mexican short story which I had started at Oxford. This was published in 1958 as *Bibliografía del cuento mexicano.*

I also began work on an anthology called *La Revolución y las letras.* This was a volume which I coedited with Edmundo Valadés, who was a critic and short-story writer in Mexico. He was the publisher of a periodical called *El Cuento.* I had just recently published my history of the Mexican short story, as well as completing the bibliography on the short story, so that I had all of the materials for this next project. But I decided to just concentrate on the period of the Mexican Revolution.

**So your anthology focused on those who were writing during the revolution or those who have written about the revolution?**
Just those who wrote during the revolution or shortly after.

**Who were some of the writers that you concentrated on?**
It included writers such as Mariano Azuela, Martín Luis Guzmán, Rafael Muñoz, Cipriano Campos Alatorre, and Francisco Rojas González.

**Was there a common characteristic to these writers?**
Most of their stories are based on episodes that these writers themselves witnessed. The stories are very autobiographical. Another characteristic is that most of these stories are written in a very rapid style, in almost journalistic style. In fact, most of these stories were first published in newspapers and then later published in books.

**Were most of these writers supporters of the revolution?**
Yes, all of them were, and most were Villistas, followers of Pancho Villa.

**And these were all male writers?**
Yes, although one exception was Nellie Campobello. She wrote a very important book of stories called *Cartucho.* She was from Durango in the north, and she witnessed the revolution as a young girl. So she presents her stories from the perspective of a young girl. She was also a Villista. She wrote another book called *Las manos de mamá,* which deals with her mother during the revolution.

**How is Nellie Campobello regarded in Mexican literature?**

Very well, although she didn't write very much. But she was considered an important writer during her time. At present, a student here at UCSB is writing a dissertation about her works.

**Is she considered an even more important writer today because of the greater recognition of women writers?**

Yes, because she was one of the few women writing at that time. There were others, but they were writing in newspapers, and many of these newspapers have not survived.

**Of the writers you included in this book, did you have a particular favorite?**

Yes, I think I preferred Rafael Muñoz. He presents the revolution from the Villista perspective and includes interesting episodes from the revolution.

**How does Muñoz compare with Martín Luis Guzmán?**

Guzmán is a better writer and stylist, but his stories—for example, his famous *El águila y la serpiente*—contain all historical characters, such as Pancho Villa. By contrast, Muñoz integrates fictional characters with real ones in a very creative way.

One of the other interesting aspects about Muñoz is that he was a bilingual writer. He lived in Hollywood for a period of time and was married to an Anglo-American woman. He knew English very well. He actually wrote some film scripts for Hollywood producers. Some of his short stories are satirical ones about American actors.

**What did he write in English?**

In 1929 he published a collection of short stories in a magazine called *Mexican Life*. It was published in Mexico by some Americans.

**Has there ever been a major study of Muñoz?**

Yes. One of my graduate students at the University of Illinois, Iris Catherine Jeffrey, wrote a dissertation on Muñoz that in 1986 was published as a book.

**Was there another major project that you commenced at Emory?**

I also was working on a long article regarding the very first Spanish-language novel published in the United States. This article was published in 1960 as "*Jicoténcal:* primera novela histórica en castellano." The novel was published in Philadelphia in 1826. But the problem with the novel is that when it was first published, no author was listed. I wanted to identify who the author was. After much research I concluded that the author was a Father Félix Varela, a priest from Cuba. It has been republished under the Hispanic Literary Heritage Project by Arte Público Press.

**What does the novel deal with?**

It is about the Spanish conquest of Mexico. It blames the Spanish and defends the Indians. Jicoténcal was the leader of the Tlaxcaltecan Indians, and he sided with the Spanish only to be executed by Cortés. It is also the first text critical of the role of Doña Marina, who has been castigated in Mexican history as *La Malinche*—the traitor who aided Cortés in the conquest of the Aztec empire and who was Cortés's mistress.

**Some feminists today would have problems with the traditional view of *La Malinche* as a traitor to her people.**

Perhaps, but you have to keep in mind that this novel was published in 1826.

**But why was no author listed for the novel?**

I concluded that Father Varela believed that he would be killed if his name were attached to the novel. Besides his anti-Spanish novel, Father Varela also published a periodical titled *El Habanero.* It appears that his life was threatened because of his attacks on Spain.

**Who published the novel?**

An American press in Philadelphia published it in Spanish.

**How did you discover the novel?**

It was known to some critics, who mentioned it in earlier studies. It was through these other critics that I first became aware of it. I saw it advertised in a catalog from Mexico sometime in the 1950s. I purchased a copy of the novel and read it. It was after this that I started my research on its authorship. I looked up the Latin American people who were living in Philadelphia in 1826. I looked in city directories and located Spanish surnames. Here I found Father Varela's name.

I also discovered that some of the other Latin Americans in Philadelphia at that time had written various texts. What I did was to locate these texts as well as examples of Varela's writings, especially in *El Habanero,* and compare these writings to the novel *Jicoténcal.* I concluded that Varela's style and images matched those of the anonymous novel. It was Varela who had written *Jicoténcal.*

**Don Luis, by this time while you were at Emory it was becoming clear that your work was linking history with literature. You were becoming a literary historian. As you know, there are some literary critics who don't appreciate the relevance of history to literature. But you do. Why did you develop in this direction?**

I think that it was born out of my study of the *cronistas* for my dissertation. There I began to work with history and fiction.

**You feel that it's important to look at literature in a historical context.**

That's right. That's the only way. For example, in *Jicoténcal* you can't fully understand it unless you understand Spanish-American colonial history. You have to go to history to understand the novel. You need to know about the conquest of Mexico. In *Jicoténcal* you have an excellent example of the relationship between history and fiction.

**Do you think that the relationship of history and literature is more of a Latin American tradition than an Anglo-American one?**

I'm not sure about that.

**During the 1950s were there other Latin American literary historians besides yourself?**

There were not many.

**So you may have been breaking new ground?**

Yes, perhaps.

**Were there other major projects that you worked on while at Emory?**

I was also working on the Mexican fables—the *fábulas*. I was collecting a great deal of information on the fables. However, I never published anything on the fables until very recently, when I wrote an article on the Mexican fable from the eighteenth to the nineteenth century. The fable was very popular during the period of the Mexican independence movement between 1810 and 1821. The first *diario* [newspaper] in Mexico was published in 1812, *El Diario de México*. Emory gave me funds to obtain a microfilm copy from the Library of Congress. Many fables were published in this paper. In every issue, at least one fable was published. Almost all were political fables criticizing the Spanish colonial administration.

**What is the definition of a fable?**

A fable is a poetic composition in which the animals as characters speak. *Aesop's Fables* is a good example. They are short and with a moral at the end. In nineteenth-century Mexico, fables were used in the school to teach morals. The great fable writer in Mexico at this time was Rosas Moreno. He published a book of fables which I read when I was in school. Fernández de Lizardi was another writer of fables in Mexico. The major period for the publication of many of these fables was between 1812 and 1830, the independence and postindependence period.

**Does the fable as a genre continue into the twentieth century?**

It continues a bit into the nineteenth century, but then it disappears.

# Chapter Four

## Illinois

*Leal in Guadalajara, Mexico, shortly after commencing teaching at the University of Illinois, Urbana, 1962.*

# Urbana

MG: **Don Luis, why did you decide to leave Emory in 1959?**

LL: It was mostly because Gladys wanted to be near her mother and sister, who lived in Chicago. In December of 1958, when I was attending the MLA convention in New York, I got together with Professor Renato Rosaldo Sr. from the University of Arizona. One evening as we were visiting the different receptions hosted by many of the big publishing houses, we ran into Professor Shoemaker, the head of the Department of Spanish, Italian, and Portuguese at the University of Illinois. He told Rosaldo, "We're looking for a Latin Americanist. Can you recommend someone?" So Rosaldo said, "Well, here is Leal." Shoemaker asked me, "Are you interested?" And I said, "Well, maybe, yes." And so he said, "Send me your credentials."

I did so after I returned to Emory and discussed the matter with Gladys. They invited me to give a lecture that next February. I remember a big storm that hit the Midwest at that time. But I gave my lecture, and soon after I had returned to Emory an offer arrived from Illinois. I accepted it.

A funny thing was that the same year, Southern Illinois University also expressed an interest in me. I sent them my papers. But they later wrote to tell me that I had been eliminated as a candidate because I had no experience directing doctoral dissertations. What's funny is that after I went to Illinois, I directed a large number of dissertations.

But the main reason we went to Urbana was to be near Chicago. Urbana is only 135 miles south of Chicago.

**Did Emory try to convince you to stay?**

Oh, yes. The dean called me. They didn't want me to leave. They offered me everything, but I said, "Well, I've already decided to go. I'm sorry."

**How much bigger was the University of Illinois than Emory?**

Much bigger. Illinois had almost forty thousand students. More importantly, it had, and still does, one of the best libraries outside of Harvard and Yale. It's a tremendous library. It is very rich in Spanish and Latin American materials. They used to send me to Mexico to buy books for the library.

**What was your department like at Illinois?**

It was quite large. It was the biggest Spanish-language department in the Midwest. Besides a large faculty, we had many graduate students. I remember one year when we had fifty students writing dissertations in Spanish alone. I taught only graduate students at Illinois, which was another difference from Emory.

**You didn't teach undergraduates at all?**

No, because I didn't have the time. I taught two graduate classes per semester. My seminars averaged about thirty students.

**Was Latin American literature one of the strengths of the department?**

Yes. There were several Latin Americanists, although the majority of the faculty in Spanish were peninsular scholars.

**What courses did you teach at Illinois?**

I was able to concentrate more on Mexican literature there. I would teach seminars on the novel of the Mexican Revolution, the contemporary Mexican novel, the *indigenista* novel, and, of course, my specialty, the Mexican short story.

**Why were there so many graduate students interested in Latin American literature at the time at Illinois?**

This interest began in the 1960s. The growth of graduate students had to do with the Russians putting up Sputnik in 1957—the first man-made satellite in space. To catch up with the Russians not only in the sciences but in other fields as well, the U.S. government sponsored new graduate fellowships. This led to an increase in graduate enrollments throughout the country.

**Were there many graduate students from Latin America at Illinois?**

There were some, but not many. There were also a few Chicanos during my years at Illinois. I directed about eight Chicano students.

**Of course, the Cuban Revolution of 1959 led to an increased interest in Latin America, did it not?**

Yes. It also led in a few years to a number of Cuban students at Illinois who were given federal scholarships. One of these students was the former head of the supreme court in Cuba, who exiled himself in the United States after

Castro took power. He was an old man. I felt sorry for him being in class at his age and having to take notes in my seminar. I once asked him, "Why are you coming back to school?"

"Well, I want to get a Ph.D. to teach," he responded.

"But by the time you finish, you'll be retired," I replied.

**Did he ever finish?**

I don't know. I don't think so.

**Did you like living in Urbana?**

Yes, even though Urbana was a very small town. You went a few blocks and you'd be in the corn fields. There were more people at the university than there were in the town. Actually, there was Urbana and there was Champaign. Urbana was on the east side and Champaign was on the west side. They were separated by the railroad tracks. There were very few industries in either place. The campus itself was half in Urbana and half in Champaign. For example, the building where I used to teach my classes was on the dividing line between the two towns.

**Were there any Latinos in either Urbana or Champaign?**

Not in the towns, but there was a good group on campus. There was a Latin American house on campus that housed the students who came from Latin America. Actually, many of these students went to Illinois especially to study in engineering and the sciences. One year we had about six hundred students from Colombia. Many others came from Venezuela.

**Did you reconnect with your friends and colleagues in Chicago?**

No. Most of the times we went to Chicago were to visit Gladys's family. Most, if not all, of the groups I had associated with in Chicago were no longer functioning.


## Synthesis in Mexican Literature

**Don Luis, in 1962 you published an article, "Contemporary Mexican Literature: A Mirror of Social Change." In this article you observe that after 1940 you see a synthesis in Mexican literature which involves the *modernista* influence on the one hand and the nationalism produced by the Mexican Revolution on the other. How exactly did this synthesis manifest itself in Mexican literature?**

Before 1940 there were two groups of writers in Mexico who were very antagonistic toward one other. One was the social-movement writers, who closely identified with the Mexican Revolution. The other was the self-proclaimed vanguard writers, who rejected the social realism of the first group. Even some of the periodicals of the pre-1940 period reflected this conflict. A journal called *Crisol* represented the nationalist writers while *El Hijo Pródigo* represented the more European-oriented, vanguard writers. However, by the 1940s this antagonism closed, and a new synthesis of these two tendencies becomes visible. Perhaps the writer who most symbolized this coming together of social themes and innovative writing technique was José Revueltas.

Revueltas wrote about Mexican social themes but used new techniques. In fact, you can see the influence of Faulkner, both in themes and in technique, on Revueltas, although he always denied that influence. Later, of course, other writers, such as Juan Rulfo and Carlos Fuentes in the 1950s, would exhibit this synthesis.

## Mexican Identity

**One of the other changes in Mexican intellectual circles by the 1940s is the emphasis given to defining the Mexican national character by intellectuals such as Samuel Ramos and Octavio Paz. How do you explain this stress? What is going on in Mexico that gives rise to this theme?**
Besides Ramos and Paz, there is also Leopoldo Zea. But what is happening is that with the involvement of Mexico in World War II—you know Mexico declared war on Japan and sent a flying squadron, the *escuadron 202,* to fight the Japanese—this engagement in the world conflict begins to raise questions for Mexican intellectuals as to Mexico's place in world politics. Who are we? This gives rise to the movement to define the Mexican.
**Is this movement also reflected in the arts?**
Yes. You have new muralists, such as Rufino Tamayo, who move away from the social murals of Diego Rivera, for example, to produce more abstract ones. José Luis Cuevas is another artist who produces abstract, even grotesque, art.
**So that by the 1940s, some two decades after the more conflictive phase of the Mexican Revolution, you begin to see a movement away from the nationalist themes generated by the revolution. You see intellectuals, writers, and artists who wish to express themselves in a more diverse way, including being critical of the revolution.**

Yes. Of course, in some way, certainly this criticism of the revolution can be traced back to [Mariano] Azuela. But such criticism and new experimentation becomes more widespread by the 1940s, and certainly by the 1950s with writers such as Carlos Fuentes.

## Samuel Ramos

**Don Luis, we mentioned Samuel Ramos and his writings on the Mexican character. How much impact did his work have in Mexico?**
It had a great influence, especially his classic *Perfil del hombre y la cultura de México* [*Man and Culture in Mexico*], which first appeared in 1934 and then went through several republications. He, of course, focused on what he proposed was the inferiority complex of the mexicano. Ramos tried to show this inferiority complex through the language used by the Mexican. This was language that few writers had ever used in print before—words such as *chingar* [to fuck]. Ramos's stress on the inferiority complex and the language that he used had significant influence on Octavio Paz's own classic work on the Mexican character, *The Labyrinth of Solitude,* and later on the work of Carlos Fuentes.

**But despite Ramos's influence on other intellectuals and writers, he did not have as much influence on Mexican politics, for example, as perhaps Paz or Fuentes did.**
That's true. What limited Ramos's impact was that he was too negative, especially about the so-called *pelado* [the uncouth one], but also the mestizo, who, of course, encompasses the majority of Mexicans. By contrast, he upheld the *criollos* [the Spaniards born in Mexico] as representing the true culture of the country and the only group without an inferiority complex. Ramos embraced European culture and rejected the Indian heritage. But in so doing, he marginalized himself not only from other Mexican intellectuals, but from the majority mestizo culture.

**Would you say that perhaps Ramos's influence may have been greater outside of Mexico than within, therefore providing a very biased and even racist view of Mexicans?**
Yes, that's right. Ramos became widely translated and provided non-Mexicans, especially in Europe and the United States, with their only perspective on Mexican culture. Within Mexico, Ramos was particularly attacked by the nationalists, who rejected his characterization of the Mexi-

can personality, at least as it pertained to the *pelado* and to the mestizo. Ramos wrote many other books on philosophy that influenced the development of Mexican philosophy, but he became famous due to *Man and Culture in Mexico*, although it was because of this book that he received much criticism.

# Octavio Paz

*Leal (left) with Octavio Paz at UC Santa Barbara, 1985.*

**In 1950 Octavio Paz published his first edition of *El laberinto de la soledad* [*The Labyrinth of Solitude*]. What impact did Paz's book have, and was it also attacked by the nationalists?**
Paz in 1950 was already a recognized poet. He had been publishing since the 1930s. Yes, he was attacked by the nationalist critics and writers for *El laberinto*, but the attack on Paz had actually commenced much earlier. You see, in the late 1930s, with the defeat of the Republicans in Spain, many Spanish intellectuals and writers found refuge in Mexico. Paz was one of those Mexican intellectuals who welcomed them and supported them. Paz himself had been in Spain during the civil war. But the nationalists, who were quite anti-Spanish, irrespective of political ideology, attacked Mexican intellectuals such as Paz for supporting the Spanish exiles. The nationalists further attacked the Spanish intellectuals when they started writing about

Mexico. They were criticized for not being "authentic" writers of Mexico.

Another Mexican intellectual who, like Paz, came under much abuse by the nationalists was Alfonso Reyes. In 1940 Reyes had established the Casa de las Españas to provide a research forum for the exiled Spanish intellectuals. This later became the Colegio de México, one of the most significant academic centers in Mexico today. But the nationalists resented this support for the Spaniards. The nationalists were still fighting the wars of independence from Spain.

**Paz's *Laberinto* was first published in 1950, and the second edition in 1957. In 1960 you reviewed the book. Did you find many differences between the first and the second editions?**

There were significant differences. In my review I compared these differences. In the first edition, Paz was much more critical of Mexico, while in the second edition he moderated his views.

**Was the chapter on the *pachuco* in both editions?**

Yes, although here he didn't make many changes.

**His essay on the *pachuco* must have been among the first on this subject published in Mexico.**

The first one, I think. Paz was in Los Angeles during the early 1940s and witnessed the zoot-suit riots in 1943. He borrowed Ramos's concept of the *pelado* and applied it to the *pachuco*. In both cases they represent the extremes of the Mexican character.

**Of course, years later, by the late 1960s when the Chicano movement developed, Octavio Paz was rediscovered, so to speak, by Chicanos. *El laberinto* was also more accessible because it had been translated into English. What I find curious is Paz's attraction to Chicanos, especially given his negative portrayal of the *pachuco*, whom the Chicano movement, in contrast, transformed into an oppositional cultural icon. How do you explain this attraction?**

It's not so much the essay on the *pachuco* which attracted the Chicanos, but the rest of the book, which provides a critical analysis of Mexico's history. It criticizes Spain's colonial rule, it points out the contradictions of Mexico's independence period, and it celebrates the Mexican Revolution of 1910, at least during its initial phases. Since there were few published Chicano intellectuals as yet in the 1960s, Chicanos turned to Mexican intellectuals and writers to give them a sense of history and of identity. Paz, [Samuel] Ramos, [José] Vasconcelos, and [Carlos] Fuentes were some of these intellectuals who filled this gap. But once Chicanos developed their own intellectuals, they soon forgot Paz and the others.

**What influences do you see in early Chicano writers that can be traced to Paz?**

The influence is that the Chicanos' reading of Paz coincided with the development of Chicano nationalism, which builds on pre-Columbian myths in an antagonism against colonialism, including Spanish colonialism, and on the nationalism of the Mexican Revolution. All of these themes Chicanos found in Paz's *Labyrinth*. For example, Paz was very pro-Zapatista because his own father had been a follower of Zapata. Chicanos, of course, identified with Zapata the revolutionary, the leader of an insurgent peasant movement to regain stolen lands. Chicanos, in a sense, saw themselves as contemporary Zapatistas struggling to regain their lost lands, Aztlán, the southwest.

## From Azuela to Fuentes

*Leal (right) with Carlos Fuentes at UC Santa Barbara in 1986. In background, Mario García.*

**In that article on contemporary Mexican literature that you published in 1962, you wrote, "From Azuela to Fuentes, we reach the full circle in Mex-**

ico's social change as reflected in the contemporary novel." What did you mean by that?

You see, Azuela was one of the first writers to criticize the Mexican Revolution, in *Andres Pérez Maderista,* which was published in 1911 and represented Azuela's first novel of the revolution. His criticisms of the revolution, of course, continue with *Los de abajo* and his other work. But after Azuela, few if any writers criticized the revolution, until Fuentes in the 1950s. Fuentes takes up where Azuela left off. In this sense, Mexican literature makes a full circle back to Azuela.

**Let's talk about Carlos Fuentes. How is it that a writer such as Fuentes, with his biting criticism of the revolution, can surface in the 1950s? Was his first novel, *La región más transparente* [*Where the Air Is Clear*], well received, or was it attacked by the nationalists?**

Fuentes could surface because the intense nationalism of the revolution had moderated itself quite a bit by the 1950s. *La región más transparente* was criticized by some, but on the whole it was well received. What Fuentes did in this novel was to take Paz's *Labyrinth of Solitude* and turn it into fiction. One character in the novel is even portrayed as carrying the *Labyrinth* under his arm.

**So that Fuentes, in your opinion, shows the influence of Paz?**

There's no question about it. You can see it in the language, in the characters, and in Fuentes's ideas.

**Except that Fuentes, one can say, is really much more critical of the revolution than Paz is.**

That's right. Paz defends the revolution and Fuentes attacks it.

**Yet you say that when *La región más transparente* was published it was not widely attacked. How do you explain this?**

Fuentes's criticisms are accepted because most Mexicans themselves had become critical of the revolution and of the PRI [Partido Revolucionario Institucional], which had governed Mexico since the late 1920s. Fuentes is not leading the criticism, he's following the people, because they had seen the failures of the revolution. The revolution had created an elite group of bureaucrats, bankers, and hacienda landowners, but most Mexicans did not benefit. The *campesinos* and the Indians, as in Chiapas, remained poor.

**How did intellectuals, critics, and other writers in Mexico respond to Fuentes's first novel?**

Very well. It's the first time that you have a history of Mexico City in fictionalized form. In the novel, everything happens in Mexico City. The novel critiques the class system in Mexico. You have the upper, middle, and lower classes. Fuentes even integrates the figure of the Chicano into the novel. There are Chicano characters who return to Mexico after emigrating to the United States. Some of these characters speak in English. Fuentes's novel was the first real Mexican urban novel. Its originality led to its being well received.

**Fuentes's third novel, *The Death of Artemio Cruz,* appeared a few years later.**

In 1962, the same year that he published his smaller novel, *Aura.* Now, *Artemio Cruz* is a much more artistic novel than *La región más transparente.*

**What do you mean by artistic?**

I mean the structure of the novel. Everything happens in the mind of Artemio Cruz before he dies. And everything is set in twelve hours, and so there are twelve episodes in his life corresponding to twelve months. Then you have Artemio Cruz speaking in three voices. You have the first person, *yo;* the second person, *tú;* and the third person, *él.* The novel is also very much influenced by *Citizen Kane,* the film by Orson Welles. In the film, you have Kane thinking about his life as he is dying.

**So, was *La muerte de Artemio Cruz* well received when it first came out?**

It was very well received. In my opinion, *Artemio Cruz* is Fuentes's best novel. It is very well structured. It contains not only the history of Mexico City, as in *La región más transparente,* but of Mexico, especially of the period of the Mexican Revolution. It deals with the various social classes in Mexico both before and after the revolution. Artemio Cruz, of course, is a former revolutionary who betrays his friends and becomes very rich. It is a novel about how the press is controlled by the politicians. Artemio Cruz, like William Randolph Hearst as depicted in *Citizen Kane,* is a newspaperman.

**Is there a connection, in their writings, between Fuentes, Revueltas, and Juan Rulfo?**

Yes, in a certain way. In *El luto humano,* published in 1943 and translated as *The Stone Knife* in 1947, Revueltas introduced a new type of novel characterized by innovative writing technique on the one hand and a strong focus on social problems on the other hand. In *El luto humano* you have the problem of the labor leader who attempts to resolve a peasant strike and is consequently assassinated. But it's not only the social issues that are important here but the way the story is told.

Social themes connect Fuentes, Revueltas, and Rulfo. Each writes about *caciques,* or political bosses, in Mexico. In Revueltas and Rulfo you see the influence of Faulkner. This influence is not as visible in Fuentes, who is influenced by a much wider circle of Latin American, American, and European writers.

Although all three employ innovative writing techniques, they don't necessarily employ the same ones. In *El luto humano,* for example, Revueltas at the end seems to forget that he is writing a novel and begins to write an essay. Rulfo, on the other hand, tells everything through his characters. Another big difference is that Rulfo employs what is called *realismo mágico,* or magical realism—that neither Revueltas or Fuentes uses.

**But what you're saying is that what connects them, despite certain differences in content and style, is that all three represent that synthesis after World War II that you earlier addressed, concerning technique and social consciousness.**

Technique and content, yes.

**Since Fuentes was the youngest writer of these three, did he represent in the 1950s a new departure in the Mexican novel? Certainly into the 1960s he is grouped together with other Latin American writers, such as García Márquez and Vargas Llosa.**

Yes. Fuentes represents a new novelist in Mexico who is more conscious of the outside world, of international trends. This is because he lived much of his early life outside of Mexico—in Washington, D.C., for example. He also lived in Europe and other parts of Latin America. This is different from Rulfo, who is entirely regional. Rulfo, despite the social themes he focused on, such as the plight of the peasant, rarely spoke out on politics. Revueltas was influenced by the socialist movements, but his stress was always on Mexican politics—unlike Fuentes, who addressed both in his writings and his essays the international scene. Fuentes, then, represents an opening up of the Mexican writer to the outside world.

# Mariano Azuela

**Don Luis, in 1961, after you arrived in Illinois, you published your book on Mariano Azuela. Was there a resurgence of interest in Azuela in the early 1960s?**

I think I began that interest. When the book came out, the reviews were all highly positive, and all this revived interest not just in my book but, more importantly, in Azuela's writings. Although there were periods in Mexico when much of his work was not available because it hadn't been reprinted, still Azuela was never forgotten as a writer. He even overcame, or his writings overcame, a great deal of criticism by other Mexican writers and intellectuals. For example, in the early 1940s Octavio Paz severely criticized Azuela and, by contrast, praised Revueltas's first novel. Azuela had not been liked by other writers and intellectuals because he remained aloof. He never wanted to be identified with a particular group of writers. He even rejected membership in the Mexican Language Academy. He also never wanted to take any governmental position, unlike other Mexican writers, because then he could not criticize the government.

**Does the success of Fuentes, who also criticized the Mexican Revolution, have a connection with the resurgence of interest in Azuela?**
Yes, because Azuela was the first writer to criticize the revolution, as early as 1911.

**So, with your book on Azuela, did people begin to read Azuela again?**
Well, by the end of the 1950s many of his books had been republished. There was always an interest in them, especially in *Los de abajo*. Actually, *Los de abajo* is still the best selling novel in Mexico, even today.

**Had you been interested in Azuela even earlier in your career?**
I always had an interest in Azuela and, in fact, wrote an early essay on him in the 1950s for the *Encyclopaedia Britannica*. What happened was that my mentor at the University of Chicago, Carlos Castillo, was a consultant to the encyclopedia, and he asked me to contribute several essays on Latin American writers, including Mariano Azuela, for a new edition. When I wrote this essay, I discovered that not a single book on Azuela existed. I said to myself, "I'm going to write a book about Azuela." I began to write it while at Emory and finished it after I got to Illinois.

It's a biography and a study of his place in Mexican literature. I studied not only his published work, but his personal papers as well. I visited his widow in Mexico City, who gave me access to Azuela's papers. I myself had never met Azuela. But I interviewed his widow and one of his sons, Enrique. After my book was published, when anyone went to the Azuela home (which is on a street named after Azuela) inquiring about Azuela, the family directed them to my book. And Arturo Azuela, a grandson of Don Mariano and a major writer himself, recalls seeing me do research in his grandfather's house when he was a little boy. Today, Antonio Azuela, another son of Don Mariano, has asked me to prepare another book about his father.

**Was Azuela an embittered man, perhaps because of a certain lack of recognition in his own time?**

Oh, yes! He was heavily criticized. Critics accused him of not knowing how to write. But the people read him and appreciated him despite the critics. He used to say, "I don't write for the critics. I write for the people." He didn't want to have anything to do with the critics or the intellectuals.

**Do you think that Azuela's novels have stood the test of time?**

Certain of his novels have, but not all. *Los de abajo,* of course, has stood the test of time. One of his other novels, *La malhora,* published in 1927, represents the beginning of a new trend in the Mexican novel that is more clearly visible by the 1940s. That is, the new synthesis of innovative technique coupled with concern for social issues. In this sense, Azuela was ahead of his time. In *La malhora* he combines the style of the surrealistic writers with a naturalistic topic: the life of a prostitute in Mexico City. He later said that he used a surrealistic style in this and a couple of other novels not because he himself favored such a style but in order to prove to the critics that he could write in this style. In *La malhora,* for example, Azuela employed a fragmented structure. The novel has five different episodes with the same main character in each.

**Did you choose to write about Azuela because you identified with him?**

Yes. I was especially attracted to his sincerity. He is a very sincere writer who presents Mexican society from, I guess, a middle-class perspective. When I read him, he made me feel like I was reading about some aspects concerning my own life.

**How influential were Azuela's writings on someone like Fuentes? Is there a connection? Is it that they both criticized the revolution?**

Well, first of all, Fuentes's influence as a writer has been primarily on the educated classes, whereas Azuela's was on the popular classes. But there is no question that Azuela had an influence on Fuentes, as well as on writers such as Rulfo. Azuela even influenced Spanish writers, such as Valle-Inclán, who received inspiration and direction from Azuela in the writing of his novel *Tirano Banderas,* which is about a dictator in Venezuela. When you read *Tirano Banderas,* it's like reading Azuela.

**And how is Azuela looked upon by more contemporary Mexican writers? Are they influenced by him?**

I don't think they read Azuela, and if they do, they unfortunately aren't influenced by him. The people read Azuela, not the intellectuals.

**About ten years after your book on Azuela was published in Spanish, it**

was published here in English. Did you revise it in any way for the English edition?

Only slightly. I eliminated some details that I thought an English-language audience would not be interested in, but there were only minor revisions.

**After the Spanish-language edition was published, you were promoted to full professor. Was the Azuela book the basis for this promotion?**

Yes, it was. I published it two years after I got to Illinois, and one year later I received my promotion. I could have insisted on going to Illinois as a full professor, but I didn't.

**So your colleagues at Illinois obviously thought well of the Azuela book?**

Yes, they did, but the system for promotion and merit increases, including salary increases, wasn't as complicated then as it is now—in the University of California system, for example. I don't even think outside evaluation letters were required. And it wasn't the department who voted on these matters, but only the head of the department, Professor Shoemaker. It was up to him to make the recommendation. They later changed the system so that the faculty of the department were also involved.

# José Vasconcelos

**Don Luis, although you didn't write very much about José Vasconcelos, I wanted to ask you your opinion of him and his influence on Mexican literature and culture. What were or are your views on Vasconcelos, and have they influenced your work in any way?**

Well, the first book of Vasconcelos that I read was his autobiography, *Ulises criollo,* which was published in 1935. It's particularly interesting to me because it deals with the U.S.-Mexico border and northern Mexico. These were topics that few people wrote about then, especially in Mexico. In the book, Vasconcelos describes growing up in Piedras Negras, on the Mexican side of the border, but going to school in Eagle Pass, on the U.S. side of the border. In school, he faced various conflicts with the Anglo students. His father was from Oaxaca, farther south in Mexico, but had been assigned to the *aduana,* the customs house, in Piedras Negras. Vasconcelos himself was born in Oaxaca but came of age on the border. In his autobiography, Vasconcelos writes about the differences in Mexican and Anglo-American culture and the conflicts between the two. He defends Hispanic culture. The book ends with the beginning of the revolution. Of course, he also wrote other important books, such as *La raza cósmica* and *Indología*. He was the only philosopher in Mexico who wrote books on each of the four major philosophical areas: ethics, aesthetics, logic, and metaphysics. Some consider Vasconcelos to have been among the most original thinkers in Latin America.

But Vasconcelos was more than a philosopher and writer; he was also politically involved in the 1920s as the secretary of education. Vasconcelos was responsible for having the great muralists, such as Diego Rivera, involved in decorating many of the public buildings in Mexico City. He also was known for his effort to establish rural schools and to acculturate the Indians into Mexican culture. In some of these efforts, he made certain errors. For example, he had many of the European classics, such as *The Odyssey* and other works of Homer, as well as Virgil and Dante, translated into Spanish and the books distributed free to all of the schools. This was fine, except that many of the school children, especially in the rural areas, could barely read!

**When did you first read Vasconcelos—in graduate school?**

No, earlier. I read him by myself.

**How influential were Vasconcelos's views?**

Early on, they were quite influential, up to the time when he became a more controversial political figure. He ran for president of Mexico in 1929 and was defeated. From there he began to turn more to the political right and by the 1930s was almost a fascist.

**When he wrote *La raza cósmica* in the late 1920s, was he already becoming reactionary?**

Yes, and this is also a time when he begins to travel extensively in Latin America and in the United States. He even came to the University of Chicago as a visiting professor some time in the late 1920s. I remember finding books in the library with his signature on them—books that he had checked out of the library.

**In your opinion, do *La raza cósmica* and Vasconcelos's views about a cosmic race in Latin America represent reactionary views?**

Not necessarily. He was appealing to a more universal perspective on issues of nationality and against a more dogmatic position on nationalism. He was especially concerned with the dominant influence of the United States in Latin America. He blamed all of Mexico's problems on the United States.

**Were his views influential on other writers?**

To some extent, yes. Octavio Paz later speaks well of Vasconcelos. On the other hand, I don't see much influence of Vasconcelos on someone like Samuel Ramos.

**But I can understand that Vasconcelos's ideas, which were antinationalist, would not go over well in Mexico in the 1920s and 1930s, when nationalism was being promoted.**

This is especially true in the 1930s under Lázaro Cárdenas. The Cárdenas administration sponsored nationalism, especially *indigenismo.* Vasconcelos, by contrast, favored the more Spanish or European side of Mexican culture instead of the Indian.

# Juan Rulfo

**What is Rulfo's place in Mexican literature?**
After the novel of the Mexican Revolution is exhausted by the 1930s, some new changes in the genre begin to take place. Revueltas's *El luto humano* is a good example of these changes. In 1947 Agustín Yáñez published *Al filo del agua,* which furthered this change. But then, in 1953, Rulfo published his collection of short stories, *El llano en llamas,* and that definitely changed everything. These stories are about the countryside. But the important thing is how Rulfo tells these stories—the style. He is the first Mexican writer to effectively employ magical realism, although it wasn't yet called that. Then, in 1955, Rulfo published his novel, *Pedro Páramo,* which is considered the beginning of the new Mexican novel. The influence of Rulfo was to be not only on other Mexican writers, such as Fuentes, but on Latin American writers as a whole, on writers such as García Márquez. In fact, García Márquez later said that he wished he had written *Pedro Páramo.* Rulfo also influenced writers in Europe and the United States. Magical realism, of course, became the distinguishing mark of Latin American literature.

Rulfo's style is steeped in the way the people of his native state of Jalisco talked, although he elevated this talk to a literary art form. It's not like the *costumbristas*—such as Azuela—who copied in their writings exactly how the people talked. Rulfo doesn't do that. He bases his writing on the vocabulary of the people, but not on the structure of their sentences. His style is path breaking, and this is his greatest contribution.

**Is the content of Rulfo's work also a break with previous Mexican writers?**
The content is magical realism. But all of his stories are very violent. In

*Pedro Páramo* the great innovation is that all of the characters are dead. He brings to life a dead town—the very town that Rulfo grew up in. He later revisited this place and found it almost a ghost town. So he used *Pedro Páramo* as a way of bringing the town back to life. You hear the souls speaking.

**You also have noted Faulkner's influence on Rulfo.**

Rulfo always denied this influence, but I think it's clear that it was there. It's not in the style, but in the way Faulkner concentrated on a small town—Oxford, Mississippi—and how he created small-town characters. Rulfo read widely, including American literature, and was well acquainted with Faulkner's writing. Faulkner, of course, had a tremendous influence throughout Latin America.

**The early reaction by critics to *Pedro Páramo* was not very positive. How is it that Rulfo is later rediscovered as a major writer?**

It's difficult to trace this. The only criticism was that *Pedro Páramo* was too difficult to read in order to get the story. But later critics came to recognize not only the importance of the story of *Pedro Páramo,* but even more the significance of its style. This rediscovery began in the 1960s but really grew in the 1970s. Up until this time, Rulfo was quite discouraged, frustrated, and even bitter that his work was not being validated at a time when other writers, such as Fuentes, were gaining international recognition.

**Is Rulfo considered part of the [Latin American] Boom writers of the 1960s?**

No. He benefits by the international discovery of Latin American literature, but he is never regarded as a member of this exclusive club of writers. In fact, at first these Boom writers, such as Fuentes and García Márquez, don't even acknowledge Rulfo's contributions. They finally begin to do so into the 1970s, and then they all—including Octavio Paz—celebrate Rulfo. But do you know that despite the exclusion of Rulfo from the Boom writers, no other Latin American writer has been written about as much by literary scholars as has Rulfo? It's incredible!

**You visited Rulfo in 1962. How did this come about?**

I was in Guadalajara as part of a summer National Defense Act Institute in Spanish. While there, I met many of the local writers, who every afternoon held a *tertulia* [social gathering] at the Café Nápoli, where they would read from their manuscripts. Rulfo often went there. I had, of course, read his work and had been highly impressed by it, although I hadn't as yet written anything on Rulfo. I began to know Rulfo and recall spending one wonderful Sunday afternoon visiting him.

**What kind of man was he?**

Very serious. He didn't talk very much, especially about his own work. I asked him about *Pedro Páramo,* but all he said was that it was a novel filled with errors. But one thing I remember was his extensive library. He had books from all over the world, and his knowledge of these books—especially the novels—was impressive.

**Why did Rulfo have such a tragic world view in his writings?**

Well, he had lived a tragic life. He was an orphan. His father had been killed. His mother died soon thereafter. He had trouble finding work. And he had difficulty as a writer early in his career.

**Region was very important to Rulfo.**

Yes. Just like the Chicano writer Rudolfo Anaya has said that a "sense of place" is important for a writer, this very well applies to Rulfo. With a few exceptions, his work is set in Jalisco. He is a regional writer, but then so too was Faulkner.

**The fact that he is a regional as well as a rural writer at a time when the Mexican novel is becoming an urban novel—did this perhaps affect why early critics didn't appreciate his work?**

I think there's no question about that. He was going against the trend of the metropolitan and cosmopolitan novel. This certainly prejudiced some of the urban critics against him.

**Why did you decide to write a literary biography of Rulfo, which appeared in 1983?**

Most everything I have written has been the result of external influences. I wrote my Rulfo book because at an MLA meeting in New York in the late 1970s, I was sitting next to Luis Dávila at a session on Latin American literature. Dávila, at the time, was editing a series on Latin American literature for Twayne. He asked me, "Would you like to write a book on Rulfo?" I immediately said "Yes." So I wrote it.

**Did you interview Rulfo for this study?**

No, but I had talked with him back in the early 1960s and had kept in touch with him.

**Despite the success of *Pedro Páramo,* Rulfo didn't publish very many other works. Do we know if he left other unpublished manuscripts after his death in 1989?**

During the early 1960s he began writing a novel, *La cordillera*, or *The Pack-train*, which he never completed, although short excerpts were published in periodicals. The subject was the history of a town in central Mexico during the colonial period, a town that he wanted to bring to life through the experiences of a family. Some have said that there are other manuscripts, but none have been published. It's possible that family members don't want to publish some of this material for fear that it might hurt Rulfo's reputation. He was a perfectionist and would not want anything of his published that was not perfect. He was always correcting and correcting.

**Is Rulfo the greatest Mexican writer of this century?**
It's difficult to answer this question. If you say the greatest fiction writer then perhaps it's Rulfo. But if you say poetry, then you have to consider Sor Juana Inés de la Cruz and Octavio Paz. If you measure greatness by productivity, then you have writers such as Carlos Fuentes.

**Well, then, can we say that *Pedro Páramo* is the greatest Mexican novel?**
I would say so. Although some critics would prefer Azuela's *Los de abajo*.

**Do contemporary writers in Mexico look to Rulfo for literary inspiration?**
No, because he's too difficult a writer. He's a hard writer to emulate. And if you try, people will immediately say, "That's Rulfo." One Chicano writer who was clearly influenced by Rulfo was Tomás Rivera.

## Essays in *El Nacional*

**Don Luis, in the early 1960s you started publishing essays for *El Nacional* in Mexico City. How did that happen?**
I can't remember exactly. I don't remember if Martínez Peñalosa, the editor, asked me to contribute these essays or if I just sent them on my own. But once or twice a month, I would send him different essays. They were usually published on the front page of their Sunday literary supplement.

**Were these book reviews or essays?**
They were articles. For example, I did a series on Mexican short story writers. Whenever I wanted to publish something right away based on my research, I would write up these short essays and submit them to *El Nacional*. Longer essays I would send to more-scholarly journals, such as *Cuadernos Americanos* or *Historia Mexicana*. Whenever I was in Mexico City, I would also stop by to talk to the editor.

**Was *El Nacional* a government-operated paper or was it independent?**

It was the government's official paper.

**Were you paid for these submissions?**

Oh, yes, but not much. When I visited their offices they sometimes paid me right there. I published these essays in *El Nacional* for a while until they changed editors and changed the format of the Sunday supplement. I didn't like the changes. The previous format was more like a separate literary magazine.

**In Mexico and in the rest of Latin America, there is more of a tradition of intellectuals writing for the newspapers or doing journalism.**

Yes, and in both Latin America and Spain, you also find literary supplements in the newspapers, usually published on weekends, and all the writers publish in these supplements. In Mexico, for example, Fuentes has always written for the newspapers.

**That's very different than here in the United States. You can send an essay to the *Los Angeles Times*, but there's no guarantee that it will be published.**

That's true. Back in the 1980s, *La Opinión* in Los Angeles published an excellent literary supplement called "La Comunidad," which was edited by Sergio Muñoz. I published several essays in it. But then after a few years they decided to do away with it.

# Jorge Luis Borges

**In the early 1960s, you also started to write a bit about Borges. But when did you first encounter Borges as a writer?**

I came across Borges in the early 1940s. At the University of Chicago, we read Borges's short stories in our seminars. In my own teaching at Chicago, I had my students read Borges. We had to prepare our own textbooks for the students, which the university published, and for mine I always included a short story by Borges. Then, in my teaching of Latin American literature at Mississippi, at Emory, and at Illinois, I always introduced Borges to my students. So as a result of my teaching Borges, I also began to write about him. I published about three articles on Borges and gave a few lectures on him as well.

**When you first started to read Borges, what was your opinion of his work?**

I was attracted to the way he told his stories, which is very mysterious on the one hand but very clear on the other. He gives you the idea that he's writing about something mysterious, but in reality it is very clear. I was also attracted to his mathematical mind. Everything is always mathematical in his stories.

**What do you mean by mathematical?**

I mean that he uses symmetry in his writing. For example, in one story he has a detective following someone. The detective comes to a door and concludes that there has to be another door related to the first door, and so on.

Another fascinating thing about Borges is that he always gives you clues about what is going to happen. The reader also becomes a detective.

In one of my essays on Borges, I wrote about why Borges never published a novel and why he always preferred the short story. This was also true of Alfonso Reyes. In fact, Borges called Alfonso Reyes the greatest writer in the Spanish language. There is a great deal of Reyes's influence on Borges.

**What was that influence?**

It was in style, in the way of presenting a story. Reyes had this influence on Borges even though Reyes himself only wrote a few short stories. He was mostly an essayist.

**So how exactly did Reyes influence Borges?**

Reyes was a very concise and precise writer, and so too was Borges. Neither wasted any words. I heard Borges give a lecture in Chicago in which he said that a writer should not use many words, only the minimum number to tell a story.

**How many times did you meet Borges?**

Only about four times. That one time in Chicago, then once in Houston, once in Los Angeles, and then the last time here in Santa Barbara.

**And when did you first meet him?**

In the 1960s. I don't remember the exact year, just when he was beginning to receive much attention in the United States, as his books were being translated into English.

**But besides by Alfonso Reyes, Borges was also influenced greatly by English and American writers.**

Well, Borges's special field of expertise was medieval English literature. In fact, that's what he taught at the University of Buenos Aires. His grandmother, you know, was an English woman. So there was a very strong English influence in Borges's life. He also knew American literature very well. In one of his first collections of stories, he quotes works from American literature and uses characters from that literature. He knew English and American literature. He didn't know the literature of Spain as well, although he did write some essays on Cervantes and *Don Quixote*.

**Did he speak English very well?**

Oh, yes. His English was excellent. As a matter of fact, when I heard him talk in Houston, he was followed by another Latin American speaker who apologized for his poor English by saying, "Unfortunately, I didn't have the luck of having an English grandmother!"

**So you wrote only about three articles on Borges?**

Yes. Even though I very much liked his stories, he wasn't one of the writers I was heavily researching. I did, however, write a poem about Borges, although I never published it. I once had a dream about Borges and then wrote a poem which I called "Borges en el sueño." I can't remember everything I said in that poem, but it had to do with the lack of social content in Borges's work—the fact that his stories are more characterized by attention to form rather than content.

**What in your estimation is Borges's place in Latin American literature?**

In Latin American literature, everyone reads Borges and everyone learns how to write by reading Borges. Everyone criticizes Borges's more conservative political ideas, and he never received the Nobel Prize for literature because of those ideas, but everyone reads Borges. He is also credited for moving Latin American literature into new stylistic directions that are more innovative, characteristics that become more predominant in the 1960s with the so-called Boom writers. In Argentina and in other parts of Latin America, up to the 1930s when Borges began to write, you found the more traditional and epic style of writing, characterized by "la novela de la tierra"—the novel of the countryside—such as *Los de abajo* or *Doña Bárbara*. Borges comes along with something very different. He has a more psychological approach and a more fragmented form of writing.

**Did Borges have much *éxito* in Mexico?**

Yes, all of the writers read Borges. Everyone admires Borges as a writer; not as a person, but as a writer. He really knew how to express himself.

# The Boom Writers

**Into the 1960s, everyone begins to talk and write about the so-called Boom writers. Who are the Boom writers?**

The Boom is the name given to four Latin American writers who achieved international recognition: Carlos Fuentes, Gabriel García Márquez, Mario Vargas Llosa, and Julio Cortázar. It was just these four, and they didn't let anyone else into what became a kind of club or clique. Other excellent writers, such as José Donoso from Chile, were excluded. It wasn't so much that these four writers got together and said, "Let's exclude everyone else," but that the international critics only recognized these four and excluded other Latin American writers from serious international recognition.

**But didn't these four have influence on which other Latin American writers were to be translated, both in the United States and Europe?**

That's right. In a sense, they had this influence, but I don't know how they used it.

**And the importance of the Boom writers is that for the first time Latin American writers received international recognition.**

Yes. These four writers were translated in many languages and were read all over the world. This was the beginning of what was referred to as the new Latin American novel. Before the Boom, the Latin American novel was seen as too regionalist, including a language with many regionalist terms that were difficult for non–Latin Americans, or even those within Latin America, to understand. The Boom writers, in contrast, abandon that tradition and begin to write with a larger Latin American and international audience in mind. They begin to use a language more common to all of the Spanish-speaking world.

**And, also, they represent more-urban writers, such as Fuentes.**

Yes, that's another characteristic. They move away from the tradition of the rural novel. In the earlier novel of *la tierra*, nature conquers man. However, in the new Latin American novel, man conquers nature. The Boom novel is largely an urban novel that has little to do with nature. I think that's why these novels became so successful.

**I understand that there is a close relationship between the rise of the Boom writers and Emir Rodríguez Monegal, the literary critic at Yale. Is that true?**

The relationship was the following: Rodríguez Monegal, who was from Uruguay, in the 1960s was in Paris, where he published a periodical called *Mundo Nuevo.* In this periodical, Rodríguez Monegal begins to call attention to Fuentes, García Márquez, Vargas Llosa, and Cortázar. It was Rodríguez Monegal who coined the term *Boom writers.* But other critics began to take up the term. By calling attention to these particular writers, Rodríguez Monegal influenced their translation into other languages, including English and French.

**So before the Boom writers, very few other Latin American writers had been translated?**

Very few were translated. I remember that around 1940 one of the New York publishing firms awarded a prize for the best Latin American novel, and this included a translation into English. Two of these prizes were awarded. One went to *El mundo es ancho y ajeno* [*Broad and Alien is the World*] by Ciro Alegría from Perú, which was an indigenous novel, and the second prize went to *Nayar*, by Miguel Angel Menéndez from Yucatán, which was also about Indians, in this case about Indians in the state of Nayarit in Mexico. Then in the early 1960s, William Faulkner set up a fund to help young Latin American writers be translated into English. But these translations were the exception. And even if they were translated, they weren't reviewed or read extensively. It wasn't until the highly successful translation of García Márquez's *Cien años de soledad,* or *One Hundred Years of Solitude,* that this begins to change. The translation of the Boom writers was also aided by the availability of very competent translators, such as Gregory Rabassa.

# Gabriel García Márquez

**You've discussed some of your views about Carlos Fuentes, but what are your thoughts about some of the other Boom writers, such as García Márquez? He is the other Boom writer, besides Fuentes, whom you have written more about.**

Mario, I have written about all four Boom writers, but in literary reviews not easily available. I think I was the first critic, at least in the United States, to discuss García Márquez in a book. In my 1966 *Historia del cuento hispano-americano,* I analyze García Márquez as a short-story writer. At this time, García Márquez was not very well known. He had published one novel, *La hojarasca* [*Fallen Leaves*] and a collection of short stories, *Los funerales de la mamá grande* [*Grandmother's Funeral*], which I discussed in my book. But he hadn't published more than this. He was then one of many other Latin American short-story writers.

**And what was your reaction to García Márquez when you first encountered his work?**

Very positive, but I never thought that he would become a famous novelist.

**When *Cien años de soledad* was first published in 1967, was that when you read this novel?**

Not only did I read it, but I used it in one of my seminars. In fact, one of the first published articles on *Cien años* came out of my seminar. This was a paper written in my class by Isaías Lerner at Illinois. He now teaches at the City University of New York. The paper was so good that I recommended that Lerner send it to *Cuadernos Americanos,* which he did, and the journal published it right away.

**What was your opinion of *Cien años*?**

I thought it was a great novel, comparable to Rulfo's *Pedro Páramo.*

**How are these two novels different?**

In many ways. *Pedro Páramo* doesn't appeal to everyone, because you have to work to get its meaning. In contrast, *Cien años* is written more like a traditional novel, with the exception that it uses magical realism.

**So when you first read *Cien años,* did you see it as a major breakthrough in Latin American literature?**

Yes. There have been several breakthroughs in contemporary Latin American literature. One of these is *El luto humano* by Revueltas. Of course, there is *Pedro Páramo.* Then there is Fuentes's *La región más transparente.* And then there is *Cien años* and at about the same time *Rayuela* by Julio Cortázar.

**In what sense did you think *Cien años* was a major breakthrough?**

Because of its use of magical realist elements. In *Cien años,* you have scenes that are hard to believe, but in the context that García Márquez provides, you do accept the reality of these scenes. I've just recently read Ana Castillo's *So Far From God,* which in a Chicano context also employs magical realism. However, in Castillo's case, where she has scenes similar to *Cien años,* although set in New Mexico, these scenes are difficult to believe. Her use of magical realism doesn't seem to work. But García Márquez puts magical realist elements in a context that is easy to believe. Whatever you read in García Márquez, no matter how extravagant, you believe that it can happen. If he tells you that someone can fly, you believe it. But García Márquez was not the first Latin American writer to successfully use magical realism. Before him, there was Alejo Carpentier from Cuba, who in his novels in the 1950s was using this literary technique. He called it *lo real maravilloso.*

**Did García Márquez borrow from Carpentier?**

There is no question about that, especially from Carpentier's *Los pasos perdidos* [*The Lost Steps*], which is a great novel. But I should mention that García Márquez was also influenced by Faulkner with respect to subject matter. García Márquez, himself, has admitted his debt to Faulkner. From Faulkner he took the idea in *Cien años* of creating a mythical town, as Faulkner did in his novels about rural Mississippi. Macondo, the mythical town in *Cien años,* is right out of Faulkner.

**When *Cien años* was published in Latin America, was it a major success right away?**

Yes. Thousands of copies were sold in his native country of Colombia and also throughout Latin America and in Spain.

**And in the United States, when it was published in English around 1970, did it also become an immediate success?**

Yes; it was a best seller in this country, the first time a translated Latin American novel was on the American best-seller list.

**How do you explain its success in the United States?**

Because the American reader thinks of Latin America in exotic terms, which is what appeals to them about *Cien años,* which is set in the rain forest and employs magical realism. American readers at that time reacted at two extreme levels to Latin American writers. At one extreme there was Borges, who appealed to the intellectuals, and at the other extreme there was García Márquez, who appealed to a more popular audience.

**In 1967 you published an article in *Cuadernos Americanos* entitled "El realismo mágico en la literatura hispanoamericana." Was that one of the first essays on magical realism? Was it specifically on García Márquez?**

It covered several writers who used magical realist literary techniques, including García Márquez and Rulfo. This may well have been one of the first articles on magical realism. It was certainly one of my most successful articles. I wrote this essay in response to another article on magical realism by Angel Flores, the literary critic from Puerto Rico. In his article, Angel Flores proposed that magical realism in Latin American literature begins with Borges and that all new Latin American literature was magical realist. His essay was influential but, in my opinion, wrong. So I wrote my article in response. In it I say that Borges is not a magical realist, but a fantastic-short-story writer. I distinguished between fantastic literature and magical-realist literature.

**And what is the difference?**

In fantastic literature, in Borges for example, the writer creates new worlds, perhaps new planets. But what is created has nothing to do with the reality of our world. By contrast, writers like García Márquez, who use magical realism, don't create new worlds but suggest the magical in this world. But it's a real world. It's our world.

**How was your interpretation received?**

Well, it caused some reaction. I made some critics upset, including Rodríguez Monegal, who wrote a countercritique, although in his essay he never defined magical realism. He titled his article "Diálogo entre sordos," or "Dialogue Between the Deaf." He criticized both Angel Flores and me for not listening or paying attention to the texts we were critiquing. Some time later I ran into Rodríguez Monegal at a meeting in San Francisco and I said to him, "And which one of the *sordos* am I, the first or the second one?"

**But your essay on magical realism still produced much response on the part of other critics?**

Yes, my article has been republished several times and has been widely quoted, and recently translated and included in a book on the subject. During this period it wasn't just the critics who were taken up by magical realism, but nonexperts as well. I remember one time being approached by a recent Cuban émigré at a meeting in Kentucky who, after I lectured on magical realism and Latin American literature, came up to me and said, "I thought that magical realism was when you take a rabbit out of a hat."

Some time later, there appeared a review of recent Latin American texts which asserted that magical realism had been created by Carpentier in his novel. I disagreed and wrote a response saying that in fact the term *magical realism* had been created in Germany in the 1920s and then translated into Spanish and that the term was first applied to painting, not literature. It was the Latin Americans who attached the term to literature around the 1930s and 1940s, but even then the term was not widely used. But I remember reading, when I was at the University of Chicago, a novel by an Ecuadorian writer, Aguilera Malta, which in retrospect contained elements of magical realism, but we didn't use the term then or recognize it as magical realism.

**Is magical realism primarily associated with a literature of the tropics?**

To a certain extent, yes. But it can also be applied to other contexts, such as the *llano,* the desert. This is the case with Rulfo's use of magical realism. But magical realism can also be applied to an urban context. It's really the attitude of the characters toward reality. But it's a literary technique that comes out of a Latin American cultural context. Once an English professor at an MLA meeting asked me, "Do you believe in magical realism?" I said, "What does it have to do with whether I believe it or not? It's just a literary trend and has nothing to do with whether I believe magical realism actually exists!"

**But what's the cultural foundation for magical realism? From what sources are these writers drawing?**

There is no question about the source. It comes from the first Spanish explorers who came to the New World and saw *lo maravilloso.*

**How do you define *lo maravilloso*?**

It's something that happens but which cannot be explained by reason. You can't explain it. So the Spanish explorers encountered natural phenomena which they had no explanations for and as a result gave to these phenomena a magical interpretation. Let me give you an example. One time I was giving a lecture in Salt Lake City on *lo real maravilloso,* and I said, "You don't have to go very far from here to understand what this term means, you just have to go over to the Great Salt Lake where things don't sink!" When the Spaniards came across phenomena like this they asked, "How is this possible?" This is something that people don't explain by scientific law. You just accept it.

**Of the Boom writers, is García Márquez the only one who uses magical realism?**

Yes, although Vargas Llosa in one novel, *La casa verde,* uses it to a certain extent.

**And with García Márquez's success, then other Latin American writers also begin to use magical realism. Is that the case?**

Yes, especially Isabel Allende, beginning with her first novel, *La casa de los espíritus* [*The House of the Spirits*]. As I mentioned earlier, even a Chicana writer such as Ann Castillo begins to use magical realism.

**Do you see any influence of García Márquez on Chicano writers?**

In *The Road to Tamazunchale* by Ron Arias, there is a section that is right out of García Márquez. It's right out of one of his short stories. Arias just translated it and put it into his story. You see some of this influence in Rudolfo Anaya's *Bless Me, Ultima.*

**García Márquez, of course, was awarded the Nobel Prize for literature. Do you agree that of the Boom writers, he was the most deserving of this honor?**

Yes, I do. Fuentes was still too young at the time. But, yes, I would agree that of the four Boom writers, García Márquez was the most innovative and most talented.

# Julio Cortázar

**Don Luis, in the 1960s you were also writing a bit about the other Boom writers, Cortázar and Vargas Llosa. Let's talk about Cortázar first. When**

did you first encounter his writings, and how does Cortázar compare with the other Boom writers?

Cortázar was not well known until he published *Rayuela,* his first major novel. When it came out, I used it in my classes. Before *Rayuela,* Cortázar had written some other pieces of fiction, but they exhibited too much of Borges's influence. Both, of course, were from Buenos Aires. To escape this influence and Borges's strong literary dominance in Argentina, Cortázar had to leave his country. He went to Paris, where, I think, he worked for UNESCO as a translator. It was in Paris where he wrote *Rayuela.* I was initially more interested in his short stories. Before *Rayuela,* he had published a book of short stories under the title *Bestiario.* In fact, one of my graduate students at Illinois, Martha Franscescato, who was also from Argentina, wrote her Ph.D. thesis on *Bestiario.* But it was *Rayuela* that made Cortázar famous and why he became part of the Boom. What is impressive about that novel is its structure. It's divided into three parts, but you can read these parts in any order. It's also characterized by its international flavor. It takes place in Buenos Aires and in Paris. In fact, in an earlier short story, the story first is set in Buenos Aires, but then he has his characters go through a tunnel and they find themselves in Paris. What's also interesting about *Rayuela* is that Cortázar comments on or includes characters from some of the other Boom writers. For example, he includes some characters from Fuentes's *Artemio Cruz.* In fact, the Boom writers in their works at the time inserted characters from or comments about the other Boom writers. Another interesting thing about *Rayuela* is that it's the only novel that mentions my hometown of Linares. Cortázar writes about a revolutionary from Linares. I don't know where Cortázar got his information about Linares, since I don't believe that he ever went to Mexico.

And you say that Cortázar, or at least the early Cortázar, was strongly influenced by Borges?

Yes. At the beginning of Cortázar's writing career, it looks like you're reading Borges. But that's one of the reasons that he left Argentina, to get away from Borges, because it would have been difficult for Cortázar to have been recognized if he had stayed in Buenos Aires. Going to Paris was liberating for Cortázar. He began to write differently. He gets away from Borges, although you can still see some of Borges's influence on Cortázar's later writings, especially in his use of fantastic episodes in his novels and short stories.

So Cortázar employs the fantastic and not magical realism?

There is no magical realism in Cortázar. There is the fantastic, however. For example, in one of his short stories, called "Casa tomada," a brother and sister are living together in a house which becomes taken over by something or someone. We never know what takes over the house.

**And this is an example of the fantastic?**

Yes. Some critics have given this story a political interpretation, suggesting that it is the Peronistas, the followers of the Argentine dictator Juan Perón, who are taking over the house, just as they are taking over the country. But I think that they're reading things in this story that aren't there.

# Mario Vargas Llosa

**You also wrote a little on Vargas Llosa. What was your opinion of him?**

Vargas Llosa became famous with his novel, *La ciudad y los perros* [*The Time of the Hero*]. This is a criticism of the military in Perú. Everything takes place in the barracks. There you see class distinctions, racial prejudice, and other social problems that affected Perú at that time. The novel is also a criticism of the political system of Perú. *Los perros,* by the way, refers to the new recruits into the army.

I'll tell you a funny story related to this novel. One summer when I was in Guadalajara, I ran into an American fellow who was translating *La ciudad y los perros* into English. For some reason he thought I could help him with some of the Peruvian terms and references that Vargas Llosa used. But I couldn't help him. These were very local and regional terms. "You have to ask a *peruano* to see what these terms mean." But actually, Vargas Llosa doesn't use that many *peruanismos.* In fact, his style is not as difficult to understand in comparison to other writers, such as Rulfo.

**Vargas Llosa was much more political in his early works, wasn't he?**

Yes, but no more than Fuentes or García Márquez. But what you find in Vargas Llosa is a more direct political criticism than you find in Fuentes and García Márquez. On the other hand, his novel *La casa verde* is a more traditional type of novel and not as overtly political. But Vargas Llosa has always been very political, although his politics have shifted from left to right. His more right-wing views, however, were discredited a few years ago when he ran for president in Perú and lost badly.

Despite his politics, Vargas Llosa is a wonderful writer. He is also a tireless writer. When he wrote the two-volume *Conversación en la catedral,* he said that he threw away almost two thousand pages that he didn't use in the novel. It's incredible, his capacity for writing long novels like *La catedral.* That's another tendency among the Boom writers. They write long novels. Before the Boom writers, most Latin American novels were short.

**How do you explain this?**
I think it was the influence of writers from other countries, especially from the United States and Europe, where long novels predominated.

**Of the four Boom writers, which one, in your opinion, was or is the best writer?**
It's difficult to say because they are all different. Probably García Márquez. On the other hand, I don't know whose work will last longer.

**But, of the four, which do you prefer the most?**
I've used all of them in my classes. But probably the one that I like the least is Vargas Llosa. I don't know why.

**And in your classes over the years, which of the Boom writers have your students preferred?**
They preferred García Márquez.


## Juan José Arreola and Miguel Angel Asturias

**One other Mexican writer whom you wrote on was Arreola. What is his particular place in Mexican literature?**
Arreola represents the opposite of Rulfo. He wrote short stories beginning in the 1940s and one short novel. The big difference between Arreola and Rulfo is that Arreola's writings are more directly influenced by his reading whereas Rulfo was inspired more by his personal experiences. For example, Arreola wrote an entire short story based on a biblical parable. Arreola read widely in French and was influenced by this reading in writing many of his stories. When I first visited him, I was impressed by his extensive collection of French books. He read something and then he wrote a story. Another difference with Rulfo is that Arreola did not use the vocabulary of the people. He used learned vocabulary.

But the importance of Arreola is that he revolutionized the form of the Mexican short story. He introduced a fragmented structure so that his stories don't even appear to be stories. His style is also very poetic. His one novel, *La feria* [*The Fair*], is also quite innovative. This novel, by the way, was the basis of a study by Professor Sara Poot-Herrera of UC Santa Barbara. Unfortunately, Arreola's novel is not widely read. Moreover, although his short stories have been translated into other languages, including English, Arreola is still not widely known outside of Mexico. He was best recognized in the 1950s and 1960s. But then Rulfo began to gain in stature. There was a kind of rivalry between the two. Some said Arreola was jealous of Rulfo. However, Arreola recently received the Juan Rulfo Prize in literature, Mexico's highest literary award.

**Was Arreola, as a person, different from Rulfo?**

Oh, yes. His personality is entirely different. He's still alive, and I was recently with him. He used to be an actor and had a television program. Unlike Rulfo, who was an introvert, Arreola is the complete extrovert. He talks and talks. You can't stop him.

**In the 1960s, you also wrote about Miguel Angel Asturias, the Guatemalan writer who won the Nobel Prize in literature in the late 1960s. What attracted you to Asturias?**

When I taught the Latin American novel at Illinois, I always used Asturias's *El señor presidente* because it's the best novel to understand how a dictatorship in Latin America functions. I was also attracted to Asturias because of his use of magical realism, such as in *Hombres de maíz*. One of the key themes of his work is the U.S. role in Central America. Unfortunately, despite the importance of his writing and its relevance even today, Asturias is hardly read. His key popularity was in the 1940s.

**Despite his use of magical realism, he is not considered one of the Boom writers, is that correct?**

He wrote in an earlier period. He is a precursor of the Boom.

**In your writing on Asturias, what did you focus on?**

In my article "Myth and Social Realism in Miguel Angel Asturias," which I wrote in 1968, I concentrated on Asturias's use of native myths in all of his novels. Yet at the same time, he is also very realistic. He combines pre-Columbian myths and social realism very well. This is difficult to do, but Asturias does it.

**Can Asturias be compared with any particular Mexican writer?**

Perhaps an early Fuentes, because Asturias used political themes as Fuentes does. There is some similarity between *El señor presidente* and *The Death of Artemio Cruz*. Cruz is not a dictator, but he acts like a dictator. He is a newspaper tycoon, and his character is based on William Randolph Hearst, the American newspaper entrepreneur.

**Was Asturias exiled from Guatemala because of his political writings?**
Yes. He lived in France for a good portion of his life.

**Did Asturias have a significant impact on Mexican writers?**
Not only on Mexican writers, but throughout Latin America.

# Chapter Five

## **Aztlán**—Part One

*Leal receiving Lifetime Achievement Award from National Association for Chicano Studies (NACS) with Mario García, 1988.*

# The 1960s and Change

MG:   Don Luis, the 1960s, of course, was a very tumultuous period, especially because of the Vietnam War and student protests against it. What was the situation like at Illinois at that time? Was there much student unrest?

LL:   When I first arrived at Illinois in 1959 and for the next few years, the campus was very quiet. It really wasn't until about 1968 that things began to change. It was in 1968 when some of our students went on strike protesting the war, as well as conditions on the campus. They held marches; they broke windows, in particular a big window in the administration building. I would go to class and only a few students would show up. But these protests, although disruptive, did lead to certain reforms on campus. For example, the students, both undergraduates and graduates, gained representation in all the committees of our department. The same was true in other departments. Before this, students hardly participated in departmental affairs. The only committee that they were not allowed on was the personnel committee. Other reforms that came in this period included curriculum changes. We completely revised our M.A. and Ph.D. programs, as well as our undergraduate curriculum. The curriculum became more innovative and less traditional.

Another change that occurred was that we dropped having a head of the department and replaced it with a chair. The difference was that a head held almost dictatorial powers, while a chair shared executive responsibilities with the tenured faculty. Shoemaker, who had been the head of the department, didn't support this change and retired rather than give up his power. Although he ruled as a dictator, Shoemaker was responsible for the tremendous growth of our department in the 1960s. We were ranked third or fourth in the nation among Spanish departments. He recruited a number of top

*Leal (left) giving lecture at Bellas Artes, Mexico City, 1960 (with Celestino Gorostiza).*

scholars, such as Marcos Marínigo from Argentina. John Kronik was, of course, there, and James Crosby in golden age. Merlin Forster was also there for a time, and Henry Kahane in linguistics.

Besides recruiting faculty, Shoemaker increased our graduate program by attracting more students. When I arrived in 1959, we had no more than about twenty-five or thirty graduate students. But by 1968, we had many more. Of course, all of this wasn't just due to Shoemaker. It was also the times. After Sputnik, the federal government greatly increased support for graduate research through the National Education Act. This support especially focused on preparing students in mathematics and foreign languages. This increased our graduate students. So it was the best of times for the department.

**When the students were demonstrating, were they demonstrating to bring about these kinds of changes?**
The principal demonstrations were against the Vietnam War; then there were the civil rights demonstrations. But as part of these demonstrations, the students also demanded that the university change and represent more of the students' needs and interests.

**When you mentioned curriculum changes, what kind of changes did you mean?**
Well, for instance, there had been too much emphasis on peninsular literature. But the students said, "We want more Latin American literature." So we began to offer a more balanced program. The students also said that the requirements for the M.A. and the Ph.D. were too demanding, and so we made changes there also, and made the program more flexible.

**Did the greater emphasis on Latin America place more pressure on you?**
Yes, I had to take on more students. But, fortunately, we had a good group of Latin Americanists.

**How many graduate students were you directing at this time?**
Well, over my seventeen years at Illinois, I mentored forty-four graduate students who completed their Ph.D.s. During one academic year, I was directing as many as eight dissertations. I felt like a barber—"Who's next?" I remember having to be part of four Ph.D. exams in one day!

**And these students who came to work under you, did they have ideas about what they wanted to work on?**
Most of them did. I didn't insist that they had to study Mexican literature. They could write on any aspect of Latin American literature. If some didn't have a topic, then I suggested one. But most knew what they wanted to do.

**What were some of the topics that they wrote on?**

There was a wide range of topics. Many of these dissertations were later published. I directed those theses on the novel and the essay, while Professor Forster took all of the poetry and drama projects.

**Did these dissertations reflect new approaches to the study of Latin American literature?**

They were more innovative and less traditional. They included a new focus on nontraditional subjects, such as gender. But they also involved new theoretical and ideological influences, such as Marxism and poststructuralism. They were also more interdisciplinary.

**Did this put more pressure on you and other faculty members? As literary criticism was changing in the 1960s, did faculty have to adjust?**

Yes. We had to try to keep up with these changes. Some, however, refused to change. Shoemaker was one of these. He would tell students who wanted to work with him, "All right, if you want to study with me you have to write on Galdós, and here is your topic." He would give them their dissertation topic. For example, Rolando Hinojosa, who was a graduate student at Illinois, studied under Shoemaker, who made Rolando write a dissertation on money in the novels of Galdós. He gave someone else the topic, the priests in the novels of Galdós. Shoemaker wouldn't change. He had another Chicano student besides Hinojosa, a fellow by the name of Victor Baptiste from Kansas. He wanted to write about poetry, but Shoemaker wouldn't let him. So he came over to me and wrote a dissertation about Rosario Castellanos's poetry. It was later published in Chile and was one of the first books on Castellanos.

**During the 1960s, were there efforts to recruit Chicano students to Illinois?**

The problem at Illinois with the Chicanos was that all of them went to the Chicago campus of the University of Illinois. They didn't want to go to Urbana, which is 135 miles south of Chicago. The Chicago campus was built in one of the Mexican barrios.

## The Chicano Movement

**Now, Don Luis, by 1965 there began the effort by César Chávez to organize the farm workers, and then by 1968 in Los Angeles and elsewhere you**

had Chicano student demonstrations and school walkouts. All of this marks the commencement of the Chicano movement. What contact did you have with this new protest movement?

Very little, since most of this protest was taking place in the Southwest. However, we did begin to invite Chicano speakers from Chicago to speak on our campus. I also remember that around 1968 I presented my first paper concerning Chicano literature at a conference about Chicanos in Chicago. What about speakers from the movement in the Southwest, did you invite any?

Yes. We invited some. For example, we invited Professor George Sánchez from the University of Texas, who had been researching and writing about Chicanos for many years and was also a strong civil rights leader. We also had Ricardo Sánchez, the poet from El Paso, come and read his protest poetry. Our contacts were more with Texas than with the California movement. We never had an opportunity to have César Chávez on our campus. The exception from California was Bert Corona, who visited the campus several times, since his daughter, Margo, was a student in the Spanish department. I had her in my classes. I remember she wrote a paper about Chicanas. Whenever Bert visited I would invite him to speak. I did the introductions.

The paper on Chicano literature that you delivered in 1968, what did it deal with?

It concerned some of the early Chicano writings, such as the poetry of Alurista and of José Montoya. But I also commented on even earlier, premovement writers, such as José Antonio Villarreal, who published his novel *Pocho* in 1959.

## Octavio Romano and "El Grito"

How did you first come across Alurista's poetry?

In the Chicano newspapers, where much of this early poetry was published. But I also began to read *El Grito,* the Chicano journal from Berkeley, which began to publish in 1967 some of these early writers of the movement. That year I met Octavio Romano, the anthropology professor at Berkeley, who was the publisher of *El Grito.* I met him in Guadalajara that summer, where both of us were teaching in a summer program for U.S. teachers sponsored by the University of Arizona. Romano came down with the first issue of *El Grito*, and that's how I learned about this journal on Mexican American thought. Later he published *El Grito del Sol* and announced that the first subscriber from each state would get a free lifetime subscription. I was the first from Illinois, and so I began receiving *El Grito del Sol* free.

**What did Romano tell you about *El Grito*?**
He said, "I have a Chicano journal." He said that it was a journal for Chicanos to present their point of view.

**What was your impression of Romano?**
He was always clashing with the students in the program in Mexico. They were teachers of bilingual education in the United States. There were fifty in all. The program, by the way, was financed under the National Education Act. But Romano was always defending Chicano culture, and many times this led to heated arguments with some of these teachers who had differing opinions.

**Who were some of the other instructors of this program in Guadalajara?**
There was Gustavo Segade from San Diego State, Seymour Menton from UC Irvine, Joseph Silverman from UC Santa Cruz, Renato Rosaldo Sr. from Arizona.

**What was your impression of *El Grito*, especially the first issues?**
Oh, excellent. It was very good. I still go back to those first issues in my own work on Chicano literature.

**I agree. Those early essays by Romano himself which deal with Chicano history, identity, and which take on the traditional views of Chicanos by Anglo social scientists are very important. I don't think enough acknowledgment has been paid to Romano's influence in the development of Chicano-studies approaches and of creating an early Chicano intellectual perspective.**
Yes, and especially the influence Romano had on the study of Chicano culture by non-Chicanos. In his criticism of the social sciences, however, Romano had been preceded by Américo Paredes, who in his studies on Mexican American folklore and culture, especially on the *corridos* of the Texas border, also was highly critical of Anglo social science perspectives on the Chicano.

**That's true. But, you know, the other thing that's important about Romano's essays is that he stresses the diversity of the Chicano experience, which went against the more essentialist and monolithic image of the Chicano produced by the Chicano movement of the late 1960s. Other writers**

and intellectuals of the movement didn't pay attention to the diversity of experiences and identity as Romano did.

But I think it's natural that the movement emphasized similarities, because if it stressed differences among Chicanos, you'd never get anywhere. You're right; in his essays, Romano pointed out some of the differences, but look at what he also did. For example, when he published Tomás Rivera's novel *. . . y no se lo tragó la tierra* [ *. . . and the Earth Did Not Part*], he omitted one chapter because he and Herminio Ríos, his copublisher of Quinto Sol Press, didn't feel that this chapter represented the "good Chicano." It was a chapter about a character, Pete Fonseca, who is a *pachuco* type who uses drugs and who deceives a girl. Rivera was being critical of some aspects of Chicano culture, but Romano and Ríos didn't want to publish it, according to Rivera himself.

**Did Tomás Rivera ever mention this to you? How did he feel about the episode?**

I think that he said that he wanted to show that not all Chicanos are good Chicanos. He wanted to represent another side of the Chicano. But I don't think that he opposed Romano and Ríos about dropping this chapter. I think that he felt that if he did, they wouldn't publish his book at all. I don't know all the details, only what I heard Tomás say about this affair.

**Still, despite this contradiction in Romano, I think that he is a very important early Chicano-movement writer who hasn't been given his full due. Neither has *El Grito* been given the recognition it deserves by historians and literary critics. The journal was ground breaking and provided a movement perspective that was lacking. I remember when I was first asked to do a course on Chicano history in the fall of 1969 at San José State, all that I had to rely on was my discovery of Carey McWilliams's seminal *North from Mexico*, which remarkably had first been published in 1949. This was the first history concerning Mexican Americans. But my discovery of *El Grito*, and especially Romano's essays, was just as important for me. His essays gave me the Chicano perspective not found in McWilliams. Romano gave me a framework to position my notes from McWilliams.**

There's no question about it. Romano's essays and *El Grito* are of major importance. Herminio Ríos, for example, published an essay in the journal in which for the first time the point is made that Chicano literature is not just something recent, but in fact can be traced at least back to 1848, when the United States conquered Mexico's northern frontier—the Southwest. This opened a whole new perspective on Chicano literature. Besides *El*

*Grito,* Romano published some of the earliest anthologies of Chicano literature in a series entitled *El espejo/The Mirror.* These were landmark publications which showed the emergence of Chicano literature.

**Don Luis, as you became acquainted with what was happening in the Chi-
cano movement, what was your own personal reaction? The movement
was certainly more militant than the Mexican American efforts you had
been associated with in Chicago back in the 1940s and 1950s.**

Yes, the movement was entirely different. The big difference was that in the
1940s, we were dealing more with Mexican immigrants, while Chicanos—
native-born Mexican Americans—were not yet as articulate nor as visible,
for example, in the universities. By the 1960s, however, you have a new generation of Chicanos who are able to express themselves. Another difference
is that in the 1940s and 1950s, we didn't have a national leader with the stature of César Chávez.

## Chicano Terminology

**What about the term *Chicano*? Were you comfortable with using this term
of identity?**

I accepted it immediately. I still defend the use of the term *Chicano.*

**Of course, the term *Chicano* was not recent. It had been used for many
years, but not in the politicized way in which it began to be employed in
the 1960s.**

Yes. It was first used to designate immigrants from Mexico. Manuel Gamio
observes this in his study of Mexican immigrants in the United States,
which was published in the early 1930s.

**And why do you think that in the 1960s the term *Chicano* was now mostly
applied to U.S.-born Mexican Americans?**

It seems to me that the term Chicano was accepted in the 1960s for two
reasons. One, it was used to reject American culture. And two, it was also
used to reject Mexican culture.

**But wasn't it also a rejection of the term *Mexican American*?**

Not completely. The intellectuals, or at least some of them, like Luis Valdez,
rejected the term *Mexican American,* but not ordinary people. But even some
intellectuals didn't reject the term either. After all, what is the subtitle of
Romano's *El Grito*? It's "A Journal of Mexican American Thought." What I
also find interesting, Mario, is comparing Chicano terminology with that of

black Americans. You see, black Americans recently changed to African Americans, but Chicano militants rejected a comparable term to *African Americans,* which is *Mexican Americans.*

**Yes, it's interesting that African Americans have abandoned the term *Black,* which is like Chicanos abandoning the term *Chicano.***

You see, Chicanos wanted to separate themselves as something different from both the United States and Mexico. When you say you are African American, you don't know if you're a recent immigrant from Africa or not. But the term *Chicano* is perfect, because you know immediately what it means.

**There's been speculation about the origins of the term *Chicano.* What's your opinion?**

Well, I comment on this in an article I wrote in 1973. I say that the word *Chicano* comes from the word *mexicano.* If you drop the first syllable of *mexicano,* you have *xicano,* and in Mexico *mexicano* is spelled with an *x,* while in Spain it is spelled with a *j.* If you pronounce *xicano* using the Náhuatl pronunciation, the *x* is pronounced *sh;* then it comes out *Chicano.*

**Is it your understanding that the term *Chicano* originates on this side of the border to refer to Mexican immigrants?**

Yes.

**But we don't know exactly when it is first used?**

The earliest that we know it was used was in the 1920s. Gamio mentions the term, although it's misspelled. Instead of *Chicano,* it's spelled *Chicamo,* with an *m* instead of an *n.* But the term might have been used earlier. We just don't know. But what's of further interest about the term *Chicano* is that it and the term *Mexican American* have been the only terms used to try to bring a unity to Mexicans in the United States. The problem with the term *Chicano* is that it was rejected by the Mexican American middle class because they thought it was a term used only by militants or by the lower class.

**What about the term *pocho*? What is its origin?**

The word *pocho* is from northern Mexico, from the Caita language, an Indian language.

**And so the term refers to these Indians?**

No, it meant something like an animal whose tail has been cut. Something incomplete.

**Was the term *pocho* brought to this country with Mexican immigrants?**

No, it was invented here by José Vasconcelos. He was the first to apply the term to Chicanos. He used it in the 1920s, but as a term of derogation, implying that Mexican Americans had been cut off from their culture.

## José Antonio Villarreal

**Speaking of the term *pocho*—as you know, José Antonio Villarreal published his novel *Pocho* in 1959. Were you aware of this novel then?**
No. I only became aware of it later, when it was rediscovered due to the Chicano movement and republished in the early 1970s.
**What was your reaction to *Pocho*?**
It was very positive. I especially appreciated how Villarreal changed the word *pocho* from a negative to a positive. The young protagonist, Richard Rubio, says, "I'm a pocho, I speak pocho, and I'm proud of it." In the novel, being *pocho* is nothing to be ashamed of. It's a positive experience.
**Did you find it remarkable that a novel like *Pocho* could be published as early as 1959? And that few people knew of its existence?**
It was remarkable, but some knew of its existence. For example, it received a very favorable review in *The Nation* shortly after its publication. I suspect that it was reviewed in *The Nation* because Carey McWilliams was the editor at that time. The only problem I have with that review is that the reviewer notes that *Pocho* is a novel concerning "a new people among us." His impression was that Chicanos were new immigrants, but, of course, Chicanos had been here in California and the Southwest long before many other Americans, except, of course, Native Americans.
**But did you find that the themes in *Pocho* fit comfortably with the views being expressed by the Chicano movement? Did the novel speak to the movement?**
I think that *Pocho* represents the end of an era. The novel ends at the conclusion of World War II. Richard goes into the military even though the war is over. But as you know, the end of the war brings on a new period of Mexican American political activity as the *veteranos* return home and deal with existing forms of discrimination against Mexican Americans. I, of course, was one of those returning veterans. So the novel really deals with the period before the war and when there was not as much Mexican American political activity.
**Richard Rubio represents a transitional figure. He is someone wrestling with his identity.**

You're right. He has a problem of identity in relation to the majority because his friends are of all nationalities.

**But Richard also faces tension within his family, especially with his father.** Richard and his father represent two cultures: the American and the Mexican. They clash.

**So it's really a novel about this clash of cultures. There is no conclusion to this clash. You're not left with a sense of what is the result of this clash.** No, because the novel ends before there is any resolution. But *Pocho* for me has another important characteristic, which is its structure. It's a structure that will influence later Chicano writers during the movement. That is, the structure revolves around a hero or a main character coming out of Mexico, or his family coming out of Mexico, as the result of the Mexican Revolution. In *Pocho* and in several other later novels or stories, the first part takes place in Mexico and the second in the United States.

**You later met Villarreal. Did he address some of these questions?** No, he never did. Villarreal is a very abrupt person who doesn't like to answer questions. I remember once going to UCLA and meeting with Villarreal, along with a few others, shortly after the publication of his third novel, *Clemente Chacón.* Those of us there talked about his novels, but he didn't answer our questions.

**But Villarreal is certainly a very important premovement writer who later is discovered by the movement. He represents a generation of other Mexican American writers who wrote before the movement and who in this time received little recognition. I'm thinking about writers such as Mario Suárez.** Suárez wrote in the 1940s from Arizona. The problem with Suárez is that he never published his short stories as a book. Some appeared in the *Arizona Quarterly,* but few people read them. But he's an interesting writer. He's the first to use the word *Chicano* in a story. He's also the first to write a short story about the *pachuco.*

## Alurista

**One of the writers you first encountered out of the movement is Alurista. What was your impression of his poetry?** I was impressed by his use of language, the combination of English and Spanish.

But it's not only his use of language, it's also his use of pre-Columbian symbols and terms. You, of course, had earlier studied pre-Columbian culture in your work. Did you find that he was using those pre-Columbian symbols and terms correctly, or was he transforming them?

No, he used them correctly. Alurista represented what could be called neo-*indigenismo*. In Mexico, the *indigenismo* movement ended around 1940. After that, few novels or poetry about Indians were published. *Indigenismo*, or neo-*indigenismo*, surfaces again in the late 1960s, but this time it is north of the border among Chicano writers, such as Alurista. I remember being invited by Professor Joseph Sommers, who had studied with me at Wisconsin, to give a lecture in his class on *la novela indigenista* at the University of California San Diego, around 1977. After the lecture, Joe asked me why the *indigenista* movement among Mexican writers no longer existed. Before I could answer, a young man in the class jumped up and said, "No, we Chicanos have *indigenismo!*" The young man was Alurista, who was in the seminar.

But the *indigenismo* of Alurista and of other Chicano writers was not the same as Mexican *indigenismo*. The difference is that the Mexican *indigenistas*, although they were not Indians themselves, wrote about the terrible conditions of the Indians in Mexico. Their writings showed the contemporary plight of Indians and had little to do with the glory years of the pre-Columbian era. By contrast, Alurista and other Chicano neo-*indigenistas* focused on pre-Columbian culture and symbols and not on contemporary Indians. Neo-*indigenismo* has nothing to do with Indians. It was an attempt to create a new consciousness among Chicanos about their part-Indian background. Alurista used symbols such as Aztlán to accomplish this goal.

**Alurista, of course, introduced the concept of Aztlán at the first National Chicano Youth Liberation Conference in Denver in 1969. He wrote the so-called *Plan de Aztlán*, or at least the preamble to it. As you know, this conference was hosted by Corky Gonzales, and he wanted to end the conference with a series of resolutions. Gonzales himself had no conceptualization about Aztlán. Alurista was at the conference, and on his own he wrote the preamble to the resolutions and called it the "Plan Espiritual de Aztlán." Corky and the other organizers liked it and said, "It sounds great! Let's go with it."**

And it caught fire. But one other very important thing, Mario, is that Alurista actually called his preamble/poem "El Plan Espiritual de Aztlán." Later, when the poem was reproduced in the new Chicano journal out of

UCLA called *Aztlán,* the editors of that journal dropped the word *Espiritual.* I think they did so because they saw a clash between the spiritual and the secular.

**That was unfortunate, because I think that by using the term *Espiritual,* Alurista was really capturing what was happening at the Youth Liberation Conference and in the Chicano movement. There was a new spirit, a kind of spiritual bonding among these Chicanos, and in some ways they were emphasizing a kind of humanism opposed to the materialism of the United States.**

But the influence for this perspective comes from *La raza cósmica,* in which Vasconcelos argued for a Latin American humanism against Yankee materialism. You can also go back further to José Enrique Rodó, the Uruguayan writer, who in the late nineteenth century, especially in his book *Ariel,* also attacks American materialism.

**So Alurista, whether conscious or not of this influence, is following in this tradition?**

Right.

**Have you ever talked to Alurista about how he came to some of these concepts?**

Not directly, but Professor Francisco Lomelí, who was an undergraduate at San Diego State when Alurista taught there, tells me that Alurista talked in his classes about Aztlán even before 1969.

**Alurista and others in the Chicano movement stressed that Aztlán, the mythic homeland of the Aztecs before they migrated to the Valley of Mexico, was geographically in the same location as the Southwest. But most scholars dispute this and locate the original homeland of the Aztecs somewhere along the Pacific coast of present-day Mexico. What is your reaction to this?**

Well, as far back as 1610, the Spanish chronicler Gaspar Pérez de Villagrá was saying that the Aztecs had originated in New Mexico. But one thing to keep in mind is that there are very few references to Aztlán in Mexican literature. You have to go back to the sixteenth-century writer Diego Durán, who writes about Aztlán in 1581. He writes about how the Aztec emperor Moctezuma sent his scouts—his *hechiceros*—to look for Aztlán in the north. They found it and reported this back to Moctezuma. Much of this, of course, is legend. But Alurista must have read Durán because that's the source for the myth of Aztlán. I myself had to study Durán for my dissertation, so I was already aware of the myth of Aztlán well before Alurista called attention to it. But for the most part, the myth of Aztlán is not discussed in Mexico. I point this out in an essay I did in 1981 called "In Search of Aztlán." I went back to see which Mexican writers had referred to Aztlán and found this reference in only one novel, called *El nuevo Aztlán*, published in the 1940s.

## José Montoya and Early Chicano Poets

**Poetry was certainly a driving force in the early stages of the Chicano movement. Were there other Chicano poets who impressed you at that time?**
After Alurista, to me the most important Chicano poet was José Montoya. He began to publish some of his early poetry in *El Grito* and in *El espejo/ The Mirror*. In one of my very early papers on Chicano literature, I refer to some of this poetry. Montoya especially became known due to his now classic poem "El Louie," which is about *pachuco* life. What's distinctive about Montoya is the rhythm of his poetry, which resembles *pachuco* slang.
**Did Montoya, like Alurista, go through a pre-Columbian phase, an emphasis on pre-Columbian influences and images?**
To a much lesser extent. The difference is that the indigenous influences in Montoya are the contemporary native peoples rather than the Aztecs and Mayas employed by Alurista.
**You mentioned the poem "El Louie." We had earlier talked about the image of the *pachuco* in relation to Octavio Paz's *The Labyrinth of Solitude*. Is Montoya's *pachuco* different from Paz's?**
There's no question about the difference. Paz gives an external view of the *pachuco*, while Montoya gives us an insider's perspective, since Montoya himself was a *pachuco* in Sacramento. Montoya's view is a more realistic one.
**Between Alurista and Montoya, who is the better poet?**
I don't think you can say one is better than the other. They are quite different. Alurista treats more mythical themes. Montoya uses more social ones. Alurista is much more of a bilingual poet. He is comfortable in both languages. Montoya, although he uses some Spanish, is more skilled in English. You can see in Alurista more of a Mexican literary and cultural influence, while Montoya exhibits more U.S. characteristics. In fact, Montoya has said that he was quite affected by reading Walt Whitman. He even has a poem about Whitman.
**It seems to me that one of the reasons that poetry is in the forefront of the Chicano artistic movement is because it could be produced faster and was**

more accessible in public places. It was a poetry meant to be recited and heard rather than read.

That's correct. It's a very collective form of literature. You had poetry festivals such as the "Flor y Canto" ones, for example, in Los Angeles and other cities, where Chicano poets read their social-protest poems to large numbers of people.

Are there other important poets that you came to recognize during the early period of the Chicano movement?

Well, there is, for example, Angela de Hoyos in San Antonio, who wrote some interesting poetry but didn't get a lot of attention. Then, of course, there are the El Paso poets: Abelardo Delgado and Ricardo Sánchez. Delgado published some of his poetry but not a lot of it. Sánchez, on the other hand, published a great deal, especially his most important collection, *Canto y Grito mi Liberación*. Sánchez is a very powerful poet and has had lasting influence. He recently died at a still-young age, but his reputation in some ways continues to increase.

Of the movement poets, would it be fair to consider Alurista as the poet laureate of the movement?

Yes. There's no question about that.

## Origins of Chicano Literature

Don Luis, in 1973 you published an article entitled "Mexican American Literature: A Historical Perspective" in the first number of the *Revista Chicano-Riqueña*, later reprinted in a collection of essays edited by Joseph Sommers and Tomás Ybarra-Frausto. In that article you argue that Chicano literature is not just the literature that comes out of the Chicano movement, but that it is a more extensive literature which can be traced as far back as the Spanish colonial period in the Southwest. Why do you think we need to look at Chicano literature in this expansive way?

I'll try to justify my point of view in this way. First of all, some critics suggest that Chicano literature begins with *Pocho* in 1959. But even before *Pocho*, there was a literature that wasn't called Chicano literature because that term wasn't used in that way. We could call it Mexican American literature or pre-Chicano literature. No literature is born out of thin air. Every literature has a background. Before 1959, there are novels, a great deal of poetry, plays, and essays, that were written by people of Spanish/Mexican descent. The problem was that no one studied that literature. But why should we omit that literature? When we study American literature, we begin with the landing of the pilgrims. When we study Mexican literature we don't say it was born in 1810 or 1821 when Mexico becomes independent. No one would say that Sor Juana Inés de la Cruz is not a Mexican writer because when she wrote Mexico did not exist, but New Spain did. I have an article also about the nature of Mexican literature in which I comment that some critics insist that the Mexican novel was born in 1815 with the publication of *El periquillo sarniento*, because before this time Mexico did not exist. But in my article I observe that if you know the history of this novel you know that the first part was published before the independence movement and the second part during the movement. So does that mean that the first part is not Mexican literature, while the second is? That's absurd!

The second point I would make is that why should Chicanos give up their literary roots? We should not give up the writers both before and after 1848 when the United States captured the Southwest. In fact, you can go as far back as the explorer Cabeza de Vaca, who wrote about his adventures in Texas in the sixteenth century.

A question arises, however, when you deal with the pre-1848 literature. The question is whether the literature of northern New Spain and later the northern frontier of Mexico is the same as the literature of central New Spain and central Mexico. If it is similar, then is it part of Mexican literature or of pre-Chicano literature? I don't think that the literature of the north is that similar to that of central Mexico. For example, if you examine Cabeza de Vaca's chronicle, you find that the attitude toward the Indians and to nature is different from that being expressed in the center of New Spain. The writers in the center are much more influenced by Renaissance images, but that isn't necessarily the case in the north. In the north, writers such as Cabeza de Vaca are much more realistic in their descriptions of the land and of the Indian inhabitants. It's because of these differences that I consider the colonial writings in the northern frontier of both New Spain and of Mexico as pre-Chicano literature.

My 1973 piece had some influence and is often quoted. For one, because, as you say, I periodize Chicano literature as far back as 1542 with Cabeza de Vaca's journal. And, second, because I have a periodization of Chicano literature that critics had not considered before, one that includes the colonial period, the Mexican period, the Mexican American period, and the Chicano period. Whenever anybody wants to talk about pre-Chicano literature, they quote this article.

**So, taking this broader historical perspective, you also suggest that Chicano literature can't or shouldn't be defined by a particular political perspective, such as a Chicano-movement perspective. Chicano literature, defined broadly, includes various perspectives, although they all address a specific ethnic experience.**

That's right. It's the Chicano experience, as you say, defined broadly, but it's not necessarily always overtly political. The political may predominate, but it's not the only influence. There are many poems written over the years by writers of Chicano background that have nothing to do with politics. Let's take a writer such as Francisco Ramírez, who published *El clamor público* in Los Angeles in the post–Mexican War period. Is he a Chicano writer or not? If you go to Mexico, nobody knows about Ramírez, yet he wrote wonderful essays defending the Mexicans in California after the Anglo conquest. He also wrote many poems in Spanish. But unlike his political essays, his poems are about love. But can we say that only his political essays are part of Chicano or pre-Chicano literature, and his love poems are not? I don't think so.

**But there are some Chicano-studies scholars who insist that whatever we include in Chicano studies, including literature, has to have a certain political perspective, which is often referred to as *Chicanismo*.**

Yes, but who is going to study the other cultural aspects of the Chicano experience that are not representative of movement politics? We need to study the full experience, not just a part of it.

**I agree. That kind of political or Chicano-studies perspective is too limiting. Who determines what is politically correct or not? If you say that Chicano literature is only the literature that conveys a certain political perspective, then you continually narrow the definition of Chicano literature.**

That's right. I'm not against studying the more political literature, but we also need to pay attention to other types of literature. Much of our folklore, for example, represents myths and legends that are not political in the sense that some use the term *political*. Are we to forget this type of literature?

**You have an interesting comment in your essay on Mexican American literature, and I'm wondering if you can expand on it. You say at the beginning of your essay, "It has not yet been determined whether Mexican American literature should be considered as an entity in itself, as part of**

American literature, or even perhaps a part of Mexican literature." So you're raising the problem of whether Chicano literature is part of a particular national literature, or a transnational literature, or a literature unto itself. Twenty-five years after the initial publication of this essay, what is your thinking now about this question?

I maintain that Chicano literature is an autonomous literature. I reached this conclusion because it is clear that even though Chicano literature should be a part of American literature, it is not accepted, or not fully accepted, as such. Part of this has to do with language. American literature does not include literature written in any language other than English. The minority status of this literature also explains its exclusion. So Chicano writers represent *huérfanos*—orphans—because nobody accepts them. But if you classify this literature as Chicano literature, then these writers have a home.

But in some ways, you can make the argument that Chicano literature is part of both American and Mexican literary traditions. It's part of both literatures. It's American literature, whether written in English or Spanish, because it is writing done within the United States about an American experience. On the other hand, it is also a part of Mexican literature because it is writing that comes from what used to be called in the early twentieth century "México de afuera," or a Mexican diaspora.

That's right, but here you face the problem of nationality. What constitutes a national literature? Some critics say that national literatures don't exist. Literature is literature. So that someone can make the case, for example, that if you read a Guatemalan writer you can't really differentiate that writer from a Mexican writer. But in contrast, other critics say that there are systems of literature: Spanish literature, English literature, Chinese literature, and so forth. English literature would include the literature of England, the United States, Australia, Canada, and New Zealand. Spain, Latin America, and the Caribbean would form another system. If you deny that there are systems of literature, then there is no problem, but then you also lose your identity as Chicano.

So you believe that there is such a thing as Chicano literature which has not been integrated into American literature. But if it were integrated, would Chicano literature cease to exist?

Mario, my answer is this: if immigration from Mexico stopped, then perhaps Chicano literature in time would cease to exist because it might be integrated fully into American literature. However, this is not the case now and probably not into the foreseeable future. As long as Mexico is next door and immigrants continue to come in, there will be something like Chicano literature.

**I think the case is clearer that at least theoretically, Chicano literature is, or should be, a part of American literature. The greater problem is whether it is also a part of Mexican literature.**

Well, here we can say that since most Chicano literature is written in English, it is not a part of Mexican literature. We come back to systems of literature, or spheres. If you take a novel, for example, such as José Antonio Villarreal's *The Fifth Horseman,* you can say this is a novel about the Mexican Revolution. But it is written in English, and Mexican critics don't accept it as part of the novelistic tradition about the Mexican Revolution. They probably don't even know about it. On the other hand, a stronger case can be made that a Chicano novel written in Spanish, like *Peregrinos de Aztlán* by Miguel Méndez, does represent a part of Mexican literature. Not only is it written in Spanish, but it's an *indigenista* novel within that tradition in Mexican literature. It's also been republished in Mexico and well received by critics. But that's the only Chicano novel that has been accepted in Mexico.

**So it's very much a language question, then. If Chicano literature is written in Spanish, then you can make a stronger argument that in some ways it's part of Mexican literature, or an extension of Mexican literature, because of the language.**

Yes. For instance, Rudolfo Anaya, or any Chicano writer who writes in English, is not considered in Mexico at all. Even if their books are translated into Spanish in Mexico, they are still seen as Chicano novels and as a literature from north of the border. The critics in Mexico don't say, "These are Mexican novels."

**Don Luis, in 1971 you gave one of the first papers on Chicano literature, entitled "The Nature of Chicano Literature," at a Midwest Modern Language Association conference. What did you mean by "the nature of Chicano literature" at that time?**

This was a meeting in Detroit. My paper was really a response to a paper given by Luis Dávila. This session on Chicano literature was one of the very first such sessions at an MLA-sponsored conference. I don't remember exactly what Dávila said, but my comments were aimed at distinguishing Chicano literature. Of course, there wasn't much yet in terms of publications. But one of the first distinctions I observed was that it was a literature written in English and Spanish. It was a bilingual literature. No other litera-ture used English and Spanish in the way that Chicano literature did. Both languages were integrated, as shown, for example, in Alurista's poetry. The other point that I made was that Chicano literature was a literature that had to be written by Chicanos and that it was a literature in which themes related to the Chicano experience.

But what's also interesting about this conference is that 1971 was an impor-tant year in the development of Chicano literature. It was a watershed year. A year earlier, in 1970, for the first time you have the awarding of the Quinto Sol literary prizes established by Octavio Romano and *El Grito*. That year the first award went to Tómas Rivera for . . . *y no se lo tragó la tierra*, a novel published in 1971. Also in 1971, Alurista published his influential book of poetry, *Floricanto en Aztlán*.

**It's true that much of early Chicano literature follows a bilingual for-mat, but that's no longer the case. Most of that literature is published in English. So how does that affect the nature of Chicano literature?**

I don't think that's exactly true. I challenge you to show me a book by a Chi-cano that doesn't use some Spanish.

**They all do, but not as heavily as in the past.**

Even Richard Rodríguez uses Spanish.

**Right, but not in the way bilingualism was used during the heyday of the Chicano movement, when it appears that there was a more conscious effort to be bilingual. Since the 1980s and into the 1990s, which I consider to be the postmovement years, it appears that writers don't feel as much the political pressure to be bilingual. There are bilingual expressions inserted, but for the most part the texts are in English. So does that change the nature of Chicano literature—the shift in language?**

Well, that's only one point. Language is not the only determinant of Chi-cano literature. If it were, then a recent novel like *The Crossing* by Cormac McCarthy might be considered a Chicano novel. In writing about northern Mexico, he uses English and Spanish very much like a Chicano writer. But it's not a Chicano novel because of the attitude of the author toward the Mexicans he writes about.

**So it's not just a question of language.**

No. It's also a question of attitude. The most important aspect is that you have to understand Chicano culture from the inside.

# Tomás Rivera

*Leal (left) with Tomás Rivera (center) and Guillermo Rojas.*

So it's really a combination of elements that make up the nature of Chicano literature. But, Don Luis, I wanted to discuss with you one of the key writers who comes out of the movement: Tomás Rivera. You earlier mentioned that you had met Rivera in the early 1960s, before he blossomed as a writer.

Yes. It was in 1962 at a bilingual teachers' institute in Guadalajara. Tomás was one of the teachers. He had written some poetry by that time. I was lecturing on the Mexican short story, and he became very interested in short fiction. After I returned to Illinois, I received a letter from Tomás inquiring if he could come study with me. He had an M.A., but I couldn't get a fellowship for him.

What do you know about the background of the writing of . . . *y no se lo tragó la tierra,* Rivera's major work?

I don't know the history of the book. He must have been working on it in the 1960s, because he received the Quinto Sol prize in 1970.

Why do you think that very soon after its publication, . . . *y no se lo tragó la tierra* became such a celebrated text among Chicano critics?

Well, there are several things. For one, it documents the life of Mexican migrant workers for the first time in a novelistic form. Second is the fact that he produced a particular style of integrated episodes that becomes somewhat of a model for other Chicano writers. Rivera also writes in a style that reflects the life of the people he writes about. And perhaps, finally, there were not many Chicano novels written yet. Rivera's was one of the first.

What do you mean by the style that represents the people?

He writes in the way the migrant workers speak. He also reflects the conditions of these workers and their families. For example, in an independent story, "Las salamandras," Rivera observes that the conflict for these people is not just with Anglo bosses, but with nature itself.

**So you accept Rivera's text as a novel and not as a series of short stories?**

Yes. It's a fragmented novel in the postmodern sense, but it still is a connected unit. The young boy protagonist connects all of the different episodes. This type of fragmented style also characterizes other Chicano novels.

**. . . *y no se lo tragó la tierra* was written in Spanish, was it not, although published in a bilingual format?**

Yes. Herminio Ríos translated it from Spanish to English.

**Why did Rivera write his novel in Spanish and not English?**

Tomás was writing poetry and some short stories in English, but they were all rejected by publishers. However, when the Quinto Sol prize was announced, it was stated that you could submit texts written in either English or Spanish. Rivera said later that hearing that he could submit something in Spanish liberated him, because he could express himself in his original language. Growing up in Texas, he had first spoken Spanish. So he wrote his novel in Spanish and won the prize.

**The text was later retranslated by Rolando Hinojosa. Did this change the text much?**

It did. Hinojosa's translation is almost a new text. He changed the structure considerably.

**Is . . . *y no se lo tragó la tierra* an example of a Chicano realist novel? Is it social realism even though it has an innovative structure? I'm thinking of texts like those of Steinbeck of the 1930s, which also deal with migrant workers. These texts bring attention to particular social problems. Is . . . *y no se lo tragó la tierra* in that tradition?**

Yes, to some extent it is a realist novel. But you also have to know that when Rivera was in Guadalajara for that summer institute, he attended my seminar where we read, among other things, Juan Rulfo, in particular *El llano en llamas*. Tomás was very impressed with Rulfo's short stories in that text, and you can see Rulfo's influence in . . . *y no se lo tragó la tierra*. It's almost the same type of writing that Rulfo did about the problems of people in Mexico and that Rivera did about Mexican migrant workers in the United States.

**The fact that Rulfo wrote about the countryside as did Rivera is still another connection.**

Yes, but in Rulfo's case, if you asked him what his purpose in writing was, he would say that it was only for aesthetic value and not to change anything. But here we have another problem: does literature change society? To what extent does literature influence society and the behavior of people? Some critics say it has no influence, others that it has a very powerful effect.

**But certainly, given Rivera's involvement in academic life and in the community, he wrote as a way of trying to influence people and bring about change. Bringing attention to the problems of migrant workers was a way of trying to achieve social change. It's interesting that his novel coincides with the efforts of César Chávez to organize farm workers. This may in fact be one major reason why early Chicano critics paid so much attention to Rivera's novel.**

Of course, he wrote the novel before he became a university administrator, including becoming chancellor of the University of California Riverside. He was a teacher in high school when he wrote . . . *y no se lo tragó la tierra.* He himself was from a migrant family.

**So is it also an autobiographical novel?**

Yes; there's no question about it. Any literature is a product of a society. Literature reflects social problems, even a fantastic novel does. This was certainly true of the novel of the Mexican Revolution. The *indigenista* novel reflected the problem of the Indians in Mexico. And the novels and poetry published during the Chicano *movimiento* reflect the problems of the Chicano people during that period.

**These writers saw themselves as people who wanted not only to reflect certain social problems, but to make change. They saw themselves as part of an effort to change society. Isn't that another characteristic of Chicano literature?**

Well, if that's true, then the writer has to begin with the premise that he's going to write a novel in order to change society. But it doesn't work that way. That's a secondary motivation. You don't write a novel to change society, because when you finish the novel the problem is already solved, at least for the writer.

**What you're saying is that a text in itself can't change society. It's whether it can influence others to do something.**

Yes. Besides, in Rivera's case the migrant workers don't read . . . *y no se lo tragó la tierra.* The novel is not written for the people who have the problems. It's written for the people who read novels.

**That raises another, related question. Who was the audience in this early period of Chicano literature that came out of the movement? It seems to**

me that it was primarily intellectuals and students. If so, what does this tell us about the nature of Chicano literature, the fact that it reached only a small segment of the Chicano population, which was literate and socially or, at least, intellectually involved?

Well, we really don't have a way of measuring reader response in the case of Chicano literature. But you're right; Chicano literature has had a very limited audience. Now, recently, writers such as Sandra Cisneros have published with national publishing firms, which gives her access to a larger audience. As more Chicano writers get published by New York publishers, perhaps we will be better able to say something about reader response. But for now, we really don't know what this response is. We know that the Teatro Campesino influenced the farm workers because its plays were performed right there in the fields. But Chicano novels and poetry published in Berkeley by students in very limited editions and with limited distribution—we just don't know the extent of reader response other than that this literature, as you say, was read mostly by professors and students.

I find it interesting that the early movement novels, such as those of Rivera, Anaya, and Hinojosa, came out in the early 1970s when the large majority of Chicanos lived in the cities, and yet these texts reflect and speak to a rural culture. They are addressing a minority experience for most Chicanos. Why didn't we get more urban novels out of this first wave of writers?

Well, that's a difficult question to answer. First of all, the problem of the *campesino* [farm worker] was still an important one in the early 1970s. But, second, there is a type of urban novel that is also appearing. Of course, *Pocho* in 1959 was an urban novel. Also you have John Rechy's *City of Night,* which critics are now reinterpreting as a Chicano novel. But you also get in the 1970s what I call the "border novel," which has elements of an urban novel. Here, for example, you have Miguel Méndez's *Peregrinos de Aztlán* and Villarreal's *Clemente Chacón,* and also urban novels such as *The Revolt of the Cockroach People* of Oscar Acosta.

In Joseph Sommers's *Modern Chicano Writers* [edited with Tomás Ybarra-Frausto], Sommers has an article called "Interpreting Tomás Rivera." Among other things, he observes Rulfo's influence on Rivera, but he also notes the influence of Faulkner, Dos Passos, and James Joyce. Do you see these other influences in Rivera?

Certainly Rulfo was influenced by Faulkner, so right there I think Sommers is correct. Rivera, of course, had read Rulfo, but Tomás had also studied

American literature and no doubt had read both Faulkner and Dos Passos, especially a novel by Dos Passos such as *Manhattan Transfer*, which is a fragmented novel and which has a little epigraph to start each chapter of the kind that Rivera used in . . . *y no se lo tragó la tierra*.

**But what about Joyce?**

Joyce is a very difficult writer. There might be some influence on Rivera, but it's less noticeable.

**Perhaps a Joycean stream of consciousness?**

But there's very little stream of consciousness in . . . *y no se lo tragó la tierra*, except in the first and last chapters when the boy is thinking. This is maybe what Sommers had in mind, but then Joyce has had this influence on many writers.

**Since the publication of . . . *y no se lo tragó la tierra*, we've had many other novels published by Chicano writers. But has Rivera's novel stood the test of time over more than twenty-five years? Is it still one of the major novels in Chicano literature?**

Yes—there's no question about it. It has been republished and retranslated. Interest in Rivera, despite his untimely death in 1984, is still there. Arte Público Press not long ago published a collection of his unpublished work. I always include Rivera in my Chicano literature courses. Where Tomás would have developed as a writer is hard to know. He was sidetracked because he became a university administrator.

**In comparison with Chicano writers who were his contemporaries, such as Anaya and Hinojosa, is Rivera perhaps considered more important because he was a better writer, or because of the particular nature and themes of . . . *y no se lo tragó la tierra*?**

I think it's both, Mario. I don't think we can separate the two. But, you know, it's not just the novel we should read and appreciate. There are his short stories, which have now been published, and his essays. Rivera was also an insightful critic.

**Don Luis, what was your reaction to the recent film version of . . . *y no se lo tragó la tierra*?**

It was very well done, although I think they could have selected a better actor to portray the young boy. Maybe it's just my reaction to seeing on film the image of the young boy in Rivera's novel. I had a different image of the boy before the film. You know, in the novel you don't know the exact age of the boy. He could be eight, or ten, or twelve. But in the film you see, more or less, the age of the boy. It's not just the age of the boy, but how I saw his personality in the novel and how the film shows his personality. The film changes some of the scenes from the novel. But no film fully reflects the written work. My only problem with turning a novel into a film is that it destroys your imagination. You read a novel and you create an image of what takes place. But then you see the film version and it gives you a ready-made image, which is now difficult to erase. On the other hand, it's good that they did the film because it will increase interest in Rivera and perhaps more people will read the novel. You have to read the novel to get everything Rivera was trying to say. You can't watch the film and say you know . . . *y no se lo tragó la tierra.*

**You published an article on Rivera called "The Ritual of Remembering." What did you mean by this?**
According to Rivera, he believed that the writer reconstructs the history of a community. The writer becomes the historian and the conscience of the community. So the writer has to remember and give expression to this past by remembering what happened and by writing about it. In this way, the writer reconstructs the past, the culture, and becomes the voice of the community.

**Do you think that Rivera was attempting to do this in . . . *y no se lo tragó la tierra?***
Yes. For example, in one chapter the boy is remembering what happened during that year. He's reconstructing the history for that year. If he doesn't, then it's a lost year. By remembering, he's creating history. There isn't a people without a history, even before there was a written text. Through oral traditions, some communities created and maintained this history. In the Mexican tradition, the best examples of this oral tradition have been the *corridos,* the ballads, which preserve historical memory. You sing the *corridos,* the people hear them, and they reconstruct their own past.

**Rivera seemed to be particularly concerned about the concept of community. Do you think that's one of the things he was attempting to do through his writings—create a sense of community?**
Yes, that was one of Tomás's concerns. He believed that you establish community by talking to each other. He recalled in his hometown in Texas as a young boy hearing a community poet recite his poetry out in the streets and, in doing so, creating a dialogue and a sense of community.

**You also gave a paper entitled "The Search and the Labyrinth: Tomás Rivera and Chicano Literature." What did you mean by the search and the labyrinth?**

I suggest that Rivera in his novel is observing that his characters are caught up in a labyrinth and that they—especially the boy—are trying or searching to find a way out. One way of getting out is to find a form to give expression to our ideas. So part of the search is to find this liberating form. Rivera credited Américo Paredes for finding such a form through his work on the *corrido*. In . . . *y no se lo tragó la tierra*, the boy is lost, but eventually he finds his way out of the labyrinth. He finds a way of expressing himself. He finds his voice. Through his particular form of writing, Rivera also found his way out of his labyrinth.

**Do you think that Rivera was attempting to talk back to Octavio Paz and *The Labyrinth of Solitude*? In fact, in some ways the Chicano movement was engaged in a dialogue with Paz. How to find the way out of the labyrinth of solitude? How to find a form, a voice, and how to create community?**

Yes, I think you're right about that.

**Don Luis, do you know anything about the last novel that Rivera was working on?**

The novel he was working on when he died was entitled *La casa grande del pueblo*. But no one knows much about it. The manuscript has never been found. Julián Olivares, who edited his unpublished work, found in Rivera's papers at UC Riverside only one chapter of this novel. It's possible that that chapter is all there is to the manuscript. Rivera once told me that the novel was about a home where poor people lived. It was a way of expressing Rivera's concern for community.

**Besides Tomás Rivera, you've written about what you call the "Quinto Sol generation." What do you mean by that?**

Well, it's the group of writers who come out of Octavio Romano's Quinto Sol Press, some of whom also received the initial Quinto Sol literary prizes. It includes writers such as Rivera, Anaya, Hinojosa, and Estella Portillo Trambley. Some, if not all, of these writers were also included in Romano's literary anthology, called *El espejo/The Mirror*.

## Rudolfo Anaya

**Let's talk about one of these other writers from that generation: Rudolfo Anaya. He won the second Quinto Sol prize for *Bless Me, Ultima* [1971]. When did you first meet Anaya?**

A few years after his book was published. Very few people knew Anaya outside of New Mexico.

**What was your reaction to** *Bless Me, Ultima?*

Very positive. I immediately associated it with magical realism because I saw various elements of this Latin American trend in Anaya's writings. In fact, I think that it's the novel's connection with Latin American magical realism, as popularized by García Márquez, that is one of the key reasons why *Bless Me, Ultima* became popular both among Chicano critics and Anglo critics. Of all the Chicano writers who came out of this period, Anaya has been the most successful and the one most often mentioned by mainstream critics.

**What was your reaction to the themes and setting of** *Bless Me, Ultima,* **which is mystical and rural? You also have in this novel, as you find in Rivera's novel, a young male protagonist.**

Yes, what you have in *Ultima* is a combination of the real, as found in the young boy, and the spiritual, as found in the old woman, Ultima. You find such a combination, for example, in *Don Quixote.* Anaya was suggesting that in New Mexico the combination of the real and the spiritual is very strong. As you know, in the novel Ultima possesses supernatural powers, and in the end she transforms herself into an owl. That kind of transformation—from a person into a bird—is very popular in Mexican and New Mexican folklore.

**It's a very New Mexican novel. It's regional literature. When I first read it, I liked the novel, but somehow it didn't seem to speak to my more urban concerns or the more political concerns of the movement. Rivera's novel, even though it was also rural, spoke more directly to the movement, because of the farm-worker connection. Anaya, on the other hand, had this more remote and mystical character. Yet interestingly,** *Ultima* **became very popular in Chicano circles. Why do you think this was? Was it because of the magical realism in the text?**

Anaya was criticized for being more aloof from what were considered to be movement political issues. However, he defended himself very well. Of course, in my opinion, you cannot reduce Chicano literature only to certain political or social themes, because there are many other themes and aspects of life among Chicanos. But Anaya defended himself by saying that he had to represent the ideas of the people in New Mexico without changing them. In his later novels, Anaya introduced more social and political themes, maybe reacting to some of this criticism.

You're absolutely right. You can't hold writers to just writing about political issues.

Also, notice that despite this criticism of *Ultima,* Romano published it, and
he, of course, was and is very political.

**But do you think that Chicano readers liked *Ultima* because in some
ways it resembled not only Latin American magical realism, but also
the writings of Carlos Castaneda, who wrote about shamans like
Don Juan?**

Yes, for those who were acquainted with Castaneda. What's surprising about
*Ultima* is how many people over the years have read it even though the
Quinto Sol edition had a limited distribution.

**Of course, it has now been republished, along with Anaya's more recent
books, by Warner Publishers.**

That's right. Many people who don't know anything else about Chicano literature mention Anaya.

**Anaya proved to be more popular than Rivera.**

Much more, yes. Rivera's novel is hardly known outside of Chicano critics
and Chicano readers.

**Is it fair to compare . . . *y no se lo tragó la tierra* with *Bless Me, Ultima*?**

Well, you have to keep in mind that Anaya wrote in English while Rivera
wrote in Spanish. And even if we compare *Ultima* with the English translation of . . . *y no se lo tragó la tierra,* there's a problem, because a translation
never fully conveys the quality and character of the original. Sometimes it's
unavoidable. You have to read the translation if you don't know the language. I read all of Dostoevsky, but I had to read it in English translation
because I don't know Russian. So with respect to writing style and quality,
it's difficult to compare because of the language difference. Another difference is in themes. Rivera is more interested in describing people, while
Anaya spends a lot of effort describing nature.

**Juan Bruce-Novoa has observed that one of the differences between Rivera
and Anaya is that Rivera writes about the migratory experience, in which
the people lack a sense of place or home, whereas Anaya writes about a
sense of permanency, of a place where people have lived for generations.
Rivera's characters are seeking a sense of place, while Anaya's speak out of
a sense of place.**

Yes, that's true.

**But that's one of the reasons why, in Anaya's case, you have to see it as**

regional literature and not just Chicano literature. It is also New Mexican literature.

And, of course, in Rivera's case, his characters are moving all the time. On the other hand, Anaya has written an essay entitled "A Sense of Place." **Anaya's second book, *Heart of Aztlán*, uses the term *Aztlán*, which may have been his way of trying to relate to the Chicano movement even more.** Not only that, but Anaya also organized a symposium on Aztlán at one of the meetings of the National Association for Chicano Studies in Albuquerque a few years ago. He and Francisco Lomelí then edited a volume called *Aztlán: Essays on the Chicano Homeland*. Even though, as you say, he might have been trying to be more political in his second novel, he maintains that interest in the mythical and the spiritual.

**What was your reaction to *Heart of Aztlán*?**

It's not as good as *Bless Me, Ultima*. *Ultima* has more depth. The mythical aspect of *Aztlán* is too obvious in the second novel. *Heart of Aztlán* is less well known than *Ultima*. His third novel, *Tortuga*, is even less well known. Tortuga is a person who is paralyzed and is covered in a cast. He can't move. He's like a *tortuga*—a turtle. But there's also a mythical element involved, because *Tortuga* also refers to a nearby mountain range in Albuquerque. The myth says that this range is called Tortuga because it's really a turtle sleeping, and one day, when the floods come, the *tortuga* will come back to life.

**Getting back to the point you made about the influence of magical realism on Anaya, do you think that he came to employ magical realism out of his own New Mexican culture, or do you think he was directly influenced by García Márquez?**

I think that he uses some elements of what we call magical realism out of his New Mexico culture, but without his necessarily classifying it as magical realism. It's the critic who identifies it as magical realism. García Márquez, for example, says that others say his novels are examples of magical realism, but that he doesn't know what magical realism is. The same thing is true with Anaya. He gives expression to the culture of New Mexico, which is a culture that contains elements of what we call magical realism.

**But do you see the same kind of magical realism in Anaya's writings that you find in García Márquez?**

Some, but not all. But then I don't see in Rulfo the same kind of magical realism that I see in García Márquez because it's a personal interpretation and each writer has his own interpretation. Without thinking of the concept of magical realism, each writer gives expression to a reality he observes in the people. To me, magical realism is an attitude on the part of the characters in the novel towards the world, not necessarily the attitude of the writer. How the people of New Mexico interpret their reality may be completely different from how people do so in Colombia or in Rulfo's Jalisco.

**But these elements of magical realism in rural New Mexico culture come out naturally in Anaya's work because he's set in a tradition where these kinds of influences are pervasive.**

Yes, because there is no theory about magical realism that he could have read about and then applied.

**So in *Ultima* you don't see magical realism being applied artificially?**

No. Magical realism is not a formula. You can't write a novel of magical realism using a formula.

**This is in contrast, you've mentioned earlier, to the case of Ana Castillo's novel *So Far From God*, which is also set in New Mexico, in which she artificially imposes a kind of magical realism on her characters. But the point I would make here is that while some critics have criticized Castillo, who is from Chicago, for writing about New Mexico, where she has not spent much time, others have said that this doesn't matter. That it's the imagination of the writer that counts and not the geographical base of the writer. Yet in Castillo's case, her lack of familiarity with New Mexico does seem to matter, because this leads to her failing to recognize certain nuances about New Mexican culture—as opposed to Anaya, who has grown up with that culture.**

I agree. A Mexican critic has said that if, for example, a Mexican poet writes a poem about Arabs, those Arabs are going to behave like Mexicans. If a non-Chicano writes a novel about Chicanos, those Chicanos are going to behave like the writer. A good example of this is John Nichols's *The Milagro Beanfield War*. If you compare *Milagro* with *Ultima*, you can see the differences immediately. Nichols's Hispanos are more Anglocized.

**But again, returning to the influence of magical realism on Anaya's writings, one characteristic of his work is this emphasis on the mystical?**

Well, you have to be careful about using the word *mystical* or *mysticism.* Mysticism means a relationship with God, which is not what Anaya is doing in *Ultima* or in his other work. Magical realism is entirely different from mysticism. Mysticism is evident in the work of Santa Teresa de Jesús in *Las siete moradas* in the sixteenth century—how she communicates with God and undergoes this mystical experience. You don't find that in Anaya. In Anaya it's more a relationship between human beings and nature that can't be explained by reason. You can't explain the way things happen. They just do. If you can explain it, then it's not magical realism. But this has nothing to do with God as divine intervention.

**Both Rivera and Anaya can be said to be Chicano writers, but Rivera is also a Texas or Tex-Mex writer, and Anaya is a New Mexican writer. Have Chicano critics taken sufficiently into account these regional distinctions in Chicano literature?**

I don't think anyone has directly written about these regional distinctions. And they're not only regional differences but cultural ones as well. Américo Paredes in his article "The Folk Base of Chicano Literature" has called attention to some of the cultural differences. He classifies three groups of Mexican Americans: the traditional people who have been in the Southwest since the Spanish colonial period, such as in New Mexico; the immigrant farm laborers who work in the fields; and then the urban Mexican Americans. Critics have addressed some of these cultural differences, but not so much the regional ones. I remember an MLA meeting in San Francisco where there was a session on Chicano literature and one person commented that when he read Miguel Méndez's work, he couldn't understand anything. This person was from New Mexico, while Méndez writes from an Arizona background.

**I think in some ways, that was my reaction to Anaya's *Ultima*. It was interesting, but I couldn't relate to it. It was something very different from my experiences.**

Well, then there are two things we can say here. First, that there is no one Chicano literature. There are several Chicano literatures. And second, we have to consider Chicano literature as encompassing a set of regional literatures. But still, I find it difficult to classify Chicano writers by region, such as a Texas writer. Rolando Hinojosa is from Texas, but he can write a novel about anything. And Alejandro Morales's last novel is about a transnational future.

**But you do have writers, such as Anaya and Hinojosa, who in fact do focus heavily on their own sense of place, even though I'm sure they're capable of writing about other places.**

Well, I would rather consider region as only one aspect of Chicano literature. Take, for example, Ana Castillo, who is from Chicago but then moves to California and then to New Mexico and now is back in Chicago. Or Sandra Cisneros, who is also from Chicago but now lives in San Antonio. In the

United States today it is becoming impossible to classify people from a particular place, since everyone moves around so much. I lived in Illinois for a number of years but now live in California. So, I guess I don't have a sense of place!

**The point I'm trying to make is that one of the characteristics of some Chicano writers is their focus on a particular area. If you don't understand that, you miss something in their work. A novel like *Ultima* can't be transposed to an urban context. It doesn't work. It is a very rural and regional piece of fiction.**

You have many novels like that. Faulkner's novels are very regional and set in Mississippi.

**That's a good comparison. Saying that Anaya is a regional writer should not detract from the fact that he's also a Chicano writer and an American writer.**

It's interesting that mainstream critics have classified Anaya as a western writer. They say Anaya is one of the best western writers.

**Anaya is the most anthologized Chicano writer in texts about the West. He is seen as a southwestern writer. But you're right that to classify Anaya only by his regional connection is too limiting. He's really more than that. What seems to be partly at work here is that mainstream critics have developed a stereotype about Chicanos as a predominantly premodern rural people, and a novel like *Ultima* plays into that stereotype. I'm not saying that Anaya is stereotyping. He's not. But mainstream critics see in Anaya's *Ultima* their justification or evidence of their biases toward Chicano literature.**

You're right. But Rivera probably does the same with his focus on farm workers. Many Anglo-Americans still have a picture of Chicanos as a rural, farm-labor population—which it isn't. But this isn't just a Chicano problem. In Europe, for example, there is a stereotype or an expectation that all Latin American fiction has to deal with social problems, especially in the rural areas.

**Of course, in Anaya's *Ultima*, even though some might suggest that it doesn't deal with social problems, in fact it does indirectly. It's a discussion of rural poverty in New Mexico and the alienation and lack of opportunity that drives younger people into the urban areas. It possesses social criticism, but not of the dramatic kind that some movement critics wanted at that time.**

# Rolando Hinojosa

*Leal (right) with Rolando Hinojosa at UC Santa Barbara in 1978.*

**I want to turn now to Rolando Hinojosa. You knew Hinojosa even before he became a writer. Tell me the background to this.**
After I arrived at Illinois, Rolando came to study for his Ph.D. in Spanish. I think he arrived in 1963. But he majored in Spanish literature, not Latin American literature. He wrote his dissertation under Professor Shoemaker. His focus was on the nineteenth century, and he studied the *costumbrista* writers, who had a great influence on his own later writing.
**Who were the *costumbristas*?**
These were nineteenth-century writers who developed not only in Spain, but in France, England, Italy, and Latin America. They broke with the neoclassicism of the eighteenth century. The *costumbristas* were interested in describing the customs of the people. This interest coincided with scholarly interest in folklore, in particular folk legends. This was the beginning of romanticism. Romanticists were very much interested in humanity, in the life of the people in the community. So they began to write what they called in Spain *cuadros costumbristas*, in which the writer described the popular customs of the people. From here, these writers went on to develop the *cuentos costumbristas*, in which they wrote stories not just describing the customs, but

adding fictional elements with a dramatic ending. These stories are about local types: the barber, the priest, the store owners, etcetera. *Costumbrista* writers in Spain, such as Mariano José de Larra, used these stories to also criticize the government and certain social customs. *Costumbristas* wrote in the 1820s and 1830s. Hinojosa read all of these writers, not only from Europe, but from Latin America, such as José Milla from Central America.

I came to know Hinojosa because I let him share my office with me. We became very well acquainted. But I had no idea that he would become a writer. He later told me that he was already writing even before he went to Illinois.

**Did he study with you?**

No, he didn't. Shoemaker was pretty strict on what his students could study. But we used to have coffee every day and discuss various literary topics. He also participated in a study group with other professors and graduate students which met once a month to discuss a certain subject. We met at different professor's houses, including mine.

**Do you remember him telling stories as a student? Was he a storyteller?**

I don't remember him telling stories. I remember him telling *chistes,* or jokes. He liked to talk.

**When did Hinojosa finish his Ph.D. work?**

Around 1969.

**Then did you lose contact with him, or did you stay in touch?**

We kept in touch. He used to write to me all the time. When he finished he went back to Texas, to Trinity University in San Antonio. From there he got a position at Texas A&I in Kingsville, where he was from. He became a dean there, and that's when he started to publish his stories. He later, of course, went to the University of Texas at Austin, where he has taught for many years.

**Were you surprised when his first book was published?**

Very much. I couldn't believe it. I didn't know he was writing a novel.

**And his first book was *Estampas del valle* in 1973, which is a sketch of the lower Rio Grande Valley in Texas and was published by Quinto Sol. Did you read it when it first came out?**

Yes. He sent me a copy which he inscribed for me.

**What was your opinion of *Estampas*?**

I had a favorable impression of it. I especially liked it because it was the only Chicano novel which had humor in its prose. No other writer had such humor. Rivera and Anaya were very serious.

**Is humor one of the characteristics of Hinojosa's writing?**
Yes.

**Is it humor or satire?**
Both humor and satire. This is what distinguished Hinojosa from the other Chicano writers of the 1970s.

**What is the key importance about *Estampas*?**
It is that for the first time a Chicano writer gives you a picture of a Chicano community apart from the Anglo world. It is the world of the Mexican American barrio.

**The book was originally written in Spanish, wasn't it?**
Yes.

**Because *Estampas* consists of a series of short sketches, critics have debated whether it's a novel or not. What's your opinion?**
I consider it a novel. All the stories have the same background. The same characters also appear in the stories. And a similar plot connects the stories. All the stories are interrelated.

***Estampas*, like Rivera's and Anaya's books, was published by Quinto Sol and also won the Quinto Sol prize in 1972, so that these three writers represent a kind of "big three" in Chicano literature for their time.**
That's right.

**In an interview with Juan Bruce-Novoa, Hinojosa says that *Estampas* and his later novels all represent one large novel. Would you agree?**
Yes. All of the characters reappear in all of Hinojosa's books. He calls it the Klail City Death Trip Series after the fictitious town on the border where his stories take place.

**You mentioned that when Hinojosa was at Illinois, he was influenced by reading the *costumbrista* writers. How is this influence seen in *Estampas*, for example?**
It's in the style and in the humor and satire and, of course, in his showing of the local customs of Klail City.

**Is it also by a focus on folk tradition or folklore?**
No. There may be some folklore, but that's not the main subject. The focus is on the customs of the people. How they do things. There's no folklore in *Estampas*.

**Is Hinojosa an innovative writer?**
Yes—in his humor, satire, the way he presents his world, the idea of using the language of the people. He presents the language of the people much better than Rivera, for example. In Hinojosa you really get a sense of how

the Mexican Americans of the Rio Grande Valley speak. Also, the fragmented nature of the structure of all his novels is innovative.

**And here again you have the example of a regional writer who writes about what he knows best, the lower Rio Grande Valley of Texas. And, Don Luis, you wrote an essay on Hinojosa concerning history and memory in his work. How did you see history and memory being reflected in *Estampas*, for example?**

In *Estampas* all of the characters remember the Mexican Revolution of 1910. They also remember how the town, Klail City, was first established during the Spanish colonial period. So you get all of this history in *Estampas,* and you can see how the town developed over time. There is always in Hinojosa's work a particular character who remembers this history, and he tells the story of Klail City.

**Through fiction, Hinojosa is functioning as a historian. He's retaining the memories of that community. For Hinojosa, history is very important in terms of storytelling.**

Yes—that's what gave me the idea of writing that article.

**Hinojosa, for his second book, *Klail City,* won the Casa de Las Américas literary prize awarded each year in Cuba. How important was this award?**

It was very important. It was the first time a Chicano had received this award, which is focused on Latin American literature written in Spanish. It was the first Chicano book to receive international recognition. As a result of the prize, *Klail City* was distributed all over the Spanish-speaking world, and Hinojosa became well known in Latin America and Spain.

**So of all of the Chicano writers in the 1970s who came out of the Chicano movement, Hinojosa is probably the best-known writer outside of the United States?**

Yes, that's right, with the exception of Mexico, where the writings of Miguel Méndez are better known. Méndez's works have actually been republished in Mexico.

**We were earlier comparing Rivera and Anaya, but is it also unfair to compare Hinojosa with these other two writers?**

The big difference certainly between Hinojosa and Rivera is the amount of production. Rivera only wrote one novel and a few short stories, whereas Hinojosa has written several novels. In his productivity, Hinojosa resembles Anaya. But a big difference between Hinojosa and Anaya is that Rolando has written mostly in Spanish, while Anaya has written only in English. Another difference between Hinojosa and Anaya is that Hinojosa's novels are all related, while Anaya's are not. Each of Anaya's novels is its own world. But what Hinojosa has done is to continue to write about the same community and people. So when he finishes his work, you will have a real view of a Chicano community on the border. And that's still another difference. Unlike Rivera and Anaya, Hinojosa is a border writer. His characters go back and forth across the border.

**So the border plays a very important role in Hinojosa's writings?**

No question about it. He's always talking about the border. In his novel, *Partners in Crime,* the police from both sides of the border, from the American border town and the Mexican border town, collaborate to catch a gangster. In fact, although the border is there in his work, for his characters there is no border. They go back and forth as if there were no border.

**All of Hinojosa's books have been published by a small press, Arte Público Press. Is that by his own choice?**

I think so. This was a question that was asked of him by students when I taught a graduate seminar at Stanford which focused on Hinojosa and Alejandro Morales. I invited both of them to the seminar and they both came. Hinojosa's response was that he was comfortable publishing with Arte Público, that he did not need a mainstream press. Of course, you also have to remember that Hinojosa has published mostly in Spanish or in bilingual editions, which New York publishers, until only very recently, have avoided.

**What were some of the other questions that these graduate students asked of Hinojosa?**

They were interested in Hinojosa's characters, why they reacted in certain ways. Some of the students wrote papers on Hinojosa while others worked on Morales. Some of those who wrote papers on Hinojosa concentrated on various aspects of his writings. I remember one paper which dealt with the picaresque elements in Hinojosa's work. In the Spanish picaresque novel, for example, the main character goes from one master to another, and the novel criticizes society. This one student believed that this is what Hinojosa did in his novels—that he sees society through the eyes of his characters who move from place to place: school, a bank, going to war. I think that there is something to what this student proposed. After all, Rolando had been a student of Spanish literature, including the picaresque genre.

**The fact that Hinojosa's books always deal with many of the same characters and the same location, does this limit his range as a writer?**

Well, for some his work would be too repetitive, but, as I said earlier, by concentrating on one community in his writings, Hinojosa provides a comprehensive and in-depth analysis of the lower Rio Grande Valley area.

**I believe some critics have compared Hinojosa's concentration on one community with Faulkner's similar technique. Would you agree with this comparison?**

Yes. Faulkner consistently wrote about the same area in Mississippi. But one difference between Hinojosa and Faulkner is that Faulkner was not humorous in the way that Rolando is. Faulkner's work is tragic.

**In the series of interviews that Juan Bruce-Novoa did with Chicano writers of the 1970s, he asked each of them if they saw their work as political. Most of them responded that they were not being consciously political in their writing. In the case of Hinojosa, is there a politics to his work?**

Oh, there's no question about it. I think that Hinojosa wants to show that the Chicanos of the lower Rio Grande Valley have a culture and a life just as valuable as that of the Anglos. And that Chicanos are just as complex as any other group in their customs, in their ideas, in their ways of looking at the world, and so forth. Through the way his characters behave, he's trying to show that one culture is not superior to another.

**Yet Hinojosa doesn't reveal his politics as obviously as, for example, Rivera does in his treatment of the migrant farm workers' plight.**

No, he doesn't. But what Hinojosa does is to take another approach. He concentrates on his characters as representing the development of the culture of the Mexican people in the lower Rio Grande Valley. It shows that Mexicans are people with a culture.

**So what you're saying is that the importance of Hinojosa's work is that it shows Chicanos as historical actors and not just as historical victims. They are involved in determining their own culture and circumstances. But do you think that in so doing Hinojosa crosses over into romanticizing that culture, or do you think he deals with the contradictions of the culture?**

No, he doesn't romanticize. All of his characters are presented with all of their faults. They are not idealized characters. You have the good and the bad. He presents the people and their customs as they are.

# Chapter Six

## Aztlán— Part Two

*Leal (center) with Antonia Hernández (left) and Blandina Cárdenas at Aztec Eagle Award presentation at Mexico City, 1991.*

# Ron Arias

MG: Let's talk about Ron Arias, whose novel, *The Road to Tamazunchale*, appeared first in 1975. He didn't publish with Quinto Sol, so he was not part of that group.

LL: He first published a few short stories. One of his first he entered into the University of California Irvine Chicano literary contest. It won first prize for fiction. I think that this was also in 1975. But he also published some stories with *Revista Chicano-Riqueña*. His novel, *The Road to Tamazunchale*, was published in 1975 by a small press in Reno. At first it was almost impossible to get a copy of the book. A second edition was then published by another small press, Pajarito Publications in Albuquerque, in 1978, and it became more accessible. A third edition was later published in 1987 by Bilingual Press in Tempe.

**And more recently a fourth edition has appeared, published by Doubleday. Which edition did you first read?**

The first.

**Has the book changed over the years with these different editions?**

No, I don't think so.

**What did you think about *The Road to Tamazunchale*? Because it's very different from some of the early Chicano novels. It's more experimental.**

My first reaction was that here you had a novel that was greatly influenced by the new Latin American novel. The others we've talked about had some of this influence, but not as much as Arias's novel. For example, there is a section of the book that is almost a direct translation from a section of García Márquez's *One Hundred Years of Solitude*. García Márquez and magical realism are important influences on Arias. The theme of death in *Tamazunchale*, through the old man, Fausto, also reveals the influence of Juan Rulfo's *Pedro*

*Páramo.* Of course, there are other influences as well. The main character, Fausto, obviously comes from Goethe's *Faust.*

**The other Chicano novels, as we've mentioned, are also very regional in character. In *Tamazunchale,* the setting is Los Angeles, but really the story could have taken place anywhere in the Southwest.**

Yes. The novel has certain local references in Los Angeles, like Elyssian Park, but then there are also references to llamas, which, of course, are animals found in Perú. So the novel has these influences from both sides of the border.

**What do you think Arias is saying about the Chicano experience in this novel?**

Well, Arias was criticized for not presenting the Chicano experience like other novelists who used obvious Chicano themes and settings. Yet Arias clearly is also presenting a Chicano experience. All of his characters are Chicanos. It's a Chicano world seen through the eyes of the novelist in close association with Latin American society more than North American society. I think that the Latin American references in the novel suggest that the Chicano experience is not a closed experience or not just a U.S. experience.

**The novel doesn't have any artificial divisions, such as borders or countries. It goes back and forth from Los Angeles to Perú. It's also interesting that Arias chose as his main protagonist an old man, Fausto. In the other Chicano novels, the main characters tend to be young boys, as in Rivera's *Tierra* and Anaya's *Ultima.* But here you have an old man. It's as if Arias is saying that the Chicano experience is not just a youthful one, but has something to do as well with older people.**

I think someone else has written about old people in Chicano literature. But, you're right, old people are not the usual central characters in Chicano literature, although many writers do include as secondary characters the *abuelitos*—the old people, the grandparents. In fact, the *abuelitos* are common characters. They are used to represent the older Mexican traditions, but they are never the main characters. However, in Arturo Islas's *The Rain God,* Mama Chona, the grandmother, has a very important role.

**Do you think that Arias's use of magical realism works? For example, he has Fausto's dead wife reappearing to him.**

Yes. He uses it in parts, but not in the total novel. It's not like in Rulfo, where you have magical realism from start to finish and it works very effectively. Arias uses it in parts.

**I was also impressed by how funny the book is. It's a funny novel. In that**

sense, with the exception of Hinojosa's, it has more humor than some of the other Chicano novels of the 1970s.

Yes, you're right.

**What about the name *Tamazunchale*? Where does that come from? I understand it's a place in Mexico?**

Yes. Some years ago Gladys and I stayed there one night, in this town. We were on our way to Mexico City from Linares. This was before they built the new highway from Monterrey to Mexico City. Along the old highway you had to go through Ciudad Victoria, the capital of Taumalipas. From there you went down into Tamazunchale, where the tropics in Mexico begin. Tamazunchale is in the state of Veracruz. It's a small town. I still remember our visit. I had papaya for breakfast. You can feel the tropics. Today very few people pass through there.

**What's the symbolism of Arias's using *Tamazunchale* for the title of his novel? Arias never explains this.**

I suppose because at some point Arias also passed through there. But the town has really nothing to do with the novel. Arias just uses the name of the town.

**Perhaps he's using it as a way of linking the Chicano experience with Mexico and the rest of Latin America.**

Yes—this is part of it. But it also symbolizes the road north. Remember that the Mexican immigrants in the novel are from Tamazunchale but they head north to Los Angeles. The other point that I think Arias is trying to make is that Tamazunchale immediately makes you think of the Indian presence in Mexico. It's an Indian name. It's similar to what Ana Castillo does in *The Mixquiahuala Letters*. This also makes you think of Indian Mexico.

**In this sense, Arias is consistent with the Chicano movement's reappropriation of pre-Columbian cultural symbols—the idea of going back to the Chicano's Indian roots. In fact, in the 1975 edition, Tomás Rivera in his introduction to the novel stresses that *Tamazunchale* is a novel about death, which is also a pre-Columbian influence through such celebrations as *Día de los Muertos*.**

Yes, I think that's true. The pre-Columbian view is that life is complemented by death.

**Arias, like Rivera, never published another novel. He's now a senior editor for *People* magazine. Still, *Tamazunchale* has remained an influential book, and this is underscored by its recent republication by Doubleday. This, of course, is part of a trend of the big New York publishers seemingly having**

discovered Latino writers in the late 1980s. But before then, they wouldn't touch Latino writers.

That's true. This started to change with the tremendous success of *Like Water for Chocolate* by Laura Esquivel, whose book is not a Chicano novel but a Mexican novel translated into English. It made the best-seller list in this country. This was, of course, also helped by the success of the movie version. But New York publishers were hoping to find another *Like Water for Chocolate* in publishing other Latino writers, especially female writers.

But these more recent novels couldn't have happened without the earlier Chicano writers and their texts of the 1970s. Without the efforts of the small presses like Quinto Sol, Bilingual Review/Press, and Arte Público, the later Latino novels would not have happened. But, I wanted to ask you, do you think the critics are still interested in Arias and *Tamazunchale*?

Yes. *Tamazunchale* represents a novel that opened a new field by its experimental character. Arias accomplished something different. I think that *Tamazunchale* is just as important as Rivera's *Tierra* and Anaya's *Ultima*.

I hadn't read Arias until very recently. I had a sense that *Tamazunchale* was perhaps too experimental and too esoteric. But I found it to be a very enjoyable novel.

Yes, it's a very easy novel to read. It's the kind of novel you don't want to stop reading.

# Miguel Méndez

Don Luis, let's turn to another Chicano writer of the 1970s, Miguel Méndez. His first novel, *Peregrinos de Aztlán*, was published in 1974 in Spanish. It's also very experimental. I've never read it in Spanish, but in English translation. Even in English, it's a difficult novel to read. It seems to have no focus. It moves back and forth, and characters blend into other characters, and scenes blend into scenes. It's much more complicated than Arias's. Is it as hard in Spanish?

Yes, it is. But it is a very important novel. What attracts you the most is Méndez's use of language. He uses the *pachuco* language of southern Arizona. A second important fact about *Peregrinos* is the naturalistic representation of the border; part of the novel takes place in a border town which is supposed to be Tijuana, but it could easily be any border town. It is a border novel. A third characteristic of the novel is that it is an *indigenista* novel. It is about the Indian world of northern Mexico—the Yaquis' world. Méndez, himself, grew up in northern Sonora and southern Arizona in close relationship to the Yaquis. Unlike Arias, who has a connection to the new Latin American novel, Méndez follows in the older tradition of the *indigenista* novel of Mexico and Latin America, which was strongest in Mexico in the 1930s under the Cárdenas administration, with writers such as López y Fuentes, who wrote *El indio*. In other parts of Latin America, you had writers such as Ciro Alegría from Perú. The *indigenista* novel, which describes the harsh realities of Indian life, dies off by the 1940s, only to have its influence revived with the Chicano movement in the United States in the late 1960s and early 1970s, with poets such as Alurista and novelists such as Méndez.

I'll tell you an interesting thing about Méndez. I first met him in the 1960s in Arizona when he was a construction worker and had just started to write. I was in Tucson attending the *Instituto Internacional de Literatura Iberoamericana* [International Institute of Latin American Literature]. At a reception, Professor Renato Rosaldo Sr. introduced me to Méndez, who told me he had written some short stories and would I like to read them. I told him to send them to me. I read them and told him they were very good and that he should publish them. One or two were later published by Quinto Sol.

**What's fascinating also about Méndez is that by his own account, he only has a sixth-grade education.**

Yes. He's self-educated, and now he's a professor at the University of Arizona in the Spanish department.

**Were these short stories similar to *Peregrinos*?**

They were the basis for *Peregrinos*. They're about Yaqui survival in the northern Sonora desert. Part of the struggle is their migration across the border into Arizona and into border towns like Tijuana. Although his writing is difficult because he blends characters together, he has some very lyrical passages, which are like prose poems about the desert.

**You're right about how Méndez represents, along with Chicano writers such as Alurista, a kind of neo-*indigenista* literary influence. But there is a fundamental difference between Alurista and Méndez. Alurista and the Chicano movement as a whole celebrated the high Indian culture of the Aztecs or, in Luis Valdez's case, the Mayans. However, Méndez doesn't celebrate high Indian culture. He writes in a very realistic or neorealistic way about the poverty and exploitation of contemporary Indian life. In**

that sense, he's really much more in the tradition of the *indigenista* movement in Latin America. Alurista and Valdez romanticize in their use of pre-Columbian symbolism to some degree, while Méndez writes realistically about contemporary Indian life.

Chicano writers such as Alurista and Valdez and, even before them, Corky Gonzales in his epic poem *I Am Joaquin* use references to pre-Columbian culture as a way of instilling pride in the past of the Chicano. Méndez, on the other hand, is interested in the history of the Yaquis and how they have been treated.

**Méndez is different because he's trying to suggest that it's not only an issue of going back in history and learning about pre-Columbian culture, but that it's about recognizing that Indians in Mexico are still alive and that their conditions are tragic.**

But I think a better term to describe Méndez is that he is a *naturalistic* writer rather than a *realistic* one.

**What is the difference?**

The difference is that a realist tries to represent society as it is, as the novelist thinks it is, but still leaves open the possibility for change. The naturalistic writer also represents society as it is, but focuses on the lowest sectors of society, where, according to the writer, there is no possibility for change. It's almost predetermined that there can be no change. The characters cannot escape their fate. If your father was a drunkard, you will be a drunkard. Méndez, at least in *Peregrinos,* is that kind of writer. The Yaquis cannot escape their trap.

**In this sense, Méndez is different from most other Chicano writers, who do have a sense of hope and of change. Méndez doesn't seem to have that. The other thing about *Peregrinos* is that it is a proletarian novel. It is about workers, in this case immigrant workers, which gives *Peregrinos* some connection with Rivera's *Tierra.* But at the same time, it's not similar to the proletarian novels of the 1930s in this country, for example, which were Marxist-inspired and were not naturalistic to the extent that they argued for social change led by the working class. Would you say that this is another way of looking at *Peregrinos*?**

Yes. Méndez sees his subjects in very fatalistic terms. But there is still one more way of analyzing the novel, and that is that in fact it is a mythical novel. Méndez inserts Yaqui mythical elements in *Peregrinos.* He's trying to preserve Yaqui myths and pass them on.

**That brings up an interesting comparison with Carlos Castaneda, the**

writer who also has written about the Yaquis and especially the character of Don Juan, who instructs Castaneda about the spiritual use of peyote. But would you say that there's a difference between the mythical elements in Castaneda's writings and those in Méndez's?

There is a difference. The difference is that Castaneda presents myths created by the Yaquis under the influence of peyote. And this is not the case with Méndez. The myths presented by Méndez are not the result of a mind that has transformed nature and society. In Méndez, you have myths that see the world as it is without changing it. I think you learn much more about the reality of the Yaquis in Méndez than you do in Castaneda.

Another thing about *Peregrinos* is that on reading it, I felt that his depiction of immigrant workers crossing the border didn't seem to conform to my own understanding of the consciousness of Mexican immigrant workers through my historical studies. That is, most Mexican immigrant workers who have entered the United States, including those at the present time, seem to possess a much more hopeful, optimistic view of the future. They represent enterprising people who hope to make a better life for themselves on this side of the border. By contrast, Méndez's characters seem more depressed and fatalistic. However, when you put his characters in context, perhaps it makes more sense. These are not just Mexican immigrant workers. They're Yaqui immigrant workers. And given the history of exploitation and marginalization of the Yaquis in Mexico, it makes some sense that these workers may have, as Méndez suggests, a more fatalistic world view. But this is very different from the perspective of most Mexican immigrant workers.

I would agree. The same thing could be said of other Indian groups in Mexico. As you know, the history of Indian exploitation in Mexico has deep roots. In the particular case of the Yaquis, this history included forced Indian removals during the Porfiriato—during the dictatorship of Porfirio Díaz [1877–1910]. The Yaquis were rounded up and sent to work in the fields of Yucatán. So in Méndez's novel, his characters are the result of this kind of exploitation and dislocation. I think that's why in *Peregrinos* Méndez displays an ambivalence about the desert. The desert can be both life and death. This is also true about his feelings toward the concept of Aztlán. For Méndez, Aztlán doesn't necessarily mean the promised land. For his characters coming into Aztlán, it means more exploitation and hardship.

That's a good point. Méndez, rather than romanticizing the myth of Aztlán, as did other Chicano writers and the Chicano movement, is in fact

problematizing the concept. He's seeing Aztlán in more dialectical terms—
good and bad, myth and reality.

## Oscar Zeta Acosta, Ernesto Galarza, and John Rechy

We've talked about some of the early movement writers, but one writer we
haven't talked about is Oscar Zeta Acosta. He, of course, wrote *The Autobiography of a Brown Buffalo* [1972] and *The Revolt of the Cockroach People*
[1973]. These two books have also recently been republished by a major
New York press. When these texts first came out, what were your
impressions?
I don't know why the critics don't write more about Acosta. Perhaps because
these texts are between fiction and nonfiction—autobiography but with
some fiction. There's also the fact that he disappeared and did not publish
more. Interestingly, Acosta is well thought of in Mexico. Whenever Chicano literature is discussed in Mexico, Acosta is mentioned. In this country,
when the Chicano novel is discussed, Acosta is usually not mentioned. And
then when autobiography is discussed, you also don't hear about Acosta.
But what are your views on these texts?
Well, there's no question that his books present the grievances of Chicanos
for that time, especially against injustices. I think this is the major contribution of the books.
That's certainly true about *Cockroach People*.
The two speak to the issues of injustice against Chicanos. As you know,
Acosta was a lawyer, so he had a legal background that he brought to his
writings. He knew the law, and, who knows, possibly this had something to
do with his disappearance around 1973. No one ever heard from him again.
That's interesting—what you said earlier about the division between autobiography and fiction—because certainly the other works we have discussed, those of Rivera, Anaya, Méndez, are very autobiographical.
All of them are.
So here you have Acosta, who writes autobiography, but the autobiography
itself is very fictional.
You take, for instance, *Barrio Boy* by Ernesto Galarza, which also comes out
of the early 1970s. It is an autobiography, and yet it can also be read as a
novel. If you didn't know that Galarza was a real person, you'd think it was a
novel. *Barrio Boy* has all of the structural elements of a picaresque novel. It is

the story of the development of an adolescent. The Germans refer to this type of novel as a *Bildungsroman*.

**When you say picaresque, what do you mean?**

It involves the character of the text. A picaresque novel is a first-person narrative. It may involve many different scenes, but what holds the novel together is the presence of the narrator—and that's what we have in *Barrio Boy*. Galarza writes about his experiences as a child in Mexico and then his coming to the United States and his development here as an adolescent. But the picaresque novel has to be a first-person narrative told from the perspective of a child or young man or young woman.

**Can you say the same thing about Acosta's two books?**

No, because he only in part relates his experiences as a child. Most of his two books deal with his experiences as an adult, as a lawyer.

**Of Acosta's two texts, *Brown Buffalo* deals more with his acquiring a new sense of ethnic identity, while *Cockroach People* deals with his activities in Los Angeles during the period of the Chicano movement. Of the two, do you distinguish one from the other in terms of quality or of importance?**

I think that *Brown Buffalo* is the more interesting and important book. It's much more original, while *Cockroach People* has much repetition of themes from *Brown Buffalo*.

**I agree with that. I like *Brown Buffalo* more because of the central theme of the search for identity. And you see how Acosta undergoes this shift of identity over a period of time. He writes about going from the San Joaquin Valley, where he grew up, to San Francisco in the early 1960s after graduating from high school, and how in the city he became associated with the Beat generation. How he gets into drugs. *Brown Buffalo* is also very much about drug culture.**

Yes, the counterculture.

**The counterculture, exactly. And then Acosta begins his search for his true self. Ultimately, the text concludes in El Paso/Ciudad Juárez, which is where Acosta was born. So he comes full circle to discover his ethnic roots. Of course, this is quite typical of Chicano writings of this period, the coming back to one's roots. In Acosta's case, he returns to the border to discover that he really is a Chicano after all. I mentioned the Beat generation earlier. I see a lot of Jack Kerouac in Acosta, a kind of *On the Road* text.**

I think you're right. You have in Acosta more of the influence of the American novel. You find the same influence in John Rechy. Of all of the Chicano writers, Rechy received the most attention by mainstream critics, first with his *City of Night* [1963].

**You mean during the period of the late 1960s and early 1970s?**

Yes, because the first Chicano novels didn't transcend Chicano readers and critics, but Rechy's did.

**Well, Rechy at the time had already reached a certain national stature.**

He wrote for a national public and not for the Chicano public.

**Rechy, of course, is an interesting writer because, at least during the period of the Chicano movement, he was not seen as a part of Chicano literature. He was seen as outside of it.**

He wasn't seen at all. It wasn't widely known that he was Chicano even though one of his early short stories is about growing up Mexican American in El Paso. More recently, because of his novel *The Miraculous Day of Amalia Gómez,* which is about a Mexican woman in Los Angeles, Rechy is now recognized as a Chicano writer. I remember, and you probably will also, when he came to UC Santa Barbara in the late 1970s when he was invited by Salvador Rodríguez del Pino, who was teaching here then. Rechy said that this was the first time that he had been invited to give a lecture as a Chicano.

**I remember his appearance very well. He was dressed all in black leather, with his muscles bursting out.**

Later there was a whole panel on Rechy at one of the meetings of the National Association for Chicano Studies. And he attended it.

**But during the 1970s and even into the 1980s, Rechy was not widely recognized as part of the Chicano literary movement.**

That's right.

**He was really seen as being part of the manifestation of gay culture, since he predominantly wrote about homosexual themes. So it's interesting that in the 1990s more literary critics are integrating Rechy into Chicano literature and that he, himself, has now associated himself by his writings with other Chicano writers.**

    **But was it the fact that Rechy didn't write about Chicanos or was it because he wrote on the controversial subject of homosexuals that he wasn't accepted as a Chicano writer in the period of the movement?**

Well, I think you touch here on two factors. One has to do with the definition of Chicano literature. And the other is the attitude of the author. Let's take the second point first. If you don't consider yourself a Chicano writer, you're not going to be included as one. Perhaps this was Rechy's attitude.

I don't know. The other point is that most Chicano literature is defined as treating Chicano life and culture. This raises the interesting question of whether a Chicano novel can be about any subject. I think that if you're not known, and if you as a Chicano write a novel about Africa, I don't think you're going to be accepted as a Chicano writer by other Chicanos. On the other hand, if you're already a well-known Chicano writer, such as Anaya, you can write a book set in China! There's no question but that Anaya is a Chicano writer. And no matter what Anaya writes about, he will still be considered a Chicano writer. But if a new writer who happens to be Chicano writes about any topic that has nothing to do with Chicanos, I doubt he or she will be included as part of Chicano literature.

**That obviously was the case with Rechy, because his novels dealt with other communities and other issues.**

**Let's talk a bit about Galarza. Of course we know Galarza as a historian, as a labor organizer, as a political activist, and we know that his early works concerned historical and sociological issues, such as his classic book on the Mexican *braceros*, *Merchants of Labor*, which came out in 1964. As you know, this was an exposé of the contract labor program which started in World War II and continued until 1964. In the book, Galarza exposed the exploitative nature of this program. But then in 1971, Galarza came out with his autobiography, *Barrio Boy*, which was very distinct from his earlier writing, not only with respect to representing a different genre, but in the higher quality of writing contained in *Barrio Boy*. It's a wonderful piece of writing and has stood the test of time. It's gone through numerous editions now. What were your own observations about *Barrio Boy*? Were you surprised that Galarza wrote such an autobiography?**

No, I wasn't surprised, Mario, because it's very common for a writer after he or she has already published several books to write about himself or herself—an autobiography. I'm thinking, for example, of George Santayana, the philosopher, who later wrote an autobiographical novel, *The Last Puritan*. The same thing happened with Galarza. By the way, besides his autobiography, Galarza also wrote a book of poems in the 1970s.

Now, I think that the idea of writing his autobiography, which reads like a novel, was to share in a personal way what happened and is still happening to Mexicans who come to work in the United States. These were the workers that he had been studying in his more historical/sociological works. Galarza could not write about these *braceros* from the inside, but, if he wrote about his own experiences, then it would illustrate, in a very personal way, what he was trying to say from a sociological perspective in his other writings.

That's right. In that sense, *Barrio Boy* is not disconnected, for example, from *Merchants of Labor*. If you read *Merchants of Labor*, you understand how these workers were victimized, but you don't get a sense of the *braceros* themselves, about their own feelings. The only way that Galarza could show these feelings was to turn to autobiography and, through the experiences of his own family, reveal at a more emotional level what it meant to be a Mexican immigrant worker. So *Merchants of Labor* and *Barrio Boy* are really the same story. And it's interesting that Galarza ends *Barrio Boy* with the same message contained in his other writings, which is that the only way these workers can combat their exploitation is to organize themselves and struggle against injustice.

Yes, to organize; that's correct.

And, of course, the organization of farm workers was so central to Galarza's own life as a labor organizer.

I think that it's also interesting that the subtitle of Galarza's autobiography is *The Story of a Boy's Acculturation*. What's interesting is that at a time when so much emphasis was being placed on ethnic/cultural differences in order to counter assimilation and acculturation, Galarza is addressing acculturation. He's writing about how immigrants from Mexico have adjusted in the United States, how their children begin to learn English in the schools, and how there is a bridging of cultures, especially manifested in Galarza's own generation. As a young adolescent in Sacramento, Galarza literally and symbolically translated for his Spanish-speaking family. Galarza, as indeed his generation—what I and others have referred to as the Mexican American Generation—became translators between cultures.

So I find that the theme of acculturation is a very important one that Galarza employs, even though it's a theme that is out of step with the movement's ethnic, nationalistic ideology. The movement is very critical of acculturation, even though almost all movement activists themselves were quite acculturated. I think that only because of Galarza's stature was he not criticized for this theme. Anyone else might have faced severe censure. As part of his acculturation, Galarza writes about his success in the public schools. In fact, he represents the original *scholarship boy* years before Richard Rodríguez, in his own autobiography, *Hunger of Memory*, uses that term to describe his educational success, interestingly enough also in Sacramento. Galarza, of course, went on to college and achieved a Ph.D. in history from Columbia University. But here again, the theme of educational success and mobility goes against the grain of the movement, which focused on the failures of the public-school system. Rodríguez, after his book came out in 1981, was harshly and, I think, unfairly criticized and even censured for his views. But Galarza was not, because in a sense, unlike Rodríguez, he had certain political credentials that made him acceptable to the movement.

Galarza's theme of acculturation, or what some would call transculturation, is a very important and apropos theme with respect to the Chicano experience. But it's a theme that was lost sight of because it surfaces during such a highly nationalistic period. In a way, Galarza's text is postnationalist and therefore postmovement.

You're right. And it's also interesting to compare Villarreal's *Pocho* with Galarza's *Barrio Boy*. They both are set in the same historical context of the Mexican Revolution of 1910 and the mass migration of Mexicans into the United States. Villarreal also stresses the process of acculturation, although he emphasizes more so than Galarza the tensions linked to acculturation. Richard Rubio, his main character, is not a scholarship boy. So it's interesting that Villarreal, or at least his protagonist, is criticized by movement critics for the focus on acculturation, while Galarza is not.

**But, you know, Don Luis, the other thing about *Barrio Boy* is that it's a beautifully written book. It shows Galarza as someone who could masterfully control the English language.**

There's no question about it. I have read the book many times, and each time I'm fascinated by the way he tells his story. It's a wonderful story and very well motivated. You identify with Galarza as a young boy, or at least I do.

**Did you know Galarza personally?**

No, unfortunately I never met him. He died in 1984. I did meet his wife at Stanford when she turned over his papers to the research library there. Stanford also has an annual Ernesto Galarza Memorial Lecture.

**I was fortunate to meet Galarza when I was a graduate student at the University of California, San Diego in the early 1970s. Galarza spent a quarter teaching there, and I sat in on one of his classes. He was very impressive, and I was struck by the various experiences that he talked about. But he was a scholar, too, and his lectures always possessed a historical and sociological perspective.**

# Chicana Writers and the Movement

**Don Luis, in this early grouping of movement writers, there are very few women writers. One of the few is Estella Portillo Trambley. How does her work fit into this picture? She was predominantly a playwright.**
She is well known as a playwright, but she also wrote some very good short stories. She never wrote a novel. But for her work, she received the fourth Quinto Sol prize in literature. She followed Rivera, Anaya, and Hinojosa. But few critics remember that she won that prize.
**What themes did she stress?**
She wrote about the problems of women, of Chicanas, and about the aspirations of women, about the dreams of women. She wrote an interesting play about Sor Juana Inés de la Cruz. But for many years now, she hasn't written anything or at least nothing published.
**But her plays are not very political, or at least not political in Chicano-movement terms. Portillo Trambley's plays are much more introspective.**
That's right. They deal with personal, gender, and sexual issues.
**And these were not issues that the movement focused on.**
Yes. And Portillo Trambley was the only real recognized female writer at a time when Chicano literature was dominated by men. Today, with so many other Chicana and Latina writers, Portillo Trambley, unfortunately, has been largely forgotten.
**How do you explain the fact that so few Chicanas were writing at this time, or at least not in a more formal way?**
I think it's the case that traditionally women in Spanish-speaking cultures did not publish at all until very recently. This also has to do with the fact that women in these cultures have not had access to university education. This is changing, and today almost all of the Chicana and Latina writers are university trained. Notice that almost all of them write in English as well. Many have graduated from English departments. Portillo Trambley wrote in English. One of the few exceptions is Lucha Corpi, who was born in Mexico and writes partly in Spanish. Lately, however, she has been writing novels in English.

But the other thing, Mario, is that although more women are writing and being published today, there has always been a history of Mexican American women writers. The first English-language novel published by a Mexican American was written by a woman, María Amparo Ruiz de Burton, who in 1872 published *Who Would Have Thought It* and in 1885 in San Francisco published *The Squatter and the Don.* Both have been recently reedited and republished by Arte Público Press.

**I recently used *The Squatter and the Don* in a seminar and found it very interesting. She's very critical of what happens to the older *Californio* families after the U.S. takeover of California following the U.S.-Mexico War. She's especially critical of the loss of the *Californios'* lands.**

Yes, of how the *Californios* were dispossessed of their lands. But I didn't like very much her attitudes toward the Indians.

**While the book is critical of the Euro-American takeover, at the same time it reflects certain elite, upper-class attitudes on the part of the *Californio* landed families toward the subaltern Indians and poor mestizos. This is a contradiction—a class contradiction—that isn't being focused on too much by some contemporary Chicana critics, who, in their enthusiasm to extend the genealogy of Chicana writers back into the nineteenth century, tend to avoid dealing with these class contradictions of these earlier writers.**

That's true, but the point I'm making is that despite such contradictions there is a longer history of Mexican American female writers. You have, for example, writers such as Jovita González in Texas and Josefina Niggli in the 1930s, 1940s, and 1950s.

**But even during the period of the Chicano movement, there were many Chicanas writing poetry and essays in the numerous movement newspapers of the period. There were even specific Chicana newspapers and journals, such as *Hijas de Cuauhtémoc* and *Encuentro Femenil.* So it wasn't that Chicanas weren't writing, but that they were not writing in some of the genres that men were writing in, such as the novel.**

One exception would be Angela de Hoyos of San Antonio.


# Chicano Literature and Publishers

**We've talked about several of the key writers who come out of the Chicano movement, but are there others who you think are also of importance?**

Well, there are many more writers. You have poets and essayists, such as José Antonio Burciaga. But for the most part, many of these lesser-known movement writers have stopped publishing. Burciaga, of course, recently died. But there's another reason for this decline in publications. During the 1970s we had several Chicano publishing houses, and it was much easier to publish. But all of these houses have disappeared, with the exception of Arte Público Press in Houston and Bilingual Review/Press in Tempe. As a result, those—I don't want to say secondary writers—lesser-known writers have stopped publishing. There's a theory of literature that suggests that the more prominent writers are the result of these other, less-publicized ones.

**Do you think this theory applies to Chicano literature?**

I think that it applies very well to Chicano literature. These lesser-known writers of the 1970s prepared the background and environment in which the more prominent writers flourished.

**And would you agree that these later writers, indeed all of the writers, would not have developed without the impact of the Chicano movement?**

There's no question about that. The movement, for example, opened up the possibility of writing and publishing in Spanish. Tomás Rivera said that when he realized he could publish in Spanish through Quinto Sol Press, that encouraged him to write his novel, which was published bilingually. But before then it was difficult to publish in Spanish unless you sent your manuscript to Mexico.

**But the movement created this bilingual and bicultural context.**

Yes. The movement stressed the nationalistic tendency based on Spanish/Mexican culture. So some of these writers began to write in Spanish. But now that's over. Now almost everybody writes in English. One thing, however, is that most Chicano/Latino writers still employ some Spanish in their writing.

**So, Don Luis, do you think that this period of the late 1960s to the mid-1970s can be considered the golden age of Chicano literature? Although, I assume, the female writers wouldn't agree with this.**

Well, Philip Ortego, one of the early critics of Chicano literature, referred to this period as the "Chicano renaissance." But my reaction was, *renaissance from what?* You must have something else before you can have a renaissance. I think it's better to say that this period sees a flourishing of Chicano literature. The term *renaissance* suggests a preceding dark age which I'm not sure is the case, as we're discovering more and more premovement writings.

## Chicano Literary Criticism

**We've talked a lot about the early Chicano-movement writers, but I want to turn now to the development of Chicano literary criticism. Of course,**

you were very much a part of this development, but how do you assess the development of Chicano literary critics in the 1970s? Did it parallel the success of the writers?

I think so, beginning with several Ph.D. dissertations completed on Chicano literature. Philip Ortego, whom I've mentioned, completed his around 1970. It was one of the first on Chicano literature. It is a survey of Chicano literature from 1848 to 1970. He then published several articles based on his concept of the Chicano renaissance. Besides the dissertations, we had journals such as *Revista Chicano-Riqueña,* which included some of this early literary criticism. Then later in the 1970s, we begin to see published texts on Chicano literary criticism. Much of this criticism is as good as the creative work. Part of this development involves competing tendencies influencing the direction of Chicano literary criticism. Those trained in English departments especially attempted to apply European-based theories to Chicano literature, while other critics attempted to come up with more original interpretations based on the Chicano experience.

This raises an interesting related question concerning where Chicano literary criticism should be based. Should it pertain to departments of English or to departments of Spanish? How did you see that question in the 1970s?

This is still a relevant question. Chicano literary criticism is divided between English and Spanish departments. For example, at Stanford you have Ramón Saldívar, who does Chicano literature out of the English department. Here at UCSB, we have Francisco Lomelí and Ellen McCracken, who teach it out of the Spanish department, while Carl Gutiérrez-Jones is in English. Adding to this dimension is that on some campuses, Chicano literature is not taught out of any language department, but out of Chicano studies. This is the case here at UCSB, with María Herrera-Sobek in the Department of Chicano Studies and Lomelí, who has a joint appointment in Chicano studies.

But I guess my point is that in the beginning of the development of Chicano literature, it seemed as if in particular the language departments, English and Spanish, didn't know how to relate to Chicano literature. Those in English felt that it belonged in Spanish. But Spanish departments said, "No, no, much of this literature is in English, so it belongs in the English department." Both couldn't deal with Chicano literature.

This is true. If you look at the MLA conferences in the 1970s, they didn't know where to put a paper on Chicano literature. Should it be on a panel on Latin American literature or should it be on a panel on American literature?

I'm not so sure that even today this issue has been resolved. I think that traditional English and Spanish departments are still uncomfortable with Chicano literature.

Then, of course, you have Chicano studies.

That's true, but on some campuses you don't have Chicano studies. But besides this question, I recall that later in the 1970s there was some controversy in Chicano literary circles over a very important article in Chicano literary criticism written by Joseph Sommers, which resulted in a somewhat tense reaction by Juan Bruce-Novoa. In his article, Sommers suggests that Chicano literary criticism can have several approaches, including a formalist one and a more Marxist one. Sommers sided with a socioeconomic or Marxist approach. Juan responded by dismissing Sommers's orientation and aligning himself with a more formalist interpretation that focused on the text without bringing in socioeconomic or historical considerations. What did you think about this debate? Was it a relevant debate? It certainly was one of the first significant debates in Chicano literary criticism.

Actually, this discussion about methodology and emphasis had an earlier history. For example, Tomás Rivera wrote an essay in the early 1970s in which he discussed the search for a methodology for the study of Chicano literature. He believed that Chicano literature was a literature in search of a form. Bruce-Novoa had also addressed similar concerns in his 1975 essay on space and Chicano literature. For Juan, the interpretation of Chicano literature was to be found in that hyphen space between Mexican and American or Mexican-American. I myself entered this discussion in my essay on Mexican American literature, where, in effect, I extended Juan's space to include pre-Chicano literature as far back as the Spanish colonial period in the Southwest. And then, of course, there was Sommers with his very influential article. As you say, he discussed various methodologies and proposed the idea of text and context. This is the idea that Chicano literary criticism should look at not only the text, but also the context out of which that literature comes. This is what Juan rejected.

Why was Juan so strong about rejecting Sommers's perspective? It seems like an obvious point.

Obvious to us, but not to others.

If you look at the writers we've been discussing—Rivera, Anaya, Hinojosa—they are all writing out of a particular historical and social context.

There are two approaches here. Some critics, such as Bruce-Novoa, focus on the form of a literary work. Others, like Sommers, analyze that work both with respect to form and to context. This synthesis Juan rejected. He stresses the form and attempts to seek the hidden meaning of a text. Juan can be considered a formalist critic.

This debate between Sommers and Bruce-Novoa certainly generated much discussion, but it was an important process. You had scholars of Chicano background being trained at various universities in very traditional and formalist ways at the same time that these scholars were attempting to deal with a Chicano literature that was very political and very social in its orientation.

Those two tendencies still exist. Some critics just want to study literature as an independent entity and only in relation to other works of literature, while other critics see literature as a reflection of society and culture.

And you can have extremes on both sides: the very strict formalist who refuses to see the social context and those socioeconomic or Marxist critics who only see the historical and social meaning of a text and who dismiss the text altogether.

That's right.

And, I guess, during the 1970s, since so much about anything Chicano always seemed to go to extremes, people tended to take sides in this debate about Chicano literature. But, as you suggest, it really should be a synthesis of these two positions.

The function of criticism should be to help the reader see the work better and to help the reader interpret the work.

I think that there are fewer extremes on such issues today and that there's more tolerance of multiple approaches. As you've often said, whatever position a critic takes, it contributes to our understanding. Irrespective of approach or theoretical perspective, all critics of Chicano literature have contributions to make. We shouldn't ever insist that all critics write in a certain way.

They all contribute.

At the time, I was sympathetic to Joe Sommers's position, but in retrospect Joe may have also been too rigid by suggesting a hierarchy of approaches and by saying that the socioeconomic or Marxist approach was superior. It might have been better to note that all approaches contributed to a better understanding of Chicano literature.

There's no question about that, Mario. Let's take a work such as Anaya's *Bless Me, Ultima.* You can interpret this text with respect to historical and socioeconomic issues, but there are still certain important, more-mythical elements that need to be considered and they cannot all be reduced to the socioeconomic factor. So everyone contributes from his or her focus. Now, of course, methodologies change over time. In certain periods, critics will emphasize certain ways of looking at a text, but these will be revised in another period. So how a text is interpreted can change considerably. For example, interpretations of *Don Quixote* over two or three centuries have changed greatly. This isn't the case yet with Chicano literature because its criticism is of recent origins, but in time we'll see the same process at work. **Different generations of critics will find different things in these texts.** Yes, because the social context will change. But we don't know what that context will be in the future. One hundred years from now, people might not even know who César Chávez was.

# Mexico: 1968

**Don Luis, in 1968, while you were in Illinois, some momentous events occurred in your native country, Mexico. That year witnessed an intense student oppositional movement to the ruling PRI political party and specifically to the administration of Gustavo Díaz-Ordaz. The government responded by suppressing the student movement that fall in what became known as the Massacre at Tlatelolco, the location in Mexico City where the students were gunned down. I want to talk about that as well as about the generation of writers in Mexico whose reference point becomes Tlatelolco. What was your reaction to those student disturbances and to the suppression of the students?**
You have to think about '68 not as an isolated problem in Mexico, because the problems were also here in the United States and elsewhere—for example, in France. Students in many places were protesting against the status quo. The student disturbances in Paris that spring had a significant influence on the Mexican students. In Mexico, the student protests were occurring at the same time that the Olympics were scheduled to be hosted by Mexico that fall. Díaz-Ordaz didn't want to have any disturbances. These student protests, which actually began with high-school students, had commenced that summer. I was in Mexico City at the time. All of this tension was building up. On October 2, there was a mass rally at Tlatelolco. Nobody knows who gave the orders for the army to intervene and begin killing the

students. Some blame Díaz-Ordaz, some blame Echeverría, the interior minister in charge of police and security forces. In any event, while the students were assembled in what is called *La Plaza de Las Tres Culturas,* the army, positioned in surrounding buildings, began shooting into the crowd. While no one knows exactly how many students and others were killed, it's estimated that it was between three and four hundred. Some claim even higher figures. There was much concern and anger to what was a military overreaction. Octavio Paz, who was Mexico's ambassador to India at the time, resigned his position in protest. Many other writers and artists, such as Elena Poniatowska and Carlos Fuentes, voiced their outrage at the government.

After the events at Tlatelolco, a group of writers emerged who began to produce what became known as the Tlatelolco novel. Sometime in the 1970s I gave a paper at a conference on Mexican literature at Yale, put together by Juan Bruce-Novoa, on the novels of Tlatelolco. In the paper I discussed works by Elena Poniatowska, who was the most important member of this group. Her book *La noche de Tlatelolco,* translated as *Massacre in Mexico,* is not really a novel but a documentary based on interviews. She interviewed students and others who were at Tlatelolco that day and gathered their testimonies about the event. Among those who wrote about Tlatelolco was René Avilés Fabila, who in his novel indirectly criticized Díaz-Ordaz, although in those days a writer could not openly criticize the government for fear of retaliation.

As a result of Tlatelolco, there was a change in Mexican literature. Before '68, that literature had attempted to stress more universal themes and fewer national ones. But after Tlatelolco, there is a return to writing about national problems. Writers wanted to know, *Why did this happen? Why Tlatelolco?* Even older writers, such as Paz, reacted to the events of '68. Paz wrote a short book of essays called *Posdata* in which he severely criticized the government. He could get away with it because of his stature and fame. Fernando del Paso, one of Mexico's most important writers today, published a novel that talks about Tlatelolco. Some, like Arturo Azuela, devote an entire novel to the events of '68, while others refer to it in part of their texts. The younger writers, many of whom had been students at the time and involved in the protests, collectively became referred to as the Generation of Tlatelolco. It is a generation of writers shaped by the events of that year.

I still don't understand why the government didn't just allow the students the opportunity to have a peaceful protest march.

**But these demonstrations brought out exactly what the students were say-**

ing—that the Mexican government, rather than being a government and a political party with a revolutionary heritage, was instead antidemocratic and authoritarian. These protests brought out the contradictions of the Mexican government.

And part of the students' criticism was that the government was spending millions of dollars for the Olympics while millions of Mexicans were poor and hungry.

**Can you say that the writing that comes out of the events of '68 represents a resurgence of the political novel in Mexico?**

Yes, I think so. There is a theory about the political novel that states that it has to deal with contemporary events. If it deals with political issues of the past, then it is a historical novel. Tlatelolco was a contemporary event. However, today if you wrote a novel about Tlatelolco, it would probably be considered a historical novel. The political novel in Mexico, of course, has a very rich tradition, especially going back to the Mexican Revolution of 1910.

**Is it also the resurgence of the urban novel, especially the Mexico City novel?**

All of these novels about Tlatelolco, by their very nature, are about Mexico City. This is still another rich literary tradition. Later in the 1970s, I wrote a paper criticizing the existing view of some critics stating that the urban novel in Mexico was a new phenomena. I said *no*. You can go as far back as the period of Mexican independence in the 1810s and find examples of the urban novel set in Mexico City. You have novels set in Mexico City throughout the nineteenth and twentieth centuries. Now what we can say is that in the 1950s there emerged the "new urban novel," with Fuentes's *La región más transparente*. It is a more experimental novel, and it deals with a greater variety of social classes.

**So is the generation of '68, or the Tlatelolco writers, in the same tradition of Fuentes and the new urban novel?**

Yes. And another connection is that like Fuentes, these new writers were also producing the so-called new novel. Theirs are novels that have a complex structure. In this sense, these Tlatelolco writers draw their inspiration less from Fuentes and more from Rulfo. As new novels they are more difficult to read, but because they are political novels, there is a limit as to just how difficult they can be. You can't write a political novel and make it too difficult. You have to write it so that it has some influence on a large reading public. The novels have to be accessible. That's the compromise. The subject matter forces the authors to compromise.

**How would you characterize these writers? Were they frustrated, cynical, or hopeful?**

Some of them, like Avilés Fabila, were quite cynical. Others, like Ponia-towska, were very angry. But they all have given up on the existing system ruled by the PRI. I think we can trace the current crisis of the PRI to Tlatelolco.

**Does Gustavo Sainz belong to the Tlatelolco group of writers?**

No, he belongs to another group of the 1960s called La Onda. These writers, like Sainz, don't stress Tlatelolco, but they write about youth in Mexico City. Sainz and the other writers who belonged to La Onda, such as José Agustín, are of the same generation as most of the Tlatelolco group, but they chose to write on less political themes and more about urban middle-class youth culture, including sex and drugs. A novel like *Gazapo* by Sainz is representative of La Onda. In this novel, Sainz writes about young people who don't care about anything except their own problems, their own rela-tionships, and their love affairs. They are rebels without a cause. There are also young people who are much less nationalistic. They accept and even welcome American cultural influences in Mexico, such as jazz and rock & roll. They reject what they consider to be older and more traditional Mexi-can customs. By contrast, they see American influences as liberating. They express the clash of generations—the children against their parents.

But there's still another group, called La Escritura, which also emerges out of the 1960s. They are also young writers, such as Salvador Elizondo. Unlike the other two groups, these writers are more concerned with lan-guage—not what you say, but how you say it. For them, everything is style.

**So what we see in the late 1960s is different groupings of writers, each with their own particular focus?**

That's the history of Mexican literature. You have what are called *capillas*. A *capilla* is a group of writers of the same generation who get together. They meet in high school or at the university and they edit a magazine or periodi-cal in which they publish their work. That's the way they begin as writers. That's the way Octavio Paz began. And that's the way La Onda and La Escritura began, by rejecting older writers, proposing a new way of writing, and publishing their own works.

**So the literature coming out of Mexico beginning in the late 1960s is a much more fragmented literature with no central focus?**

That's right. There's no central focus among all of these writers—unlike with the revolution of 1910, which served as a central focus.

**You mentioned Elena Poniatowska, but were there many other female writers who belonged to these groups?**

Very few. Elena Garro is one. She published a novel in 1963 called *Los recuerdos del porvenir* [*Recollection of Things to Come*], which is a story about a small town. She became very popular. But women writers in large numbers in Mexico begin to surface more in the 1980s.

**Were there any contacts in the 1970s, for example, between the Tlatelolco writers and Chicano writers?**

Unfortunately, there was no relationship. These contacts come later in a series of *encuentros,* or meetings, in the 1980s, especially concerning border literature.

# Chapter Seven

## Santa Barbara

*Leal (right) with Bert Corona at UC Santa Barbara, 1995.*

# Retirement

MG:   Don Luis, you decided to retire from Illinois in the mid-1970s. Why did you decide to do that at that time?

LL:   Actually, I didn't have a choice. Unlike today, when there is no mandatory retirement age, there was one then at Illinois and all other universities. You had to retire at sixty-eight. I turned sixty-eight in 1975, but because my birthday was in September after the academic year began, I was allowed one more year. So I actually retired at sixty-nine.

**How did you decide to come to Santa Barbara?**

In December of 1975, when I was attending the annual MLA convention in San Francisco, I happened to be sitting at a dinner next to Winston Reynolds, who was teaching in the Spanish and Portuguese department at UC Santa Barbara. We started talking, and when I mentioned to him that I was retiring, he suggested that I come to UCSB as a visiting professor the next year. I told him that I would speak to Gladys and get back to him. Gladys thought that it was a good idea. So we came on a visiting basis, but we never returned to Illinois.

   After I taught that one year at UCSB, I was invited to be a visiting professor at UCLA the next year. So I commuted from Santa Barbara to UCLA. I went there once a week to give a seminar on Latin American literature. The first semester I taught the contemporary novel and then the nineteenth-century novel in the second semester. The following year, Fernando De Necochea, the acting director of the Center for Chicano Studies at UCSB, asked me to join the center as a researcher. I did this, and then I was also asked to teach Chicano literature, as well as Mexican cultural traditions, in the Department of Chicano Studies, where I've taught at least two courses per year since then.

*Top: (From left to right): Victor Fuentes, Leal, Elena Poniatowska, Mario García. Santa Barbara, 1988.*

**You obviously liked living in Santa Barbara.**

I had never been to Santa Barbara before. I didn't even know where it was. We decided to stay here because we couldn't maintain two households, one in Santa Barbara and one in Urbana. But I missed Urbana, especially living within a fifteen-minute walk to the library. I missed the library there. However, we were attracted to retirement in Santa Barbara because our two sons, after attending college in the Midwest, decided to move to California to pursue graduate work in engineering at UCLA and then got jobs with firms in southern California. So a part of me missed Illinois, especially the library, but we were also glad to be away from the snow and cold.

**What did you think about the library here at UCSB?**

I wasn't impressed with it. It was much smaller, and at the time a new addition was being added, so there was much construction. What I did like was the availability of the Colección Tloque Nahuaque, the Chicano Studies library collection within the main library. One of the problems I faced in the early 1970s in beginning to write about Chicano literature at Illinois was the lack of library materials on Chicanos. The library there had an extensive collection of Mexican and Latin American material, but almost nothing on Chicanos. On the other hand, while UCSB had a big Chicano collection, it didn't have very much on Mexico or Latin America. So one of the big reasons I mostly shifted to writing on Chicano literature by the late 1970s was a matter of available research materials.

**In the early 1980s, you also took on the role of acting director of the Center for Chicano Studies at UCSB, which is a research unit. Why did you do this when you were retired?**

Well, I wasn't fully retired, since I was still doing some teaching and maintaining a full research agenda. But I agreed to direct the center because De Necochea had left for another position at Stanford and the administration here was threatening to close the center unless a reputable director was found. I didn't want the center to close, so I agreed to step in. I served as acting director for three years. After a couple of searches, Juan Vicente Palerm was appointed director.

## Alejandro Morales

**Don Luis, let's talk about some of the Chicano writers of the 1980s and 1990s. Let's begin with Alejandro Morales. He is certainly one of the most**

productive writers of this period. Do you see Morales as a different writer compared to some of the early movement writers such as Rivera, Anaya, and Hinojosa? Or is he still in the tradition of the early movement writers?

I think that Alejandro began in the tradition of the early movement writers, but he has changed more recently, especially in his latest novel, *The Rag Doll Plagues*. His first two novels were written in Spanish and published in Mexico. His first novel, *Caras viejas y vino nuevo*, is particularly important because it introduces a hard-hitting urban setting to Chicano literature, since it deals with the dark side of barrio life in east Los Angeles. In his second novel, which was translated as *Death of an Anglo*, Morales cuts new ground by introducing an academic environment into Chicano literature. In his other novels, he set out to write the Chicano history of southern California, such as in *The Brick People*, a history of a Mexican working-class community wholly dependent on one brick factory. When the factory goes out of business, the community disintegrates. So some of the key themes of the early movement writers also are visible in him. What's interesting about Morales is that in all of his novels one character always reappears, which gives them continuity. This character has the same surname in each of the novels; he is the one who recalls the history of the community.

**Morales is a writer who is very much interested in history.**

Yes. Although in his most recent novel he's also very much interested in the future, and that is very different from anything we have in Chicano literature. The first part of *The Rag Doll Plagues* takes place in colonial Mexico. The second part is set in contemporary Los Angeles. And the third part is in the future, when the American Southwest and northern Mexico, both with majority-Mexican populations, fuse into a new country.

**As you noted, Morales's first two novels were written in Spanish, but his more recent work is in English. Is he a better writer in one language than the other?**

Well, his novels in Spanish were very strongly criticized in Mexico for what the critics considered the use of slang Spanish. But what the critics didn't understand was that Alejandro was using the barrio Spanish of Chicanos. The Mexican critics don't know how Chicanos speak and don't care. But *Caras viejas y vino nuevo* was published by one of the most prestigious editors in Mexico, Joaquín Mortiz.

**What impressed me about *Caras viejas* was how depressing a novel it is in subject matter, dealing with gang types who have lost any hope for a future. It seems to me that that's one difference between Morales and early**

movement writers. These other writers also critiqued society, yet remained somewhat optimistic about the possibility of social change.

There's something else about *Caras viejas* in the structure of the novel, at least in its English translation as *Old Faces, New Wine*. When Alurista arranged to get it translated and published through Maize Press in San Diego, Alurista, for whatever reason, put the end of the novel at the beginning. I don't know why Alejandro allowed him to do this, or if he even had any control over it. Maybe Alurista thought the novel was too difficult to read, and he tried to make it easier by changing it.

**What are Morales's strengths as a writer?**

I think his ability to document Chicano life in the cities and, especially, his looking at the history of certain people. I think that's his strong point as a narrator. As I mentioned, in *The Brick People*, for example, he gives us a whole history of southern California going back to the nineteenth century and how the Anglo-American takeover changed the use of land and employment patterns. Mexicans lost their lands and became, along with new immigrants from Mexico, a mostly working-class population. This history of Chicano workers, in particular those associated with the brick industry, is also partly family history, since Alejandro's family were workers in this industry.

**In *The Brick People*, Morales employs what can be considered magical realism in some sections. I'm thinking in particular of when insects, in this case cockroaches, start coming out of the mouths of some of the characters.**

But this is not magical realism. It's the fantastic. Cortázar, for example, has one story where rabbits come out of the mouth of one character. Magical realism doesn't change reality, whereas the fantastic does. Cockroaches coming out of your mouth is a change in reality. Magical realism sees something beyond reality, but doesn't create a new reality.

**So does Morales in *The Brick People* employ the fantastic effectively?**

In part he does, but I think on the whole that Morales's use of the fantastic in *The Brick People* and in his last novel, *The Rag Doll Plagues*, detracts from the more effective realist nature of these works. Morales is at his best when he writes in a hard-hitting, realistic style. A realistic novel is not easy to write because, as you yourself have noted in a criticism of *The Brick People*, if you make a mistake or the critic believes you have made a mistake in accuracy, then it throws open to question the credibility of the whole work.

**I can see that. My criticism of *The Brick People* was that there was some**

distortion of history, particularly in Morales's choosing to suggest that one
of his key protagonists was willing to sell out his workers, or at least to give
up the struggle in the 1930s to achieve social justice. I thought that that
particular depiction went against the grain of the more historically accurate
portrayal of many Mexican American labor leaders at that time, who did
not give up and who helped advance the cause of Mexican American workers. Of course, when I wrote that criticism in the late 1980s, I was working
on my oral history, or *testimonio*, of Bert Corona, one of the giants among
Chicano labor and community leaders.

Your criticism is a good one, although on the whole Alejandro has done a
tremendous service in documenting in fictional form the history of Chicanos. He's also been one of the most prolific authors in Chicano literature.
I don't think that critics have fully appreciated his work. While I was at
Stanford, however, Jesús Rosales wrote his dissertation on Morales, and I
understand it is going to be published. It will be the first in-depth study of
Morales's novels.

# Richard Rodríguez

*Leal (left) with Richard Rodríguez at UC Santa Barbara, 1995.*

Another writer who appears in the early 1980s is Richard Rodríguez, whose
autobiography, *Hunger of Memory*, didn't receive much attention from

Chicano critics and, in some ways, was even boycotted by Chicano-studies scholars. His book, however, did receive much national attention. What were your reactions to *Hunger of Memory* and to Rodríguez as a writer?

To me, Rodríguez is probably the best writer in English of Chicano literature. His style is impressive. But his ideas are not directed to a Chicano audience. They are directed to the larger community, and as a result he has some severe critics among Chicanos. Rodríguez is controversial because he has criticized issues such as affirmative action and bilingual education. He has even suggested that there is no such thing as Chicano literature. So, naturally, he has received criticism for these positions. However, I think he has changed his views on some of these issues.

**If you put aside the more controversial essays in *Hunger of Memory*, it is a very moving story about identity.**

It's a wonderful story. And he handles English so well. You can disagree with some of Rodríguez's ideas and still enjoy the use of language. As you know, Rodríguez was trained in English literature and uses some of this training to write about pastoral society in his book. Of course, the controversy that went with the book only helped Rodríguez to become better known. *Hunger of Memory* was the first book written by a Chicano to be reviewed on the front page of the *New York Times Book Review*.

**Rodríguez, in my opinion, has come under unfair criticism by some Chicano-studies scholars because of how he deals with issues of identity. What these critics fail to acknowledge is that many of the insecurities and ambivalences concerning ethnic identity that Rodríguez writes about, many Chicanos have also experienced, including, I suspect, many of his critics.**

I think that most of this criticism came not so much from literary critics as it did from more political critics. Their criticisms had nothing to do with the artistry of the book and more to do with the politics of it. They reacted to, among other things, Rodríguez's contention that Spanish represents a private and more intimate language for Chicanos, while English represents a more public language.

**But this was part of the unfair criticism. I think that Rodríguez creates an unreal binary here between both languages. On the other hand, many Chicanos who have grown up in this country have always known that Spanish was the language of home and of family, but that outside of that there was English, which you had to deal with.**

This happens to everyone, not only the Spanish-speaking. Some people from the South, for example, when they leave that region, begin to speak what is considered to be standard English. But when they go back home, they once again use a southern dialect. It's a general reaction that you usually try to adapt the way you talk to the circumstances. You don't talk to your mother in the same way that you talk in public.

**What about some who say that you shouldn't read Rodríguez because of his views and you shouldn't invite him to your campus because of his views on affirmative action and bilingual education?**

I think that's wrong. We need to have a broad attitude to accept or deal with many views. You cannot limit yourself to just one. When I had an NEH summer session here at UCSB a few years ago, I had the participants read and compare *Hunger of Memory* with Ernesto Galarza's *Barrio Boy*. No one complained because I used *Hunger of Memory*, and these were all college teachers, most of them Latinos.

**This comparison between *Hunger of Memory* and *Barrio Boy* is an interesting one because, among other things, they are probably the two best-known autobiographies in Chicano literature. Ramón Saldívar in his book on Chicano literature compares the two books, and it's very clear that he favors Galarza's. I think he does this because he's more comfortable with Galarza's politics than he is with Rodríguez's. Do you think it's fair to compare these two texts?**

I think so. In the first place, the big difference is that Galarza was born in Mexico during the period of the Mexican Revolution of 1910 and came to the United States as a young boy. Rodríguez, of course, was born in the United States at a much later time. These differences in background affect their ideas and attitudes. Galarza, for example, experienced a rural life in Mexico and worked as a farm worker in this country. Rodríguez, by comparison, has had an urban experience. He writes about the pastoral in his book, but this doesn't come from a lived experience. It comes from his reading of English renaissance literature. So I think there are many comparisons that can be made between these two writers.

**Interestingly, both Galarza and Rodríguez grew up in Sacramento although, of course, at different periods. One other difference is that Rodríguez's autobiography is in the more traditional introspective and individual style. It is very focused on his individual life. This contrasts with Galarza's, which represents what can be called the "collective self." Rather than just focusing on his life, Galarza links it with community. His text becomes the autobiography of his family and of the Mexican immigrant community in Sacramento.**

Yes. Rodríguez sees the world from a personal perspective, while Galarza sees it from how events and conditions affected not only him, but others as well.

Another, more recent aspect of Rodríguez is that he has now openly come out as being gay. Some critics are saying that they knew this all along, but I'm not sure that they're being completely honest in saying this. Now that we know that Rodríguez is gay, we can go back into *Hunger of Memory* and see the hints about his sexuality. But a lot of this is hindsight. In the last chapter, for example, entitled "Mr. Secrets," we can now interpret it as revealing that his tensions with his family have more to do with the author's hidden homosexuality and his inability to discuss this with his own family. What I find interesting is that as critics and readers, especially Latinos, are rediscovering Rodríguez as a gay writer, they seemingly are now less willing to be critical of him, despite his positions on affirmative action and bilingual education. In other words, Rodríguez's gayness has now disarmed his politically correct critics, who feel timid about criticizing a gay writer for fear of being accused of being homophobic. However, this smacks of hypocrisy.

The same thing happened with John Rechy. But if writers like Rodríguez and Rechy are now being accepted as Chicano writers, it doesn't mean that they, especially Rodríguez, are comfortable with this acceptance. For example, Rodríguez always says, "We Americans." When he writes about Mexico, it's always, "We Americans" think this or feel this way about Mexico. For Rodríguez, the Chicano and the Mexican is still the other and not a part of him.

**Ten years after *Hunger of Memory*, Rodríguez published his next book, *Days of Obligation*. Do you see important similarities and/or differences between the two?**

There are some major differences. The first is an organic work. It was prepared from the very beginning as a unified book. However, the second is a collection of essays, most of which had already been published in newspapers or magazines. The other important difference is that in *Days of Obligation*, Rodríguez now openly writes about his sexual preference, which in retrospect he only hinted at in *Hunger of Memory*. There is no longer a Mr. Secrets. He is out of the closet. In ten years, society has changed enough so that Rodríguez can admit his homosexuality. A third difference that I see is that I don't think the writing in *Days of Obligation* is up to the level of that in *Hunger of Memory*. This has to do, I think, with the fact that the essays in the second book were written at different times and under different circumstances. When you write an essay for a newspaper, you generally have to do it quickly and you don't have much time to polish it. Finally, one additional difference is that while there is only one basic theme in *Hunger of Memory*, the issue of identity, in *Days of Obligation*, Rodríguez covers a greater variety of topics, jumping from his own father to Joaquin Murrieta.

**But isn't Rodríguez still obsessed with identity, even in the second book?**
Yes, which is why he discusses his relationship with his father and his conflict with his parents. I don't think that he has gotten over this.

**Isn't there an inconsistency in Rodríguez in that earlier in his writing career he did not want to be considered as an ethnic writer, yet in his second book he is writing about Mexico, Mexican immigrants, and about Chicanos?**
There is some inconsistency. But at least in the second book he is now conscious that his parents from Mexico had something important to contribute, while before, I don't think he had considered this. Rodríguez's dilemma is that he doesn't want to be identified as a Mexican, but he's not accepted as an American because of his physical appearance. But despite this continued personal conflict over identity, Rodríguez has changed over the years. He has written strongly against immigration restrictions and against immigrant bashing. He has also softened his positions on affirmative action and bilingual education.

**I find it interesting and somewhat disturbing that a major newspaper such as the *Los Angeles Times* over the last several years has turned to Rodríguez in its opinion section to interpret events in Mexico. Rodríguez is not an expert on Mexico and doesn't really understand Mexico. It's as if the *Times* believes that any Chicano can interpret Mexico simply on the basis of being Chicano, which is ridiculous and, more importantly, wrong.**
Well, most of his ideas about Mexico come right out of Octavio Paz. Everything that Rodríguez writes about the Mexican character you can find in Paz, especially in *The Labyrinth of Solitude*. Like those of Paz, Rodríguez's interpretations are philosophical, but like Paz's, they are also stereotypical.

## Gary Soto

**I think that a writer who hasn't really been given his due, especially by Chicano critics, is Gary Soto. As a poet and as a story writer, he has been extremely productive. Would you agree with this assessment?**

I agree. Gary's work represents a new trend in Chicano literature, especially in poetry. Unlike other Chicano poets, he published his poetry through a major university press known for its poetry series, the University of Pittsburgh Press, rather than through a small Chicano press. This brought him national attention, but not necessarily Chicano attention. What was also different in Gary's poetry was that unlike other Chicano poets, he uses very few, if any, obvious Chicano images, nor does he employ a bilingual style. And because his images are more accessible and familiar to non-Chicano critics, the mainstream likes him. These critics can understand his poetry better than they can that of Alurista or José Montoya. However, more recently he has been writing stories for young adults in which he does use his own experiences growing up Chicano in Fresno. He has become very successful in this form of writing.

**We've talked about this earlier: whether it's fair to establish certain criteria for what represents Chicano literature. In this regard, I don't think that Soto, especially in his poetry, has been judged fairly by Chicano critics.**
You're right. But what Chicano critics were reacting to was that Soto introduced a new trend away from the more traditional Chicano-movement poetry. He was turning away from ethnic, nationalist themes and toward what some would consider more universal ones. His poetry, unlike movement poetry, is not critical of society. When I taught a graduate seminar on Chicano literature at Stanford a few years ago, the students complained about having to read Soto. "Why are we reading Soto? What does he have to tell us?" they asked. I told them that we couldn't continue to read the same movement poets and writers over and over again. Today, in fact, we have other, younger poets who have gone even farther away from movement themes than Gary did. But I don't think that the criticism of his work by Chicano critics or, even more important, the neglect of his work by Chicano critics has affected Gary. I agree that it's unfair to demand that Chicano writers only write about Chicanos. I've always said that Chicanos should write about more universal themes and not only on social issues in a Chicano context. Of course, the response is, "What is universal?" So you have a conflict of interpretations.

**I think the issue is less about what is universal and more about that Chicano writers should feel free to express themselves over a range of themes and issues, some of which may be more specific to the Chicano experience and some which may be more in common with other experiences. In Soto's case, for example, his poetry represents his own personal feelings and aes-**

thetic expression, which on the surface lacks a Chicano context but which still can be interpreted from a Chicano perspective. What I find interesting is that some years after the movement, you still find graduate students, like the kind you described in your Stanford seminar, who retain this strong cultural nationalism and who seem to insist that Chicano writers only write about Chicano themes. How do you explain this?

This is still a big problem, especially for writers. Some writers say, "If I don't write about Chicanos, I may be accepted in mainstream literature, but I may not be read by Chicanos. But if I write about Chicanos, it won't sell, but I will be accepted by Chicanos." So it's a dilemma. What are you going to do? Some mainstream writers, of course, have written about Chicanos, but to do so they have changed their names. The most controversial case was of "Danny Santiago," who wrote *Famous All Over Town* a few years ago, which was widely praised. Then it was discovered that the writer was really an Anglo journalist.

**What was your initial reaction to *Famous All Over Town* before that revelation?**

I think I didn't read it until after the controversy. I think the novel gives a good depiction of the Chicano community in east Los Angeles. However, when he writes about the family making a visit to Mexico, you can tell by the way he writes about Mexico that he doesn't know much about it. This doesn't mean that Anglos shouldn't write about Chicanos, but that there should not be a deception. Another case like this was of the writer "Amado Muro," who wrote stories about Chicanos in the 1950s and early 1960s. It was discovered later that he also was an Anglo writer.

**What if these stories deal well with certain Chicano realities? Even if we know that the writer is not a Chicano, does this discredit the text?**

I don't think so. Postmodern literary criticism suggests that the author doesn't matter. This signifies the death of the author. We should only be interested in the text, not in the author. If you accept this, then we consider a text a Chicano text as long as it deals with Chicano life. But these types of conditions are not very widespread. Almost all Chicano literature is written by Chicanos. I don't think that anyone is going to do a literary study of Amado Muro when we have so many Chicano writers to study. No one discusses or studies *Famous All Over Town*.

# Arturo Islas

**Another important writer in the 1980s is Arturo Islas, who published two novels: *The Rain God* [1984] and *Migrant Souls* [1990]. What are your views of Islas's work?**

When I first read *The Rain God*, I was very impressed, and I used it in one of my classes. I also invited Arturo to come and speak to the class, which he did. When he came, besides talking about *The Rain God*, he read from the second novel he was working on, *Migrant Souls*. You know that Islas mentions me in *Migrant Souls*. After the novel was published, he called me to ask if I was angry because he had used my name for one of the characters. I said no, on the contrary, that I was very flattered. He told me at that time that he was writing another novel in which he mentioned me even more. But, as you know, Arturo died of AIDS shortly after *Migrant Souls* was published.

But I think that *The Rain God* is his best work. It is superior to *Migrant Souls,* which is a continuation of *The Rain God.* It's concise, has a good structure, and utilizes symbolism very effectively. He told my class that the original title of the novel was *The Day of the Dead,* but that his publisher told him that if you have the word *dead* in a book title no one will buy it. So Arturo changed it to *The Rain God.*

There are several important contradictions in the use of the title *The Rain God.* First of all, the title refers to the Aztec rain god, Tláloc. But Tláloc stands for life, while the desert, in the way Islas portrays it, stands for death. Death is a very visible element in the novel. A second but related contradiction is that there is in fact very little rain in El Paso, where the novel takes place. I expand on some of these contradictions in a paper I wrote called "Tláloc en el desierto." There are still other contradictions in the novel. For example, the family in the novel is the Angel family. However, some members do not act angelic. Mamá Chona, the matriarch of the family, has very elitist and even racist views toward those lower-class Mexicans whom she refers to as *indios* even though she herself is part Indian, or mestiza.

Another significant aspect of *The Rain God* is that in one small book Islas manages to discuss some of the most important ideological influences on the Chicano experience. For example, Mamá Chona and those of her generation who came out of the Mexican Revolution as political exiles represent a conservative and pretentious class of people. Some of them were followers of Porfirio Díaz. Then that part of the family who are first-generation Mexican

Americans exhibit assimilationist, pro-American views. This is the role of Miguel Grande, who is a policeman. Then you have Miguel Chico and those of his age, who reject or question the older generations. Miguel Chico, although an acculturated Stanford professor, symbolizes the new Chicano generation of the 1960s and 1970s. What is impressive is that Islas is able to manipulate these complicated generational tensions all within one novel.

**Is *The Rain God* well written? Is Islas a good writer?**

It's very well written. I don't think that there's any other Chicano writer, with the exception of Richard Rodríguez, who can write in English as well as Islas.

**You would agree that *The Rain God* is very much an autobiographical novel?**

Yes—there's no question about it. This is Islas's family in both novels.

**On my mother's side, I am distantly related to Islas. But more importantly, I recall growing up in El Paso and being aware of some of the incidents that Islas writes about in *The Rain God*, such as the murder of his uncle by a young Anglo serviceman. This became a big crime story with an unspoken background *escándalo*, or scandal, involving homosexuality. My mother, when she read the novel, immediately recognized many of the characters.**

What about *Migrant Souls*?

It's a continuation of *The Rain God*. It's not as well crafted. The critics didn't praise it as much as the first novel. But Islas does add to the story of the Angel family. He clarifies the identity of the characters much more.

**One of the things that impressed me about *Migrant Souls* is just how much it is filled with religious themes.**

That's also true of *The Rain God*, but, you're right, there is even more religious symbolism in *Migrant Souls*. It reminds me of Agustín Yáñez's *Al filo del agua* [*At the Edge of the Storm*], which is structured around religious themes. It's possible that Islas was very much influenced by Yáñez's novel.

**In *Migrant Souls*, the generational tensions within the Angel family seem to be centered around religion. There are the believers and then the non-believers, or, at least, those who express some ambivalence about their Mexican Catholicism. I don't believe that most other Chicano writers, male or female, have so centrally dealt with religion in the way that Islas has.**

The other thing that I like about Islas is that he is one of the first Chicano writers who wrote about middle-class Mexican Americans rather than just on farm workers or working-class experiences. Islas's novels explore class differences within Chicano life and the importance of the middle class. It's in this sense that his works are post–Chicano movement.

Hinojosa also has a focus on the middle class, but more from a business or merchant perspective and less from the religious one that Islas uses.

What Islas further suggests is that conflict, differences, alienation, etcetera in the Chicano experience are not just Mexican-Anglo phenomena. They're also within the Chicano community. There are very few Anglo characters in Islas's novels.

It's generational differences that produce a great deal of conflict. The women in his novels in particular reveal these tensions.

That's still another important aspect about Islas. He does an excellent job of portraying female characters. The figure of Mamá Chona may well become one of the major Chicano literary figures.

But, Don Luis, I get the impression that Islas has not been given his full recognition as an important writer, even among Chicano critics.

The problem here is that you either write one very ground-breaking novel, like Rivera did, or many novels, like Anaya and Hinojosa did, to get much attention. Islas is somewhere in between. On top of this, *The Rain God,* although now republished by a major New York press, was first published by a small Bay Area one with little distribution. It's very difficult to become a recognized writer. But despite these early publishing problems, Islas with these two novels is becoming more recognized, although, of course, this has come after his unfortunate death.

One additional aspect about Islas is that in his novels he introduces the issue of homosexuality within a Chicano context through the character of Miguel Chico. Obviously, John Rechy had done this more dramatically years before, but not within a Chicano context. Richard Rodríguez, as we now know, also injected a gay theme into his writings, but not in fiction. Islas is, I believe, the first Chicano male writer who does this.

I think you're right, Mario. Islas without question is a major writer who deserves much more attention by scholars.

## New Chicana Writers

Don Luis, into the 1980s Chicano literature is characterized by the growing visibility and importance of women writers, or the new Chicana writers. How do you explain this change?

I think that it's a fact that before the 1980s very few Chicanas went to the universities. Some of the Chicano men did, but most women did not. Men, for example, had the advantage of the GI Bill, like I had after World War II, but also after Korea and during Vietnam. Out of this greater movement of Chicano men into higher education from World War II to the 1970s, you get a group of Chicano writers, but very few women writers. It's not until the 1970s and into the 1980s that for the first time important numbers of Chicanas are in the colleges. Some begin to take courses in creative writing and in English and begin to write and to publish. Of course, you have some women who are writing essays and poetry for movement periodicals and newspapers, but this is not writing at the level we will see in the 1980s, with writers such as Sandra Cisneros and Ana Castillo. Cisneros and Castillo are both products of a university education. Some of these emerging women writers out of the 1970s also began to form groups and associations of women writers.

They encouraged each other to write and to publish. Some even published their own literary journals, such as *Mango*, published by Lorna Dee Cervantes here in California. You could see by the early 1980s that Chicano literature was changing from a largely male-dominated field to one, at least in the novel and short story, dominated by women.

**I recall sometime in the mid-1980s Norma Alarcón visiting UC Santa Barbara and from her perspective as a literary critic suggesting that the new Chicana literature represented an extension of the Chicano movement. I disagreed with her and noted that, in my opinion, this new writing was really a postmovement expression.**

The question is, when does the movement end? I think that it ends by 1980 with the new Reagan administration and the coming to power of ultraconservatives in this country. Before 1980, the few Chicanas who were writing were reflecting social-protest themes like the male writers. But after 1980, the new Chicana writers are more concerned with other issues, especially those related to women. So I would agree that this new writing is more postmovement.

**If we agree that this new Chicana writing is really more postmovement, then what, in a collective sense, distinguishes this writing in the 1980s from movement literature?**

It's the particular themes. For example, in the 1970s Ana Castillo was writing some movement poetry. She has a poem about César Chávez. But when she published *The Mixquiahuala Letters*, there's a complete change. She is now writing about the defense of women against men. It's not the social protest themes of the movement years. So the heavier concentration on gender themes is one characteristic of this new writing. Another is that some of these new Chicana writers also begin to address broader Latino issues rather than just Chicano ones. Some, like Ana Castillo, begin to experiment with magical realism techniques. But at the center of all of their writing is a more personal concern with gender issues. This attention had not been very visible before 1980, at least not in fiction. Another characteristic is that this new fiction introduces for the first time in Chicano literature characters who represent artists and poets. It resembles in this sense the earlier modernist literature of Latin America. You find new characters in the new Chicana writings.

**I remember that one of my reactions when I first read Ana Castillo's *The Mixquiahuala Letters* was that although she was employing a movement theme—in this case the Chicano pilgrimage to Mexico—she was doing it in a very different way. During the movement, Chicanos made their pilgrimage to search for their ethnic roots, to rediscover their identity. But in Castillo's case there is no search for roots or for ethnic identity in the protagonist's visit to Mexico. It's a search for gender identity. It's to work out her relationship with men back at home, only to confront more problematic relationships in Mexico.**

This is also the case with Sandra Cisneros in her latest book, *Woman Hollering Creek* [1991]. Mexico is in some of her stories, but more in gender terms than in ethnic ones.

**Is the difference between this new postmovement Chicana writing and movement literature just a matter of themes, or is it also stylistic?**

It's both. The writing of the 1980s and into the 1990s, especially of the Chicana writers, is more polished and poetic. It also includes much less Spanish than in movement literature. There is some Spanish—a word here and there—but not much in comparison to movement writers.

**How do you explain the greater use of English into the 1980s?**

Well, as Richard Rodríguez has said, these new Chicana writers speak less Spanish at home, and since most have gone on to the university, they have lost much of their Spanish.

**But it also might be that these writers are trying to appeal to much larger audiences.**

Not only that, but the new Chicana writers have done what the male Chicano writers were unable to do—to break into mainstream publishing houses. Few had done that before with much success. But now in the 1980s and 1990s you have Sandra Cisneros and Ana Castillo being published by big New York firms. Each of them is represented by a professional agent. By contrast, a male writer like Morales has had to go to Mexico to get his work published, or have it published by a small Latino press such as Arte Público or Bilingual Review/Press. Hinojosa, for example, has never published with a big press.

**What we're seeing is the first generation of professional writers among Chicanos. We've never had a generation of writers who could survive on their writings. As you say, these are writers who have agents, who are receiving substantial advances for their books, and whose books are obviously selling well, since the New York publishers seem to be publishing increasing numbers of Chicana and Latina writers.**

There's no question about this change. These writers have been accepted by the mainstream publishers, and their books are being reviewed in the *New York Times* and the *Los Angeles Times*. We didn't have this before, with the exception of John Rechy. The only male Chicano writer who has gotten similar attention is Richard Rodríguez.

**I agree with you that the Chicana writers have broken barriers by being published by the big presses, but their attraction is still linked to their ethnicity. The reason they're being published is because New York publishers feel they can bring in new markets and a new reading public. If they didn't feel these books could sell, they wouldn't publish them. These writers are being accepted but as hyphenated writers, as "Hispanic-American" writers. They're not just simply being accepted as American writers, not yet anyway. On the other hand, Saul Bellow, despite his strong Jewish American identity, is more comfortably accepted as an American writer. This same new marketing of hyphenated writers, of course, also extends to other minority groups, such as Asian Americans and African Americans, especially female writers.**

You're right. Before, when Chicano writers sent their manuscripts to big publishing houses, they were told that there was no market for their books. Now this is changing. Why? Why all of a sudden this interest in new ethnic writers? Does it represent just the fact that publishers feel they can now make money from these books or is it because there have been pressures from these ethnic writers and from these ethnic communities on the publishing world? I think it's both.

**I've heard it said that one of the reasons more Chicana and Latina writers are being published by big firms—as opposed to the male writers—is that**

publishers believe that female novelists sell better, based on surveys that indicate that women buy the majority of published novels in this country. That was true also in the nineteenth century, when novels were directed at female readers. This was particularly the case in the Spanish-speaking countries. The publishers are also reacting to the huge success recently of Laura Esquivel's *Like Water For Chocolate*. It was on the *New York Times* best-seller list for months. But since then, the publishers have been hoping to find another equally successful Latina writer.

**Some have suggested that there may be a danger with respect to these writers publishing through the big New York firms, that some level of authenticity will be lost or co-opted in this relationship. Do you share this concern?**

I don't think that there's a danger, because first of all, almost all Chicano writers have hoped to reach larger audiences, not just the recent Chicana writers. Will this mean that the ethnic group will disappear and be integrated into the national culture? I don't think this will happen soon or easily. But even if it does, you can't blame the writers for this integration, because it will be the result of larger forces, such as economic ones. The fact is that if you read a writer such as Sandra Cisneros, you see that there is still very much of an ethnic identity to her writing. For example, in *Woman Hollering Creek* there are some stories that contain many Mexican references. Those readers with a greater familiarity with Mexican history and culture will get even more out of these stories. Sandra is not compromising her ethnic identity. The same thing with Ana Castillo. Much of *The Mixquiahuala Letters* takes place in Mexico.

**I agree with you. I don't share that concern that has been voiced by some. The fact is that the New York firms don't want these writers to lose their ethnic identity precisely because it's that identity that they want to market. Sandra's publisher doesn't want Sandra to write something other than about Chicanos. So this means that these writers can continue to write about Chicano themes, but at the same time reach larger audiences. I think that's positive.**

The same thing has happened to Jewish American writers. They have been able to maintain their ethnic identity while becoming very successful writers.

**I think that the concern over the possibility of these writers losing their ethnic identity or of selling out to the establishment comes from a certain attitude of ethnic purity that wants to force these writers to only publish with Chicano presses.**

The problem here is that there are very few Chicano presses. In fact, there are only two. But even here, it's interesting that a press such as Arte Público has made arrangements to sell the paperback rights to some of its texts to the big eastern firms. I don't think that anyone can or should tell a Chicano writer, "Don't publish with this or that publisher."

## Sandra Cisneros

**Let's talk specifically about some of the key Chicana writers who bloom in the 1980s and 1990s. Let's start with Sandra Cisneros. How do you see her work, particularly her two main books of stories, *The House on Mango Street* and *Woman Hollering Creek*? How do you see her evolution as a writer?**

There's no question that there is a great advancement from *Mango Street* to *Woman Hollering Creek*. In *Mango Street* you still have a very limited world—the world of the adolescent protagonist. On the other hand, in *Woman Hollering Creek* you have a greater variety of characters and environments. It is a more powerful and sophisticated text. To me, Sandra has crossed the border in literature from a writer who just writes short stories to a writer who has written something of permanent value.

**In *Woman Hollering Creek*, Cisneros takes off in the title story on the legend of *La Llorona*. How successful do you think she is in interpreting, or reinterpreting, this legend?**

She handles it very well in the way she applies it to a woman from Mexico who finally liberates herself after an exploitative marriage relationship with this Chicano fellow. Sandra is very creative in that she doesn't just repeat the legend, but reinterprets it to symbolize the liberation of women from a macho culture. She links the mexicana's liberation with Chicana feminism in that the mexicana is helped in getting away from her husband by a Chicana. Here, Sandra is expressing the influence of Chicano culture on more recently arrived Mexican women.

**But what about those stories in *Woman Hollering Creek* that are set in Mexico? I'm thinking especially of the story "Eyes of Zapata." Does Sandra really understand Mexican history and culture?**

I actually not too long ago gave a paper in Tijuana about myths and the creation of new myths in Chicano literature. I referred in particular to Sandra's story "Eyes of Zapata." I said that for the first time Zapata as a hero had been demythified. Some in the audience didn't like to hear this. But in Sandra's story, Zapata is no longer a mythic hero; he's now seen from the perspective of a woman.

**This is a good example of how and why the new Chicana writings after 1980 are really postmovement writings. You would never expect to hear such criticism of heroic figures such as Zapata during the heyday of the movement. In fact, Zapata was recreated as a Chicano hero during the movement years. But, in my opinion, what Cisneros does in this story is not so much to demythify Zapata, but to demythify the macho Chicano-leader types that came out of the movement. Sandra's story has less to do with Mexican history than it has to do with Chicano history. She's commenting less on Zapata and more on Chicano *caudillo* figures.**

Yes, I think you're right, but there's another angle to Sandra's criticism that has more to do with Zapata as a Mexican historical character. Sandra is pointing out something in her story that isn't often stressed about Zapata. That is that although he has been associated with the struggles of the *campesinos,* or peasants, in Mexico, in fact Zapata himself was not a *campesino.* He was a *charro,* or a Mexican cowboy. Zapata never dressed in the traditional white-pajama-type garb of the *campesino.* He dressed as a traditional Mexican *charro.* These are entirely two different cultures. Sandra is bringing out these contradictions of Zapata. Zapata was transformed into a *campesino* leader by later politicians, artists, historians, and writers who began to mythologize Zapata and the Mexican Revolution. Sandra demythologizes this. The other important aspect of Sandra's story is that this is the first time that Zapata has been interpreted from the perspective of a woman, in this case the girl he refused to marry.

**What are some of the influences you see on Cisneros's writing? Is there another author whom she seems to correspond to?**

Well, I definitely see some influence from the Mexican writer Elena Poniatowska. For example, Poniatowska's first book, *Lilus Kikus,* is a collection of short stories with the protagonist a young girl. We see the world or, at least, her world through her eyes. This is, of course, exactly what Sandra does in *Mango Street,* which is also her first collection of stories. And even some of the stories are similar. Interestingly, Poniatowska has just recently translated *Mango Street* from English into Spanish for publication in New York. I believe she also translated it into Polish.

So in a sense, Poniatowska is reciprocating Cisneros's testimony to her—Sandra's patterning *Mango Street* after *Lilus Kikus*.

Yes. *Mango Street* is the type of literature that Poniatowska favors. It's very much like her own first book.

## Ana Castillo

**Of the Chicana writers, there's no question that Ana Castillo has produced the most. Besides her early poetry, which you mentioned, she has published three novels: *The Mixquiahuala Letters*, *Sapogonia*, and *So Far From God*. How do you see her evolution as a writer?**

Her evolution is much more striking than that of Sandra. There's a big difference from her early poetry to her novels. For one thing, she, at least in *Sapogonia*, expands into a larger Latino world—not just a Chicano one. She is also a writer for whom, although gender is one of her central themes, it's not her only one. In *The Mixquiahuala Letters* she has these two women who go to Mexico, and the perspective of male and female characters is very well done. But in *Sapogonia* she takes on a larger canvas with more characters and less emphasis on gender conflicts and more on other problems. And in *So Far From God,* she pays particular attention to regional themes, in this case to New Mexico. So her range is much broader than, for example, that of Cisneros. Castillo has also accomplished what the other Chicana writers have yet to do. She has published three successful novels.

**Do you see any particular influence on her from another writer?**

Yes, especially in *The Mixquiahuala Letters,* which she dedicates to Julio Cortázar. She herself has admitted Cortázar's influence in her writing. I find it interesting that *The Mixquiahuala Letters* is a defense of women and yet it's dedicated to the great male master, Cortázar. But I think that this type of Latin American influence is healthy for Chicano writers.

**I think it's also healthy that Castillo was not intimidated by a certain kind of political correctness that would argue that a book about women should not be dedicated to a man.**

Another noticeable influence on Castillo is García Márquez. This is clear in *So Far From God* where Castillo attempts to imitate his style, especially in her employment of magical realism. However, although the book as a whole is very good, the use of magical realism doesn't work too well, as I've mentioned before. You can also see in *So Far From God* the influence of John Nichols's *The Milagro Beanfield War.*

**Is it fair to compare Cisneros with Castillo? Are they similar or different writers?**

The big difference is that while both are excellent writers, Cisneros to date has only published collections of short stories while Castillo has already published three novels. We have to see if Sandra is capable of producing an integrated novel as has Ana. By an integrated novel, I mean a narrative that is not fragmented like a collection of short stories, such as *Mango Street,* but which has greater unity to it, such as *Sapogonia* and *So Far From God.* Sandra has to prove that she can do this also. She could continue to write short stories, but then she will not be able to achieve a higher position in both Chicano literature and in American literature as a whole.

## Denise Chávez

**Denise Chávez, of course, is still another important Chicana writer of the 1980s and into the 1990s. She first published a series of short stories called *The Last of the Menu Girls* and more recently a novel, *Face of an Angel.* What is your opinion of her work?**

Her *Last of the Menu Girls* is similar to Cisneros's *House on Mango Street.* It is a collection of fragmented stories with the same narrator, who, as in *Mango Street,* is a young female. I think that Chávez in *Menu Girls* employs symbols in a better and more sophisticated manner than does Cisneros in *Mango Street.* In *Face of an Angel,* Chávez proves that she can write an extensive narrative. One of the characteristics of her writing is her use of dramatic techniques and other elements based on drama. Denise is also an actress, and that's why there is a sense of the dramatic in her writing. Even some of her characters are actors.

**What kind of themes are visible in Chávez's work?**

The concern with gender issues, of course, and the theme of how women in Chicano communities have performed indispensable service to their families and to others. But I don't think that Chávez has the same range of themes as does Cisneros. While Sandra in *Woman Hollering Creek* goes from Zapata to *retablos,* Chávez tends to repeat similar characters and even places.

**Certainly Cisneros, Castillo, and Chávez have reached a certain level of**

national attention higher than other Chicana writers, but are there some other writers who you feel also deserve such attention?

There are many other writers who are coming along, but the problem is that most of them at this point only have one book, which limits the attention they get. You cannot stop with just one book. You have to continue to publish. However, one of the most important, it seems to me, is Lucha Corpi, who began writing poetry and changed to the novel with three successful works: *Delia's Song* [1989], *Eulogy for a Brown Angel* [1992], and *Cactus Blood* [1995]. These last two are clever detective stories, a subgenre that has become popular with younger Chicano and Chicana writers.

# Chapter Eight

## Work and
## Reflections at
## Ninety

*Leal with President and Mrs. Clinton at the presentation of National Humanities Medal at the White House, September, 1997.*

**MG:**   I want to discuss your own most recent work. I understand you've written a book on Joaquin Murrieta. Why did you decide to do a book on Murrieta?

**LL:**   I've always been interested in Murrieta as a popular hero. Some time ago, as I was collecting recordings of *corridos,* I found one on Murrieta. I think it was the very first *corrido* recorded about Murrieta. It was done in the 1930s in San Antonio. This began my interest in Murrieta. I then later came across the novel about him written by John Rollins Ridge in 1854. I began reading everything I could find about Murrieta. I became fascinated about his identity. Who was he? According to the California newspapers of the early 1850s, when Murrieta was alleged to have been a bandit, there were actually five Joaquins. At first I thought I would only do an article, but I collected so much material that I decided to write a whole book. For example, there were many dime novels written about Murrieta in the late nineteenth and early twentieth centuries.

   Another interesting thing that I discovered was that Ridge's book on Murrieta was later published in different languages and in different countries, and all of these books claimed to be original versions and ascribed to Murrieta a different nationality. For example, shortly after the publication of Ridge's book in 1854, it was reproduced in a publication in San Francisco called the *Police Gazette.* This version was then translated in 1862 into French and published in Paris. Following that, someone from Chile translated the French edition into Spanish, published it in Chile, and claimed that Murrieta was really a Chileno who had come to the gold fields of California during the gold rush after 1848. It's possible that the French edition already claimed that Murrieta was Chileno. I've discovered that there is a copy of the French translation in the National Library in Paris, and I'm trying to get a copy of it. To make matters more complicated, the Chilean edition was reedited in Mexico by Ireneo Paz, the grandfather of Octavio Paz. People began to assume then that the true author of the Murrieta book was Irineo Paz rather than Ridge. Paz's version was then translated back into English, crediting Paz as the author. In fact, of course, it was Ridge who all along was the original author. Finally, a second edition of Ridge's book on Murrieta was published, which many in this country have accepted as being the original. But in other countries, they still accept either the French version, the Chilean version, or the Mexican one. Part of my work is to definitely prove that all of these editions are simply copies or versions of the original Ridge one.

**So is your study an examination of these different publications?**
Part of it is. My study is entitled *Joaquin Murrieta in Literature*. Part of it is to deal with just who Joaquin Murrieta was, since, as I mentioned, five Joaquins are referred to by contemporary newspapers and all are linked with so-called bandit activity. Only one of them has the surname Murrieta. But why, for example, was this Joaquin selected by Ridge to be transformed into a folk hero and into what later scholars would refer to as a "social bandit"? The story goes that when Murrieta or one of these Joaquins is eventually captured, his head was cut off. However, some claimed that the decapitated head later exhibited was not the head of Murrieta. One anecdote actually says that Joaquin Murrieta himself went to see his own head! Father Alberto Huerta at the University of San Francisco wrote an article a few years ago in *The Californian* about his research concerning the head of Murrieta. He claims that it had been deposited in a museum in San Francisco, but that in the 1906 earthquake the jar containing the head broke. Father Huerta goes on to say that he actually discovered the head in Berkeley, where some antiquarian has it. Richard Rodríguez in *Days of Obligation* has written about Father Huerta's search for the head of Joaquin Murrieta.

I'm also showing that Murrieta was definitely not Chileno. You know, Pablo Neruda also claimed that Murrieta was from Chile. Neruda wrote a play about Murrieta's exploits in the California gold fields. But I've determined that Murrieta was from northern Mexico, probably Sonora. But the story is complicated, because what we really have is a myth based on scattered historical evidence. There will probably never be a definitive account of who the historical Murrieta was. In the myth, he is really a composite of the alleged other Joaquins. So while my book in part discusses the historical background of the myth, it really deals much more with how the myth has been employed over the years. The myth has been used in dime novels, in fiction, in *corridos*, in the theater, in legends, in movies, etcetera.

**How early does the myth appear in the movies?**
The first movie based on Joaquin Murrieta was in 1936. It was called *The Robin Hood of El Dorado*. I actually saw it in Chicago. Other later films, both in this country and in Mexico, also used the myth.

**What about *corridos*? Have there been many about Murrieta?**

Over the years there have been about eight different *corridos*.

**And in looking at all of these different genres that have incorporated the Murrieta myth, do you find that the myth has changed over time?**

It's constantly changing. In every dime novel, for example, it's different. In one novel published in English, Murrieta is even fighting against Mexico in the U.S.-Mexico War. In another novel, he's a Spaniard. This is similar to the Zorro story, which is actually based on the Murrieta myth.

**Is Murrieta portrayed in some cases as a hero and in some cases as evil?**

In a few cases there's a negative portrayal, but for the most part, as in the dime novels, he is shown as a Robin Hood type.

**If you look at the Ridge book, you can actually read the text either positively or negatively. You can see Murrieta as a violent cut-throat or as a social bandit, a Mexican rebelling against the conquering Americans. How do you interpret the Murrieta of the Ridge book?**

As a social bandit. I don't think there's any question about it. You see, Ridge was part Cherokee on his father's side. His father suffered discrimination, and Ridge identified with his father and with the Mexicans in post–1848 California.

**How do you explain all this interest in Murrieta over the years? Why are people still fascinated with him?**

There are many attractions. One is the mystery of Murrieta's identity. We are all interested in mysteries. Two, there's the element of the hero, just as we are interested in Robin Hood. Three, Murrieta's identification with the oppression of Mexicans in California. Certainly for Chicanos that's one of the key attractions.

**Is Corky Gonzales's poem "I Am Joaquin," written during the Chicano movement, related to Joaquin Murrieta?**

Yes. Gonzales's Joaquin is Murrieta. Joaquin, and in this case Joaquin Murrieta, represents all Chicanos.

**I understand that you're also now working on still another project concerning the Chicano short story. Can you tell me about this?**

Recently I taught a course on the Chicano short story, and in doing so I realized that there is no substantive study of that genre. For the Chicano novel, there are various studies, but not so for the short story, similar to what I did many years ago for the Mexican short story. So since I already have a good deal of material for the Chicano short story, I have decided to write a book on this subject.

My first chapter will deal with the short story from before 1848 and the annexation of the Southwest by the United States. Very important in this period is the role of the *cuento oral,* the oral folk stories passed on from one generation to another. Here you have some very important studies that I can draw upon, such as those by Aurelio Espinosa and Arthur Campa, especially for New Mexico and Colorado. Then I will have a chapter on the short story as it appeared in late-nineteenth-century Spanish-language newspapers in the Southwest. For example, in the *Gaceta de Santa Bárbara,* published here in Santa Barbara in the post–Mexican War years, there are several short stories. My third chapter will focus on writers from Mexico who came during the period of the Mexican Revolution of 1910 and who wrote short stories in immigrant newspapers in the United States. But in addition to those writers, there were also a small group of Mexican Americans writing in English who published short stories in important American magazines. One such writer was María Cristina Mena. She was born in Yucatán, but came to New York as a young girl, where she grew up. She later married a famous theater critic by the name of Chambers. She wrote as María Cristina Chambers, but she was in fact a Mexican American writer. All of her stories have to do with Mexico as a way of teaching Americans about that country. I then will deal with the Mexican American short story from the Great Depression years to the post–World War II era—the era that you discuss as the period of the Mexican American Generation. Writers here will include Fray Angelico Chávez of New Mexico and Mario Suárez from Arizona, as well as many others. Finally, I will deal with the short story during the Chicano-movement years and the postmovement years.

The project should keep me busy for at least a year or two. But I'm doing this because of my special interest in the short story.

**In addition to this new project, you've also started a new literary journal with Professor Víctor Fuentes of UCSB called *Ventana Abierta: Revista Latina de Literatura, Arte y Cultura*. Whose idea was it to start this journal?**

One night there was a function at La Casa de La Raza in Santa Barbara. Víctor and I attended. Someone there told us that he was interested in publishing a periodical if Víctor and I supplied the content and served as editors. We agreed and started to gather material for a literary journal in Spanish. But then this person backed out of the project. Although we were disappointed, Víctor and I decided to proceed anyway to raise the funds for the publication. But first we had to come up with a name. One day we were talking and Víctor mentioned the possibility of *Ventana Abierta*. After more discussion, we agreed that this was a good title. It means in English *Open Window*, and we thought that this expressed the openness to new literary expressions that we wanted to promote in the journal.

After contacting potential contributors, we had sufficient material for the first volume, although we still did not have the funding. Fortunately, we had many sympathetic friends on campus at UCSB. We first talked to Ray Huerta, the coordinator of affirmative action, who without hesitation thought that the journal was a great idea and would contribute some of his funds through the Center for Chicano Studies for the publication. Vice-chancellor for Public Affairs Ernest López also was very supportive, as was Professor Denise Segura, the director of the Center for Chicano Studies. As a result of their enthusiastic help, we were able to come up with the funds for the initial issue.

From here we arranged the printing of the journal by Words Worth of Santa Barbara, a local printing company headed by Sasha Newborn. Sasha did a wonderful job in designing the issue. The first issue came out in the spring of 1997 and our second in the summer of that year. To date, we have published six issues.

**What is the content of the journal?**
We publish original stories and poetry and a few essays, all in Spanish, although occasionally we publish some material in English, such as the poetry of Ernest López. Our third issue focused on California writers who write in Spanish.

**What is the philosophy of *Ventana Abierta*?**
It is to give the opportunity to those writers who write predominantly in Spanish to publish their work. We publish new writers, but also commission contributions from more established writers, such as Fernando Alegria. Our journal is the only literary journal published in Spanish in the United States. Our other objective is to showcase young Latino artists by publishing illustrations of their artwork.

**Why did you subtitle your journal a *Revista Latina* instead of a *Revista Chicana*?**
Because we want to include a variety of Latino writers and artists and not just Chicano ones. We would be excluding a large number of writers if we only used the term *Chicano* in our title. By using *Latina* we increase our cir-

culation. We have high hopes for *Ventana Abierta*, but we're just beginning. **Don Luis, you turned ninety in 1997, and your career spans some six decades. Is there anything you would do differently if you could?**

For the most part no. I am very satisfied with my life and work. However, I would have liked to have studied more languages. I think this would have made me a better critic and scholar. For example, I would have liked to have studied Náhuatl because all Mexican writers use words whose origins are in that Aztec language. I had begun to study Italian, but eventually had to drop it due to my concentration on teaching in Spanish. I also would have liked to have had more time to devote to all of Latin American literature. But it's hard to keep up with the literature of some twenty countries. As far as a specific project is concerned, I would have liked to have written an update to my 1956 study of the Mexican short story. But it's too late for me to do that now. On the whole, however, I don't regret what I have done. I have lots of notes on unwritten projects. But you can't do everything you want to do.

**Do you think that if you would have stayed in Mexico that you would have become a literary critic and scholar?**

I don't know, Mario. I don't think so.

**When you look back on your education in this country, would you go back and change anything?**

For that time, it was as good as it could be. The University of Chicago under Robert Hutchins was as good a university as you could find. All of the professors were up to date on the literature and criticism of that period.

**When you see recent graduate students today, as you have recently at Stanford, what are some of the differences you see in their training as compared to yours?**

It's very different. The students reflect the age in which they study. In my time, the outlook on literature was broader and more historical. Today the focus is very narrow. There is also more interest in theory now than in my time. We were more interested in the literary works themselves and the history associated with that literature, and less on abstract theory. Today many students don't have that big panoramic view that we had. They know their narrow specialization very well, but not the big picture. Some don't even know the literature itself!

**Are these changes good or bad?**

I don't necessarily say that they are either good or bad, although I have my doubts about recent trends. But these differences reflect the thinking of each period. In the nineteenth century, the literary world was affected by positivism. This was followed by modernism, then Marxism, and more recently by poststructuralism. I don't say one influence is more important than another, but each has to be put into historical perspective.

**Do you think that the current obsession with theory in literary studies makes for better critics?**

I recently read a paper at a UCLA conference on Latino studies precisely on this point. I observed that too many Chicano critics are attempting to impose or force certain contemporary European theories onto their analysis of Chicano texts. The danger here is that they don't allow the texts themselves to determine the application, or nonapplication, of these theories. They come to the texts already with prescribed theories or formulas. It becomes a static rather than a dynamic and original encounter with the text. My views, however, didn't go over very well with younger scholars and graduate students. Many of them are coming out of English departments where these postmodern theories have come to dominate, so it's not surprising that they reflect this training.

**What do you think are the implications of this stress on theory rather than on the literature itself?**

The implications are that in ten years these theories are going to be forgotten, and then you have to have new ones. To me, the purpose of literary criticism is to assist readers and students to better understand the text and not to see how a text serves a particular theory. If I write a paper on a text that helps you, the reader, understand that text, then I'm happy. The purpose of the critic is to enlighten and to clarify, not to confuse.

**Is this heavy focus on theory also happening in Mexico?**

Unfortunately yes, especially at the elite Colegio de México.

**If an aspiring graduate student comes to you for advice on pursuing a degree in literary criticism, what would you say to such a student?**

I would tell that student that in addition to studying literature that he or she also study history, sociology, anthropology, and other areas so that his or her analysis of literature is multidimensional. The second thing I would suggest would be to apply his or her own ideas rather than just those of his or her mentors or the theorists. I am not a person who tells someone else to follow this idea or that one. I prefer for others to develop their own ideas.

**Another current emphasis in the academy is that of being interdisciplinary, at least in the humanities. Do you consider yourself interdisciplinary?**

Oh yes! I have always been interested, for example, in the relationship of history and literature. But I've also had an interest in linguistics and psychology.

**On another theme, do you have any reservations about concentrating primarily on Chicano literature during the last three decades?**

No. I had already done a great deal of work on Mexican and Latin American literature, and there were many more critics in these fields. I felt the importance of doing whatever I could to promote Chicano literature. I don't regret this decision at all.

**As you look at Chicano literature today, what would you say have been the most important developments?**

That's a difficult question. One very positive development has been the emergence of women writers since the 1980s. Another is the discovery of earlier, pre–Chicano movement writers, so that we have a sense of a literary heritage. Still another is the evolution from poetry to fiction during and after the Chicano movement. Finally, I would say, is the important flowering of Chicano literary criticism.

**Do you see a positive future for Chicano literature?**

Definitely. We'll continue to have more and better writers and critics.

**Thank you, Don Luis.**

*Leal (center) with María Herrera-Sobek (holder of the Leal Endowed Chair, UC Santa Barbara) and Mario García at UC Santa Barbara at a conference honoring Leal on his 90th birthday, 1997.*

# Notes

## Introduction

1. For a now dated but still useful bibliography of Leal's work, see Salvador Güereña and Raquel Quiroz González, eds., *Luis Leal: A Bibliography with Interpretive and Critical Essays* (Berkeley: Chicano Studies Library, University of California Berkeley, 1988). Also see Luis Leal with Víctor Fuentes, *Don Luis Leal: una vida y dos culturas* (Tempe, Ariz.: Bilingual Review/Press, 1998).

2. See Mario T. García, *Memories of Chicano History: The Life and Narrative of Bert Corona* (Berkeley: University of California Press, 1994).

## Chapter Three

1. Mario T. García, *Mexican Americans: Leadership, Ideology and Identity, 1930–1960* (New Haven: Yale University Press, 1989).

# Selected Bibliography of Luis Leal's Works

## Books

*Aztlán y México: perfiles literarios e históricos.* Binghamton, N.Y.: Bilingual Review/Press, 1985.
*Bibliografía del cuento mexicano.* México: Editorial Studium, 1958.
*Breve historia de la literatura hispanoamericana.* New York: Alfred A. Knopf, 1971.
*Breve historia del cuento mexicano.* México: Editorial Studium, 1956. 2d ed., México: Universidad Autónoma de Puebla, 1990.
*Corridos y canciones de Aztlán.* Santa Barbara: Xalmán 1980, 2d ed., 1986.
*El cuento hispanoamericano.* Buenos Aires: Centro Editor de América Latina, 1967.
*Historia del cuento hispanoamericano.* México: Editorial Studium, 1966, rev. ed., 1971.
*Juan Rulfo.* Boston: Twayne Publishers, 1983.
*Mariano Azuela.* Buenos Aires: Centro Editor de América Latina, 1967.
*Mariano Azuela.* New York: Twayne Publishers, 1971.
*Mariano Azuela, vida y obra.* México: Editorial Studium, 1961.
*México, civilizaciones y culturas.* Boston: Houghton Mifflin Co., 1955, rev. ed., 1971.
*Panorama de la literatura mexicana actual.* Washington: Unión Panamericana, 1968.
*No Longer Voiceless.* San Diego, CA: Marin Publications, 1995.
Leal and Edmundo Valadés. *La Revolución y las letras.* México: Instituto Nacional de Bellas Artes, 1960. 2d. ed., México: Consejo Nacional para la Cultura y las Artes, 1990. "Lecturas Mexicanas," 3a. Serie, Número 14.

## Anthologies and Books Edited

*Antología del cuento mexicano.* México: Editorial Studium, 1957.
*El cuento mexicano. De los orígenes al modernismo.* Buenos Aires: EUDEBA, 1966.
*El cuento veracruzano.* Antología. Xalapa: Universidad Veracruzana, 1966.
*Cuentos de la Revolución.* Biblioteca del Estudiante Universitario: México: UNAM, 1971.
*Leyendas mexicanas.* New York: Regents Publishing Co., 1985.
Leal and Frank Dauster, eds. *Literatura de Hispanoamérica.* New York: Harcourt, Brace and World, 1970.
Leal, et al. *A Decade of Chicano Literature (1970–1979).* Santa Barbara, CA: Editorial La Causa, 1982.
Félix Varela. *Jicoténcal.* Eds. Luis Leal and Rodolfo J. Cornina. Houston: Arte Público Press, 1995.

# Contributions to Books

"Alfonso Reyes." *Gran Enciclopedia Rialp.* Madrid, 1974 ed. Vol. 20, pp. 249–250.

"Apéndice bibliográfico." In *Antología de la literatura mexicana.* Ed. Carlos Castillo. Chicago: University of Chicago Press, 1944, pp. 403–424.

"Azuela, Mariano (1873–1952)." *Encyclopaedia Britannica.* 1960 ed., vol. 2, p. 834; rpt. ed. 1967, vol. 2, pp. 939–940.

"Carlos Fuentes." *Contemporary Literary Criticism.* Detroit: Gale Research, 1987, pp. 166–168.

"El *Cautiverio feliz* y la crónica novelesca." In *Prosa hispanoamericana virreinal.* Ed. Raquel Chang-Rodríguez. Barcelona: Borrás Ediciones, 1978, pp. 113–140.

"La estructura de Pedro Páramo." In *Anuario de Letras.* Ed. Juan M. Lope Blanch. México: UNAM, 1994, pp. 287–294.

"Female Archetypes in Mexican Literature." In *Women in Hispanic Literature.* Ed. Beth Miller. Berkeley: University of California Press, 1983, pp. 227–242.

"The First American Epic: Villagrá's History of New Mexico." In *Pasó por Aquí: Critical Essays on the New Mexican Literary Tradition, 1542–1988.* Ed. Erlinda González-Berry. New Mexico: University of New Mexico Press, 1989, pp. 47–62.

"El hechizo derramado: elementos mestizos en Sor Juana." In *Y diversa de mí misma entre vuestras plumas ando.* Ed. Sara Poot Herrera. México: El Colegio de México, 1993, pp. 185–200.

"Hispanic-Mexican Literature in the Southwest, 1521–1848." In *Chicano Literature: A Reference Guide.* Ed. Julio A. Martínez and Francisco Lomelí. Westpoint, Conn.: Greenwood Press, 1985, pp. 244–260.

"Historia y ficción en la narrativa de Alejandro Morales." In *Alejandro Morales: Fiction Past, Present, Future Perfect.* Ed. José Antonio Gurpegui. Tempe, Ariz.: Bilingual Review/Press, 1996, pp. 31–42.

"History and Myth in the Narrative of Carlos Fuentes." In *Carlos Fuentes: A Critical View.* Ed. Robert Brody and Charles Rossman. Austin: University of Texas Press, 1982, pp. 3–37.

"Interpretaciones de la literatura mexicana." In *Humanitas.* Monterrey: Universidad de Nuevo León, 1968, pp. 259–273.

"José Martí." *Encyclopaedia Britannica.* 1965 ed., vol. 14, pp. 974–975.

"Juan Rulfo." In *Narrativa y crítica de nuestra América.* Ed. Joaquín Roy. Madrid: Editorial Castalia, 1978, pp. 258–286.

"La literatura mexicana del siglo XX (1930–1963)." In *Panorama das literaturas das Américas.* Ed. Joaquim de Montezuma de Carvalho. Angola: Ediçao do Municipio de Nova Lisboa, 1963, colofón, 1965, vol. 4, pp. 1997–2050.

"Magic Realism in Latin American Literature." In *Magic Realism: History, Community.* Eds. Lois Parkinson Zamora and Wendy B. Faris. Durham, N.C.: Duke University Press, 1995.

"Mexican-American Literature, 1848–1942." In *Chicano Literature: A Reference Guide.* Eds. Julio A. Martínez and Francisco Lomelí. Westpoint, Conn.: Greenwood Press, 1985, pp. 280–299.

"Mito y realidad social en *Peregrinos de Aztlán.*" In *Miguel Méndez in Aztlán: Two Decades of Literary Production.* Ed. Gary D. Keller. Tempe, Ariz.: Bilingual Review/Press, 1995, pp. 38–45.

"El movimiento estridentista." In *Memoria del Undécimo Congreso del Instituto Internacional de Literatura Iberoamericana.* México: Editorial Cultura, 1965, pp. 77–87.

"El nuevo cuento mexicano." In *El cuento hispanoamericano ante la crítica.* Ed. Enrique Pupo-Walker. Madrid: Editorial Castalia, 1973, pp. 280–295.

"El pachuco: de la realidad al mito." *Proceedings of the First Annual International Conference on the Emerging Literature of the Southwest Culture.* El Paso, Tex.: The University of Texas at El Paso, 1995, pp. 100–104.

"El paso y la huella: The Reconstruction of Chicano Cultural History." In *Estudios Chicanos and the Politics of Community. Selected Proceedings,* National Association for Chicano Studies. Eds. Mary Romero and Cordelia Candelaria. Ann Arbor, Mich.: McNaughton & Gunn Lithographers, 1989, pp. 19–30.

"Poetic Discourse in Pérez de Villagrá's *Historia de la Nueva México.*" In *Reconstructing a Chicano Literary Heritage: Hispanic Colonial Literature of the Southwest.* Ed. María Herrera Sobek. Tucson: University of Arizona Press, 1993, pp. 95–117.

"The Problem of Identifying Chicano Literature." In *The Identification and Analysis of Chicano Literature.* Ed. Francisco Jiménez. New York: Bilingual Press, 1979, pp. 2–6.

"The Rewriting of American Literary History." In *Criticism in the Borderlands.* Héctor Calderón and José David Saldívar, eds. Durham, N.C.: Duke University Press, 1991, pp. 21–27.

"Sor Juana Inés de la Cruz." *Encyclopedia Britannica.* 1960 ed., vol. 6, p. 806.

"Tomás Rivera." In *Dictionary of Literary Biography: Chicano Writers.* Vol. 82, first Series. Ed. Francisco A. Lomelí and Carl R. Shirley. Detroit: A Bruccoli Clark Layman Book, Gale Research Inc., 1989, pp. 206–213.

"Truth Telling Tongues: Early Chicano Poetry." In *Recovering the U.S. Hispanic Literary Heritage.* Ed. Ramón Gutiérrez and Genaro Padilla. Houston: Arte Público Press, 1993, pp. 91–105.

Leal and Pepe Barrón. "Chicano Literature: An Overview." In *Three American Literatures.* Ed. Houston Baker Jr. New York: The Modern Language Association of America, 1982, pp. 9–12.

## Articles and Essays

"Agustín Yáñez y la novela mexicana. Rescate de una teoría." *Revista Iberoamericana* 48, Nos. 118–119 (1982), pp. 121–129. Rpt. *Mester* 12 (1983), pp. 18–25.

"The American in Mexican Literature." *Melus* 5, No. 3 (1978), pp. 16–25.

"Américo Paredes and Modern Mexican American Scholarship." *Ethnic Affairs* 1, No. 1 (1987), pp. 1–11.

"Aportaciones de Hispanoamérica a la cultura de los Estados Unidos." *Hispania* 3 (1951), pp. 245–250.

"*La araucana* y el problema de la literatura nacional." *Vórtice* 1, No. 1 (1974), pp. 68–73.

"Borges y la novela." *Revista Iberoamericana* 36, No. 70 (1970), pp. 11–23.

"La caída de Alfonso Reyes." *El Rehilete,* No. 4 (1962), pp. 5–8.

"El Códice Ramírez." *Historia Mexicana* 3, No. 9 (1953), pp. 11–33.

"El concepto de Aztlán en la poesía chicana." *Imagine* 1, No. 1 (1984), pp. 118–131.

"Contemporary Mexican Literature: A Mirror of Social Change." *Arizona Quarterly* 18, No. 3 (1962), pp. 197–207.

"El contenido literario de 'La Orquesta'." *Historia Mexicana* 7 (1958), pp. 329–367.
"Un corrido cervantino." *Revista Universidad de México* 9, No. 2 (1955), pp. 21, 32.
"Cuatro siglos de prosa aztlanense." *La Palabra* 2, No. 1 (1980), pp. 2–12.
"La Cucaracha." *Revista Universidad de México* 8, No. 5 (1954), pp. 15–17.
"El 'ejemplo', género literario popular." *Revista Universidad de México* 8, No. 9, (1954),
     pp. 14–17.
"La elegancia española de 'I Promessi Sposi'." *Italica* 21 (1954), pp. 74–82.
"En torno a *Cien años de soledad*." *Caribe* 1, No. 2 (1976), pp. 117–119.
"Entre la fantasía y el compromiso: los cuentos de Fernando Alegria." *Nueva Narrativa*
     *Hispanoamericana* 1, No. 2 (1971), pp. 65–71.
"Escritores del México actual." *La Nueva Democracia* 40 (1960), pp. 16–21.
"F. N. Gutiérrez, poeta barbareño del siglo XIX." *Xalmán* 5, Nos. 1–2 (1983–1984),
     pp. 23–26.
"*La feria* de Juan José Arreola: tema y estructura." *Nueva Narrativa Hispanoamericana*
     1 (1971), pp. 41–48.
"La función de los personajes españoles en *Il Fu Mattia Pascal*," *Forum Italicum* 1,
     No. 4 (1967), pp. 325–335.
"*El gallo de oro* de Juan Rulfo: ¿Guión o novela?" *Foro Literario*, Montevideo, 4,
     Nos. 7–8 (1980), pp. 32–37.
"El héroe acosado." *Revista Universidad de México* 33, No. 8 (1979), pp. 25–28.
"History and Memory in *Estampas del Valle*." *Revista Chicano-Riqueña* 12, No. 3–4
     (1984), pp. 101–108.
"In Search of Aztlán." *Denver Quarterly* 16, No. 3 (1981), pp. 16–22.
"La leyenda guadalupana." *ABC* (Chicago), 12 Dec., 1942, pp. 3, 6.
"El libro XII de Sahagún." *Historia Mexicana* 5 (1955), pp. 184–210.
"La licantropía entre los antiguos mexicanos." *América Indígena* 20 (1960), pp. 111–119.
"Literatura de frontera." *Tierra Adentro*, No. 27 (1981), pp. 36–39.
"[Miguel] Méndez y el *Calila y Dimna*." *La Palabra* 3, Nos. 1 and 2 (1981), pp. 67–76.
"Mexican-American Literature: A Historical Perspective." *Revista Chicano-Riqueña* 1,
     No. 1 (1973), pp. 32–44.
"El norteamericano en la literatura mexicana." *The Bilingual Review* 6, No. 1 (1979),
     pp. 31–38.
"Octavio Paz and the Chicano." *Latin American Literary Review* 5, No. 10 (1977),
     pp. 115–23.
"Realism, Myth and Prophecy in Fuentes' *Where the Air is Clear*." *Confluencia* 1, No. 1
     (1985), pp. 75–81.
"Situación de Julio Cortázar." *Revista Iberoamericana* 39 (1973), pp. 399–409.
"*La sombra del caudillo*, roman a clèf." *Modern Language Journal* 36 (1952), pp. 16–21.
"A Spanish-American Perspective of Anglo-American Literature." *Revista Canadiense de*
     *Estudios Hispánicos* 5, No. 1 (1980), pp. 61–73.
"Tlatelolco, Tlatelolco." *Denver Quarterly* 14, (1979), pp. 3–14.
"El tocotín mestizo de Sor Juana." *Abside* 18 (1954), pp. 51–64.
"Tomás Rivera: The Ritual of Remembering." *Revista Chicano-Riqueña* 13, Nos. 3–4
     (1985), pp. 30–38.
"Unamuno y Pirandello." *Italica* 9 (1952), pp. 193–199.

# Index